D0152038

5

*Duquesne Studies*

# LANGUAGE AND LITERATURE SERIES

## VOLUME FIFTEEN

# THE WITNESS OF TIMES

# The Witness of Times

## Manifestations of Ideology in Seventeenth Century England

*edited by*
*Katherine Z. Keller*
*& Gerald J. Schiffhorst*

DUQUESNE UNIVERSITY PRESS
Pittsburgh, Pennsylvania

Published in the United States of America by
DUQUESNE UNIVERSITY PRESS
600 Forbes Avenue
Pittsburgh, Pennsylvania 15282-0101

Library of Congress Cataloging-in-Publication Data

The witness of items : manifestations of ideology in
    seventeenth century England / edited by Katherine Z.
    Keller and Gerald J. Schiffhorst.
            p.    cm. — (Duquesne studies. Language and
    literature series ; 15)
        Includes bibliographical references and index.
        ISBN 0–8207–0252–8
        1. English literature—Early modern, 1500–1700—History
    and criticism.   2. Great Britain—Politics and government—
    Stuarts, 1603–1714.   3. Politics and literature—England—
    History—17th century.   4. England—Civilization—17th
    century.   I. Keller, Katherine Z., 1942–   .   II. Schiffhorst,
    Gerald J.   III. Series.
    PR438.P65W57   1993
    820.9'358—dc20                                      93–34481
                                                        CIP

# Contents

# Acknowledgments

We are indebted, first of all, to the 70 participants in the University of Central Florida's first biennial Conference on the Arts and Public Policy, "Literature and Politics in the Seventeenth Century," at which abbreviated versions of the following essays were first presented in 1991. We are grateful to the Chair of the English Department, John F. Schell, and to the Dean of Arts and Sciences, Edward P. Sheridan, for invaluable support. As both dean and political scientist, Stuart Lilie helped us not only in the development of the Conference but also in formulating an appropriate notion of politics in the context of seventeenth century literature. We appreciate the expert assistance of Irene Lee and Karen Lynette in preparing the manuscript. Finally, we thank the general editor of the *Language and Literature Series* at Duquesne, Albert C. Labriola, for his guidance and support, and our editor at Duquesne University Press, Susan Wadsworth-Booth, for her fine work with the text.

Material contained in Annabel Patterson's essay was included in a different form in her book, *Reading between the Lines* (1992), and is reprinted here with the permission of the University of Wisconsin Press. A forthcoming volume by Louise Schleiner, *Tudor and Stuart Women Writers*, contains a different form of her essay, and is here published with the permission of Indiana University Press.

Orlando, Florida                    Katherine Z. Keller

November 1992·                    Gerald J. Schiffhorst

# Introduction

*Katherine Z. Keller*

I n 1599, James VI of Scotland wrote *Basilikon Doron* as a gift for his son, Henry. In 1603, upon ascending the throne of England as James I, the thrifty Scot presented the same work as a gift to his new people. The gift may have been of more use to the English people than to Prince Henry, who did not live long enough to require a treatise on kingship. Often identified as a justification of divine right and royal authoritarianism, *Basilikon Doron* in fact establishes the bipartite nature of the sovereign: the authority derived from divine selection and the humanity essential to the successful execution of that authority. The seventeenth century thus begins in England with a legacy of the consciousness of duality at the "head" of the polity, a metaphor that James, and later his younger son Charles, would use repeatedly in an attempt to give coherent shape to an institution increasingly perceived as fragmented.

Charles II—unhampered by his grandfather's parsimony, but called, like him, to reign over a not entirely united and not entirely enthusiastic people—prepared a more extravagant gift that became, in effect, a legacy: the city of London, new-built to accommodate and symbolize the now

1

triumphant liberal ideology of contractual polity and capitalist expansion, privacy of conscience and conformity of culture. The new capital city was dominated by Wren's St. Paul's Cathedral, a monument to the "Anglican compromise" and the first public building in Europe whose design and execution were entirely under the control of a single individual. In 1599, James's gift had been prepared in the expectation of Henry's personal inheritance of the monarchy of Scotland and subsequently of the united kingdoms; the expectation was thwarted initially by Henry's death and later by the intervention of a people who took seriously one half of James's theory of kingship. When St. Paul's was finally complete in 1710, Charles II's expectations of personal inheritance had also been thwarted by public intervention. The events of 1688 that drove Charles's younger brother, James II, from England were less bloody than those that interrupted the inheritance of his father, but they were no less definitive. The significance of Charles's gift to his people precluded his bequeathing his kingdom to his brother and marked, for all practical purposes, the end of the seventeenth century.

Along with their perfervid and conspicuous consumption of Chinese luxury goods, especially porcelain and silk, Europeans of the seventeenth century appear to have come under the proverbial Chinese curse: they lived in painfully interesting times. Deprived of the medieval or even the humanist consensus, as yet unaccustomed to individual determinism and the choices it requires, unprepared for the relativism of an unstable community and social opportunism, they faced the redefinition of almost every significant area of their lives. It is our belief, and that of the contributors to this volume, that in reading seventeenth century writers, we are, in fact, reading ourselves. In confronting their choices, we confront our own materialization of those choices. Were it not for the cultural and financial imperialism of the London merchant, the political role of the United States in the world would not be what it has been. Were it not for the pugnacity of the poets and dramatists, we would not have the concept of art as the property of its creator, of art as commodity, that governs so much of our current artistic production. Were it not for the persistent examinations of sexuality as cultural relationship on the Jacobean and Restoration stages, our reexamination of marriage and family life would be diminished.

When a sixteenth century translator of Cicero used the phrase, "the witnesse of tymes," he was referring to written history, among whose attributes were included "Mistresse of Lyfe," and "light of trueth."[1] With equal validity, and clearly articulated if methodologically divergent historicist inclinations, the contributors to this volume have applied those attributes to literature of all kinds, finding it the best manifestation of "that image of the past which unexpectedly appears to man singled out by history at a moment of danger."[2] For seventeenth century man, and woman, the moments of danger were ubiquitous and predicated on the need to define a viable polity, a "public policy" that enabled social control but did not intervene in those areas privatized by Reformation religion. Politics, the implementation of power in an institutional context for the mutual and deliberate pursuit of the good life, had hitherto been reserved to a small group. Ideology, the articulation of a rationale for the methods to be used to implement power, had to be made known, visible, and available as history for a much larger group of citizens. While the polity was being shaped by an interplay of forces that included the realities of electoral policies, financial manipulation, military allegiances, and transfers of land that now reached a much larger proportion of the total population of England, an ideology had also to be invented that would enable the implementation of power rather than the affirmation of authority.

No discussion of ideology in seventeenth century England is possible without some recognition of the ideology of twentieth century literary study. The historicist view that informs all of the essays included here suggests that the chronological period under study is itself, perhaps, the best example of discursive narrative: a series of sociopolitical ruptures—a civil war or a revolution, the assassination of a monarch or the assertion of popular morality, a rational religious accommodation or a heretical apostasy—to be written and rewritten. Althusser and Machery have established for us the context of ideological investigation and posed the central question of whether the representation of ideology inevitably transforms it, just as ideology interpellates the individual into a social subjectivity. The authors of the essays in this book examine, through a variety of venues, the extent to which ideological representations interact with what is arguably the radical dialectic of the period: the increasing significance of power rather than authority as an ideological framework.

Some of the basic theoretical issues that are inherent in this dialectic are examined in the first essay in this volume, Michael Bristol's "Sacred Culture and Profane Religion: The Modernity of Herbert of Cherbury." Arguing that Herbert's "views do not reflect an 'emergent' consciousness and that he is not a representative of the 'rising bourgeoisie,'" Bristol nonetheless locates in Herbert's works solutions to the problems of legitimation that plagued the Stuart monarchs, as well as a theory of a private religiosity in which no one tradition can claim sovereign authority. Herbert's works reveal an ideology little removed from the pure authoritarianism of James I. The polity is still limited to the literate elite who formulate authority and implement power; Herbert was no more ready than his monarch to envision a world in which power is consensual and negotiable. Within the authoritarian context, however, Herbert's willingness to envision an "ecumenical tolerance" connects him with what were to be the lasting effects of the ideological battles of the seventeenth century.

Perhaps the best manifestation of the dynamics of empowerment in seventeenth century England is the landscape architecture that alternately reassured viewers with classical symmetry and astonished them with fantastical discords. At one extreme of the public mind, a comfortable sense of received authority persisted; at another, a sense of authority widely dispersed caused agitation: *Basilikon Doron* was soon confronted by *An Agreement of The People*, whose efforts to define and locate authority represented the first step in what became the intensely practical issue of establishing and operating a viable polity. As the century progressed, authority came increasingly to be viewed in contextual rather than abstract terms, but the arrival of James Stuart in London and the early years of his reign were marked by a widespread deference to received thought about authority. However tenuous the hereditary rights of the Stuarts, they were founded upon absolutes that were subject to subversion but not challenge: the legitimacy of inheritance and the divinely bestowed powers of the monarchy. Supported by a hereditary aristocracy and an episcopal church, the monarchy could easily project itself as the splendid and essential head of a "body politic." The instruments of projection were readily available: control of the mass media of the day through licensing of press and theater and control of public occasions through the power of money and the law.

Even before the advent of the Stuart monarchy, which became the most visible icon of an authoritarian ideology, the Tudors had recognized the value of the public occasion as an ideological locus. In the Stuart seventeenth century, investitures, such as those of Prince Henry as Prince of Wales in 1612, royal marriages, executions, as well as the more overtly propagandistic royal progresses, continued to provide frames for the reification of the authoritarian ideology. Thomas Nowak's "Propaganda and the Pulpit: Robert Cecil, William Barlow, and the Essex and Gunpowder Plots" illustrates both the Crown's strategic subversion of the church, and the increasingly relational dynamic by which manifestations of the monarchy's authority were created. Barlow's sermon at Paul's Cross on the arrest and execution of Essex, bespoke by the throne through Cecil, presents in the person of Elizabeth a monarch intensely human yet untouchable. In the response to the Gunpowder Plot only four years later, Barlow, again under orders from the crown, initiated a rhetoric of deification, necessitated in part, Nowak argues, by a need to unite monarch and people in a sense of being God's chosen and therefore subject to biblical injunctions concerning authority and power. Such sermons, while they did much to invent the religious prejudice that was subsequently institutionalized in England, were also responses to culturally covert attacks upon the expectation of ideological conformity.

The sermons at Paul's Cross were public occasions, essentially political and as much theatrical as religious, although they adhered to orthodox, traditional forms. Other occasions, public and ostensibly ceremonial, also supplied through their theatricality a venue for the public performance of ideology. The Lord Mayor's pageants and the royal masques presented competing interpretations of authority and power. Not surprisingly, those who wrote for the theater found themselves writing also for these entertainments with their overtly political intentions. If King James and his court employed Jonson to create masques that confirmed them as the wellspring of authority, the Lord Mayor's pageants of Thomas Middleton could, as Ray Tumbleson shows in "Lord Mayor's Day Pageants and the Rise of the City," promote an alternate sovereignty, albeit one that is itself problematic. Two central issues are raised by the recognition that the Lord Mayor's pageants embodied an authority alternative to the king's. First, the "city," the new "sovereign," is not monolithic; city sovereignty can be commercial or parliamentary. In the early years of the century, Parliament was without authority: it met infrequently; it was unable to apply financial pressure because the king could rely on essentially feudal sources of income such as wardships and the royal prerogative to levy taxes; and it lacked, finally, the conviction of authority granted by divine right and biblical precedent only to the monarch. In this vacuum, commerce came to represent a viable institutional source of authority and, ultimately, of power. Later, combined with the moral force of a nonepiscopal Christianity and the political force of a more widely representative and more fully empowered Parliament, the commercial "city" interests would prove increasingly a threat to Charles I and an insurmountable obstacle to his sons.

The second issue raised in Tumbleson's consideration of the Lord Mayor's pageants stems from the first, which is one manifestation of it: that the tension among the commercial, the Puritan and the urban is one example of the relational nature of power. "By its nature possessed by one and exerted over another, power is not a freestanding artifact but a relation," Tumbleson writes. Increasingly, historicist readings, new or old, are revealing the magnitude of concern with the dynamics of power in literature of the seventeenth century. And increasingly, that dynamic is seen in the necessity of each party in the power relationship to invent the other. The London merchants commissioned pageants filled with silent and acquiescent "Indians" who represented their sovereignty over the world beyond England, thus giving themselves a realm far more extensive than the king's. Theirs is a relatively simple assertion of power in a relatively safe and circumscribed venue. As is the case with the Essex and Gunpowder Plot sermons, the Lord Mayor's pageants were intended to legitimize institutional authority, whether of court, church or city. Both Nowak and Tumbleson locate their readings in Stephen Greenblatt's deconstructionist, historicist concept of power that is perpetuated by the invention of what Tumbleson calls "a demonized opposition," which legitimizes the valorized source of authority at the expense of the other. In this respect, the institutional manipulation of public performance for an ideological end is, at one level, always dialectical rather than relational. The institution asserts its right to power, its authority, in the face of a discredited opposition.

The translation of the assertion of authority into the search for workable power required a more flexible format and a larger arena than Paul's Cross or the City of London pageants. Victor Turner makes the distinction between "social drama," the "primordial and perennial agonistic mode, by which contests for power are performed in the 'known world,'" and the theater, which allows us to reflect upon those contests and suggest remedies without resorting to transcendent authority.[3] For the London theater of the seventeenth century, this distinction was, in fact, a connection. In the liminality of the stage, the dynamics of power not only reflect the social drama, they invent it. On the public and private stages of London, the transmutation of abstract ideas of authority into the relational dynamic of power occurred daily.

In "Bringing Forth Wonders: Temporal and Divine Power in *The Tempest*," Heather Campbell argues that Prospero's attempt to assert his authority founders—as surely as does the Neapolitan fleet—through the inevitable subversion of even the most patently ideological of forms: the masque and the triumph. While inscribing the authoritarian assumptions of the Stuart monarchy, Shakespeare has also provided a subversive subtext. The powers Prospero assumes over nature, time and the polity are called into question precisely by the extent of his control and by the sterility of his creation. In the "second-degree process of figural articulation,"[4] the audience is able to see the illusion, the distance between Prospero's avowed motives and actions and their actual results, especially in his treatment of Miranda's marriage and the masque he arranges to celebrate it. We question both Prospero's and the Stuart court's political and aesthetic ideology. The failure to reify authority in *The Tempest*, a work initiated by the court, emphasizes how effectively the dynamics of the theater deny a dialectical representation of ideology and enable a more subtle and complex presentation of the relations of power.

Whatever the critical perspective from which the case may be argued, there is general agreement, from Tillyard to the present, that the theater of seventeenth century England was an ideological space, a venue for the invention and objectification of authority—and, increasingly, of power. The transfer of royal authority from Elizabeth to James was universally acknowledged by contemporaries, as it is recognized by historians, to have been a "moment of danger" for the seventeenth century English, a moment when history came to them through the theater. That blank space between monarchs, when time and the continuity of authority were suspended, was seen in the Stuart monarchist ideology as potentially anarchic. The analogical liminality of the theater enabled a revisioning of authority and its concomitant power in the civil realm. Douglas F. Rutledge in "The Politics of Disguise: Drama and Political Theory in the Early Seventeenth Century" explores the transforming nature of theater by examining the structures of ritual, where power may be transferred or invented. In this respect, Rutledge argues, theater's common bond with rituals of inversion and initiation makes it the ideal liminal space for the rehearsal of authority, as the disguised ruler passes through the stages of initiation—chaos and the acquisition of new knowledge—to be reinvented as worthy of authority and capable of exercising power. In the "absent ruler plays" of Middleton and Marston that appeared between 1603 and 1605, the transfer of power in rituals of initiation can safely figure a situation of transient authority and an accessory ideology that encompasses the open exercise of power. The return of legitimacy, of monarchical authority, is assured in these plays, but not before the embodiment of authority has been tested, as Prospero is. That Rutledge sees a more conservative outcome than Campbell may be due in part to his merging of structuralist and historicist methodology. Authority, like ritual, consolidates; power, such as Prospero assumes he has, deconstructs into potentially unstable relations.

While royal authority might be subverted when represented in the masque of Prospero, the monarchy was still monolithic, a single institutional voice. The authority of the city, on the other hand, was fragmented among sometimes overlapping elements of the population. Under Elizabeth and James I, city power was largely commercial power, and commercial interests rarely spoke with a single voice. Lacking the long royal tradition of authority divinely bestowed, the merchants, more than any other group in this period, found themselves with the power to pursue the good life in an institutional context, but without an adequate rationalization for the methods they could best employ. The ideology of capitalism had to be invented and valorized. In "Angels, Alchemists, and Exchange: Commercial Ideology in Court and City Comedy, 1596–1610," Catherine Gimelli Martin mediates between dialectical and revolutionary Marxist historicism and Greenblatt's unitary theory of containment-displacement and absorption[5] to read two works that appear to reject the bourgeois, capitalist ideology. Rather than viewing *The Alchemist* and *The Merchant of Venice* as portraits of pathological acquisitiveness, Martin argues that these works establish the value of exchange, which is essentially the medium of the rising bourgeois ideology and, significantly, a relational medium wherein "worth alters according to circumstance." Essential to exchange, and indeed to capitalism, is the liberal concept of individual autonomy, which also informs Arthur Kinney's reading of *Macbeth* in "Imagination and Ideology." Kinney sets out to examine not the absent but the self-authorizing monarch, showing us the imagining of history by Macbeth who, before "rehearsing authority," invents and appropriates it. According to Kinney, Macbeth's formulation of his ideology of authority is safely situated within the context of rebellion against tyranny, an idea long validated by the English tradition, that is liberated by the dynamics of theater, by the interaction between what is acted and what is known by the audience.

While Kinney establishes the necessity of a preexisting ideology in an apparently autonomous individual, the need of the imagination for "some culturally shaping beliefs in order to exist," Sharon Achinstein approaches the issue of cultural icons and their effect on the individual imagination from the perspective of the institution. In "The Uses of Deception: From Cromwell to Milton," she documents the considerable attention paid to shaping the imagination by exposing the individual to a correctly figured ideology. Specifically, she directs our attention to the images of sight, the emphasis placed by the "pen men" of the English Revolution on having readers see the "true" story among the many conflicting ideological configurations of events. This rhetorical strategy is based on the presupposition that the individual is a "site of conflict" whose critical reading of authority needed to be controlled if power were to be exercised within the constraints of a given ideology. The individual's power to imagine experience based on what she/ he reads is central to the relational manipulation of power that would characterize post-Reformation/post-Cromwellian society. Public writing, the exercise of propaganda, served as a focal point for the struggle to control the individual's choice.

The creation of propaganda is one half of the dialectic that concerns us now, just as vitally as it engaged those who experienced it in the years between 1590 and 1688; the other half is censorship. Along with its contemporary broad application that encompasses any attempt to silence or control public utterance, censorship in the seventeenth century was dominated by the attempt to prevent the perception that the exercise of power by the individual could be efficacious without the authority of the institution. The propaganda examined by Achinstein is to a large extent "mainstream"; that is, it originates centrally, is clearly identified with a specific ideological stance, and is disseminated throughout the population with the support of whichever group or institution it represents. It is public and overtly motivational and seeks to shape the amorphous power of newly enfranchised groups. In "Lady Falkland's Reentry into Writing: Anglo-Catholic Consensual Discourse and her *Edward II* as Historical Fiction," Louise Schleiner traces consent and subversion in Lady Falkland's works, looking at the private and largely suppressed writings of one who was at once an insider and a marginal member of her world. Lady Falkland's translations, the drama *Mariam*, the prose history of *Edward II* and the poetry are all in some form manifestations of the dialectical confrontation between the powerful and the powerless, both at the level of discourse and in their relation to the events reported as history. Silenced because she was a woman and a Catholic, Lady Falkland began to write at that point when the "consensual discourse" of her aristocratic Catholic circle began to disintegrate. Through such "paratextual" forms as the translation of religious polemic and the "historical relation," she is able to iterate the ideology of monarchist authority, while subverting that ideology through a self-censoring discourse of analogy and irony. Schleiner places Lady Falkland's writings in the context of her periods of depression, responses to a loss of control over her life and even her person, thus locating in her work the absorption with the individual which is characteristic of much seventeenth century English literature, both public and private.

Increasingly, as practical power is seen to be based in individual choice rather than institutional authority, issues of control become central. Foucault's disconcerting question, "what is an author?" seems not so new if we consider the response of Bunyan to the discipline of "authority." Sid Sondergard, in "'This Giant Has Wounded Me As Well As Thee': Reading Bunyan's Violence and/as Authority," argues that Bunyan, imprisoned for his faith, makes of the assault upon his body a source of authority, an opportunity to signify his participation in the transcendent, to "compensate for prior authority displaced by his imprisonment." Bunyan's need to empower himself—and through art, his coreligionists, by exploiting his experience of the pain of imprisonment in Restoration England represents a self-censorship of a far more subtle kind than Lady Falkland's placing her writings among her husband's papers. The violence to which he is subjected becomes in his writings a statement of Radical Protestant Christian ideology; control of his physical body by the state is merely a sign of his control over his immortal soul. Power exercised over the physical body is irrelevant to the pursuit of the good life, which is to be found only in the triumph of the righteous, a triumph described by Bunyan in terms of a violence that obliterates his enemies. In Bunyan's opposition of the powerful and powerless, each derives authority from a different source, civil law or religious faith, and directs power toward a different end: civil order or eschatalogical reassurance.

Like Bunyan's, John Milton's life spanned the years of greatest ideological uncertainty in England. Authority is increasingly problematic, but the ideology of political power is still not well understood, and his temperament responded to the fundamental political shifts of the period. As Milton's career provided a template for the changes that he saw and in which he participated, Annabel Patterson's essay, "Imagining New Worlds: Milton, Galileo and the 'Good Old Cause,'" is in many ways the keynote of this volume. Analyzing Milton's persistent, undefeated republicanism,

Patterson contends that the events of 1640–1660 extend in implication and significance far beyond those dates. The ideological struggles of seventeenth century England, triggered in large measure by the pressures of radical Protestantism on monarchical authority, have presented us with a vision that has become our own: "the transformation of the many-headed multitude into a large, literate, industrious, self-determining working class." Milton, Patterson argues, was sensitive to the difficulty of integrating "the extreme complexity of political theory, and the functional difficulty of founding a better society," and yet persisted in seeing the republican movement as the means to that end, "as valuable in the past and potentially recoverable." If The Good Old Cause validates the persistence and triumph of the liberal ideology that shapes our public policy and private culture, it also serves as a methodological paradigm.

As the essays in this volume show us, the ability to see through a multiplicity of perspectives is possibly the seventeenth century's greatest gift to us. Thus, we have not asked that all our contributors read historically in the same way; we have not demanded ideological purity. The reading of literary texts is now a house of many mansions, and while the general principles of historicism pervade the majority of these essays, it may be the case that we may see most clearly if, unlike Galileo, we do not first have to refute other ways of seeing.

# 1 • Sacred Literature and Profane Religion
## The Modernity of Herbert of Cherbury

*Michael D. Bristol*

"Aye, Policy, that's their profession, and not simplicity as they pretend" (Marlowe, 161–62).[1] For Marlowe's Barrabas the notion of policy suggests the deliberate calculation of material self-interest as well as the practice of malicious deception. Barrabas, himself an accomplished politician, is concerned here to draw attention to the Christian Governor of Malta's "policy" concealed behind a facade of private virtue and commitment to the public good. The contemporary usage of *policy* is, of course, rather different, indicating something like a plan or course of action, usually with the added sense of prudence, foresight, and so on. A public policy would be one oriented to the public interest, rather than to the private interests of the politicians. It would also be public in the sense that it is enunciated publicly rather than concealed behind a deceptive facade. In our contemporary usage of the word *politician*, however, we retain much more of the unsavory, Barabassian sense of *policy*.

One can get the full sense of this equivocal term by

considering the proverbial expression, "honesty is the best policy." Does this mean that honesty is the best, i.e., the most prudent overall plan, or is this a paradoxical statement to the effect that honesty is the best mode of deception?[2] Framed in this way, the notion of policy as it would have been understood in the sixteenth and seventeenth century is linked in important ways to the contemporary notion of ideology. Ideology is, of course, a way to make "policy" in the Barabassian sense of deception appear to be a matter of policy in the sense of action taken or proposed in the public interest.[3] Honesty, in the sense of functional equivalency to truth or plausibility, really is the best policy, in that the most effective ideology is one that appears to provide a coherent framework for effective actions.[4]

The study of sixteenth and seventeenth century literature as a function of ideological practices has become increasingly influential in recent scholarship.[5] There are a number of distinct questions implicated in this research agenda, however. First of all, it is possible to analyze the instrumental function of literature vis-à-vis the formal institutions of authority and social control. This would entail research into the way specific texts or specific authors may advance, impede or simply interpret various public policy agendas. Many of the studies that we label *new historicist* explore this question, and, at their best, these help to reestablish the worldliness of literary texts.[6] A second, more explicitly sociological orientation, takes up the question of literature as an institution and considers the system of constraints and opportunities in which literature is produced and distributed, as well as noting the effects of its circulation.[7]

A third orientation, which is the one I have adopted for this essay, explores the broader theoretical dimensions of the problem by investigating how various writers in the seventeenth century tried to answer questions about how society holds itself together over time, how it stabilizes regional disparity and other inequalities, and finally, how it regulates its own dysfunction.[8] Taken at this level, we would have to specify two preconditions for any meaningful discussion of the topic of public policy or ideology. First, the notion of public policy already presupposes a large-scale, multilayered, and contradictory social organization. More specifically, it implies some considerable degree of territorial expansion. Second, as a corollary to this, public policy presupposes some form of effective administrative and communications apparatus such that policy agendas can actually be implemented. In other words, an effective ideology requires both a set of substantive themes, images, doctrines— in short, an intellectual content of some kind—and an elaborate institutional infrastructure.[9]

In order to pursue a research agenda of this kind, it can be useful to consider marginal figures like Edward, Lord Herbert of Cherbury. As I hope to sketch out, however, the fact of his "marginality" can be a bit puzzling in that his ideas anticipate many of the widely shared norms (and contradictions) of contemporary liberal political culture. Herbert's modernity is apparent in his focus on a doctrine of *natural reason* and his rejection of revelation as a source of authority. Unlike his contemporaries, Descartes and Bacon, Herbert of Cherbury has not figured prominently in contemporary accounts of *modernism* and *modernity*.[10] And yet Herbert developed, in his varied writings, a complex, and in some respects, a highly advanced solution to the legitimation problems typical of Jacobean society. Although his approach to these legitimation problems was not taken up during his lifetime, Herbert's elaboration of a reconciliatory hermeneutics, together with his attempt to formulate a sociology of religion, anticipates the pluralism typical of contemporary bourgeois society. Herbert advocated a cultural policy of secular humanism that has become current orthodoxy, and it therefore deserves serious consideration in any discussion of early modern society and culture.

Herbert at one point aspired to a career in politics, and he served for a time as James I's Ambassador to France, but he was not an effective "politician" in the Barabassian mold.[11] Because of his failures at "policy" in this sense, Herbert devoted considerable time to the elaboration of a "public policy" organized around the key notions of religious tolerance and liberal education. The history of the publication of his works is perhaps indicative of his modernity. At least two of his important writings, the *Autobiography* and a treatise on pedagogy called *A Dialogue Between a Tutor and His Pupil*, were first published in the last third of the eighteenth century, and the autobiography has been frequently reprinted from 1764 right up to 1976.

Herbert has been styled the "father of Deism." Whether or not this epithet correctly summarizes his doctrine, it is clear that many of those who did consider themselves Deists in the eighteenth century thought of him as an early exponent of their ideas.[12] Herbert's popularity as a thinker at the time of the Enlightenment is, I think, suggestive in many ways, but I will be less concerned with a description of his metaphysics than with an attempt to understand the sociological concerns that motivated his philosophy. In the discussion that follows, I present a very brief sketch of the typical legitimation problems faced by James I during his reign. I then move on to discuss certain aspects of Herbert's *Autobiography*, in order to clarify just where he was situated in the complex social landscape of Jacobean England. Finally, I will analyze the salient features of Herbert's philosophy, with the aim of clarifying how his views on the common notions found in all world religions represent a type of cultural policy that is still widely prevalent in the contemporary world.

I

The typical debates on public policy in the Jacobean regime were related to problems of legitimation and specifically to the task of legitimating a new dynasty committed to far-reaching political innovation.[13] James I pursued a successful policy in securing the succession to the Crown, but this was only the beginning of his problems. The territorial expansion of the English nation and the extension of the authority of the English Crown into the northern hinterland had to be carried out—by a Scot, no less—as a narrative of the restoration of a United Kingdom.[14] In addition, he was faced with increasingly exacerbated social and economic tensions.[15] Finally, both the political and the religious institutions of the nation were sites of potentially explosive disagreement.[16] At a very basic level, I believe James understood the problems of public policy that this situation entailed for his administration. In other words, he knew that *policy* in both the modern and in the Barabassian sense would be needed if the latent and very precarious instabilities in his society were to be regulated in any kind of long-term way. One way to interpret James's varied pronouncements on royal authority is to see his career as an attempt to build and maintain what we would now call an ideological state apparatus.[17]

James understood, in the way that politicians do, the fundamental importance of religion in preserving social stability. Chronic social antagonisms could not be eliminated simply by royal decree. Ethnic differences were more amenable to adjudication, however, and James took particular care to ensure the peaceful integration of the Scottish nobility into his new United Kingdom.[18] Differences in basic beliefs were, at least in James's own mind, subject to administrative regulation, and so he adopted the policy whereby he would unify his kingdom in and through the medium of religious doctrine. His primary strategy as the builder of an ideological apparatus, however, was to make a centralized church the exclusive institutional embodiment of religious authority. James counted on this policy as a way to achieve the peaceful integration of the many disparate elements of his kingdom, but in the end the coercive means he adopted to achieve his ends intensified an already divisive and violent religious conflict. Here public policy as ideology proved inadequate, and in the end James did not have sufficient resources to enforce uniformity of belief, even by coercive means. The legitimacy of absolute rule was actively contested throughout James's reign primarily as a matter of religious principle, or, to put it another way, religion became increasingly politicized.

James's difficulty with respect to religion was compounded by his tendency to rely on the court—that is to say, the traditional aristocracy—for the formation of his elite cadres.

Many of the legitimation problems of Jacobean England stem from the difficulty of integrating a traditional elite, who enjoyed considerable local political autonomy, into a centralized state apparatus. On the face of it, such integration would seem an ill-advised project to attempt, not only because the local barons would have something to lose with the advance of the administrative state, but also because the political sensibility of a traditional aristocracy—its preoccupation with social precedence and personal dignity, for example—is incompatible with the norms of rational efficiency required by the managerial function.[19] The demands of the public policy mission make it seem unlikely that most aristocrats could ever become reliable and effective managers. The theory of absolute monarchy that we associate with James, if fully carried out, would really demand the *suppression* of a traditional aristocracy in favor of a more disciplined and uniformly trained bureaucracy.

James was himself a traditional aristocrat, and his difficulties as a politician are directly related to the typical political sensibility of his own social class. That sensibility entails, among other things, exaggerated sexual egotism, a clannish sense of loyalty, and the proliferation of impulsive, irrational rivalries. In her extensive and detailed study of James's court, Linda Levy Peck has shown that the system of patronage that was used to organize and manage relations among the governing elite was based on fundamental contradictions. The most fundamental of these structural rifts was the tension between the notions of *office* and of *gift*.[20]

The main practical duty of the aristocracy was to act as local magistrates and to administer justice. This obligation was defined as an *office* and required that judges refrain from partiality and the taking of bribes. To discharge an office, the magistrate had to distance himself from friends and, in fact, from all feelings of personal obligation and indebtedness. At the same time, however, the local magistrates were also deeply involved in complex networks of gift exchange, the primary means through which power, status and affiliation were acknowledged, confirmed, and at times re-negotiated. The *gift* was of fundamental importance as a social ligature, but the relations created in and through this medium of exchange were fundamentally at odds with the principles of *office*. Because James's court was a particularly dense and complicated network of patronage relations, the corruption of office became endemic. The difference between a gift required by the hierarchical systems of precedence relations and a simple and direct bribe of a public official had always been a sensitive matter. Under James, however, the sale of offices became much more a matter of public scandal than in earlier reigns, and this was partly a result of the conflict between the customary practices of an aristocratic court culture and the increasingly complex demands of the administrative state.[21]

Finally, there was a lack of clarity with respect to the purpose of the state apparatus that James wanted to create. James had many specific policy aims in view, such as building up the Royal Navy and negotiating advantageous marriages for his children. His only consistent public policy, however, was to assure peace and harmony throughout the United Kingdom. For James the question of legitimacy had nothing whatever to do with notions like the *consent* of the governed. Since James, like a number of his predecessors, believed that his authority came directly from God, the only serious question of public order was how to guarantee the *obedience* of the governed, with or without their consent. In the end, the policy of absolute rule and enforced consent proved absolutely catastrophic, and an alternative foundation for legitimacy had to be constructed. One such alternative proposal can be found in the writings of Edward, Lord Herbert of Cherbury.


## II


Edward, Lord Herbert of Cherbury was the eldest son of Richard and Magdalen Herbert, and the older brother of George Herbert. His family held important estates in Wales, and Herbert was extremely proud of his lineage.[22] Like his younger sibling, Edward was a poet, and indeed to many literary scholars he is best known as a significant "Minor Poet of the Seventeenth Century." For Edward, however, poetry was strictly an avocational interest, though not a trivial one, since the writing of poetry proved to be an important form of socialization as well as the medium in which he could express his somewhat atypical philosophical interests.

Edward Herbert belonged to the cadet branch of the illustrious Herbert family, and so he was not a lineal descendant of the Earls of Pembroke. His father, though very prominent in Montgomeryshire, was untitled. Herbert's somewhat limited prospects improved considerably when, at about the age of 15, he was married to Mary Herbert, the heiress of "the old Earl of Pembroke." Sir William Herbert, Mary's father, had made a will leaving all his estates in Monmouthsire and Ireland to his daughter on the condition that she marry someone with the surname Herbert.[23] By this provision, Sir William could assure that both the Herbert name *and* the Herbert estates would remain in his posterity through his own daughter. Although his eventual children stood to benefit from these arrangements, Edward Herbert himself did not. However, he was evidently quite satisfied with this marriage of convenience, and in his own mind at least, he "lived most honestly" with his wife for many years (*Autobiography*, 47).

Shortly after his marriage he returned to Oxford, accompanied by his wife and his mother to resume the studies that had been interrupted by the death of his father in 1596. Although he was devoted to his mother, his feelings for Mary Herbert were chilly at best. This was a marriage of convenience in more ways than one.

> . . . I went again to Oxford, together with my wife and mother, who took a house, and lived for some certain time there, and now, having a due remedy for that lasciviousness to which youth is naturally inclined, I followed my book more close than ever, in which course I continued until I attained the age of eighteen, when my mother took a house in London, between which place and Montgomery Castle I passed my time till I came to the age of one-and-twenty,

having in that space divers children, I having now none remaining but Beatrice, Richard and Edward. (*Autobiography*, 23)

Although he appears to have been a faithful husband and a conscientious provider for his family, never once, as far as I can discover, does he express any affection for Mary Herbert. By providing him with a solution to the problem of his sexual needs, Mary Herbert allowed him to focus more effectively on his education, which seems to have been a central interest throughout his life.

In 1608 Herbert approached his wife with a proposal whereby each of the partners would provide a substantial amount of property to their son. Mary Herbert refused, saying "that she would not draw the cradle upon her head," (*Autobiography*, 47). Herbert persisted, however, and shortly afterward renewed the proposal, this time in the form of an ultimatum:

> About a week or ten days afterwards, I demanded again what she thought concerning the motion I made; to which yet she said no more, but that she thought she had already answered me sufficiently to the point. I told her then, that I should make another motion to her; which was, that in regard I was too young to go beyond sea before I married her, she now would give me leave for a while to see foreign countries; howbeit, if she would assure her lands as I would mine, in the manner above-mentioned, I would never depart from her. She answered, that I knew her mind before concerning that point, yet that she should be sorry I went beyond sea; nevertheless, if I would needs go, she could not help it. This, whether a license taken or given, served my turn to prepare without delay for a journey beyond sea, that so I might satisfy that curiosity I long since had to see foreign countries. (*Autobiography*, 47)

Herbert is not entirely candid about his real motives in this affair, although it does appear that the proposal about the lands and estates was a strategic move on his part to compel Mary's agreeing to his departure. Despite the unfeeling calculation that apparently characterized his relations with his wife, however, Herbert was evidently satisfied that he left her "as little discontented as I could," that is, with both posterity and "the rents of all the lands she brought with her" (*Autobiography*, 47).

Herbert himself now enjoyed a remarkable degree of personal autonomy and independence. His brothers and sisters as well as his wife and children were fully provided for. In addition, he no longer felt obligated to perform any unwelcome domestic or conjugal duties. Nor did Herbert have any compelling sense of vocation. Unlike his brother George, he was not imbued with any passionate faith, and wasted little time in anguishing over his religious doubts. The details of Christian belief and observance were a matter of almost complete indifference, although he was evidently satisfied to conform with the Anglican religion. However, to judge from his *Autobiography*, Herbert's primary vocation was not religion but a type of sexual egotism or gallantry in which he styled himself as the defender and champion of ladies who were insulted by what we might today regard as sexual harassment.

During his first visit to France, Herbert had occasion to exchange visits with the Duke and Duchess of Ventadour at the country estate of the Duchess's father. One evening a small company of courtiers and young women took a walk in the meadows, where "a French chevalier" took the liberty of snatching the hair ribbon of the young daughter of his host and fastening it to his hatband. She was offended by this, and asked Herbert to intervene on her behalf.

> Hereupon, going towards him, I courteously, with my hat in my hand, desired him to do me the honour, that I may deliver the lady her ribbon or bouquet again; but he roughly answering me, "Do you think I will give it you, when I have refused it to her?" I replied, "Nay then, sir, I will make you restore it by force," wherupon also, putting on my hat and reaching at his, he to save himself ran away, and, after a long course in the meadow, finding that I had almost overtook him, he turned short, and running to the young lady, was about to put the ribbon on her hand, when I seizing upon his arm, said to the young lady, "It was I that gave it."

"Pardon me," quoth she, "it is he that gives it me." I said then, "Madam I will not contradict you; but if he dare say that I did not constrain him to give it, I will fight with him" . . . . I proceeded in that manner, because I thought myself obliged thereunto by the oath taken when I was made Knight of the Bath, as I formerly related upon this occasion. (*Autobiography*, 49–50)

The episode is clearly intended to advertise Herbert's boldness and gallantry, and he goes on to recount three similar episodes. The real focus throughout these incidents is on his ability to triumph over a male rival, all of whom decline Herbert's challenge to fight. Incidentally, Herbert seems to have had a bit of an obsession about hair ribbons, as he evidently became embroiled in a similar affair "in a back room behind Queen Anne's lodgings in Greenwich" a number of years later (*Autobiography*, 51).[24]

Serious religious vocation is absent in Herbert, although he does show genuine interest in a secular career, but he does not seem to have had some of the skills needed to sustain his ambitions as a courtier. He had been well received as a young man at the court of Elizabeth. His career at the court of James also began well, and at one point he emerged as a rising star with his appointment by James as ambassador to the French court. But courtiership requires skillful compromise, an ability at intrigue and a significant degree of self-effacement. Herbert was himself more sovereign than courtier, and so his diplomatic career was destined to be abruptly curtailed. According to Sir Sidney Lee, who wrote a continuation of Herbert's *Autobiography*, Herbert was too outspoken a critic of certain international policies devised by James, which he regarded as "fatuous" (*Autobiography*, 136). The same unrestrained "freedom of speech" was equally annoying to the French (*Autobiography*, 137). In 1624, during the complex and sensitive negotiations over the marriage of Prince Charles to Princess Henrietta Maria, James suddenly decided to dismiss his overly candid minister. Herbert spent the latter part of his life trying to recoup his political fortunes and composing the various philosophical treatises, the basis for his very belated reputation as a philosopher with decidedly "modern" views.

In speaking of Herbert's modernity, I do not want to imply that he was in some self-conscious way ahead of his time, or that he was motivated by a utopian wish for social amelioration. There is no meaningful sense in which he could be described as progressively minded. And, in fact, a reading of his autobiography reveals the same aristocratic political sensibility that I have already described in connection with James I. The personal vanity expressed here in the affair of the ribbon is related to a more diffuse vanity of family prestige. Herbert, greatly preoccupied with the dignity of his ancestors, cherishes a sense of grievance for any and all slights to family honor committed in the past.

Herbert's obsessive concern with the honor of his lineage is equally apparent in the way he talks about the achievements of his own brothers, Henry (the courtier), George (the saint), Richard (the sea captain) and so on, as if to say, "We Herberts still count for something in this world!" (*Autobiography*, 11). I stress these aspects of Herbert's political sensibility because I want to insist that his views do not reflect an "emergent" consciousness and that he is not a representative of the "rising bourgeoisie" that figures so prominently in the Marxist account of the early modern subject. The elements in his philosophical outlook that appear to be typically modern are derived from an exacerbated aristocratic *ressentiment* and from a desire for recognition and personal vindication.

Herbert's individual autonomy, his ability to achieve an unusual level of self-government and of self-determination, are clearly the product of his aristocratic circumstances. Unlike his bourgeois contemporaries, Herbert displays neither loyalty to the work ethic nor any interest in economic accumulation. His highly developed sense of personal freedom is used in the interests of personal self-development and self-actualization, which Herbert understood primarily as a search for knowledge and for truth.

## III

The various treatises produced by Edward Herbert after his enforced retirement from his diplomatic career have neither the rigor nor the clarity of his better-known contemporaries in philosophy. His arguments are often diffuse, and they are based on somewhat eclectic sources. There is apparently not much doubt, however, that Herbert, despite his arrogance and his quarrelsome disposition, had a philosophical temperament, even as a child.

> The very furthest thing I remember, is, that when I understood what was said by others, I did yet forbear to speak, lest I should utter something that were imperfect or impertinent. When I came to talk, one of the furthest inquiries I made was, how I came into this world? I told my nurse, keeper, and others, I found myself here indeed, but from what cause or beginning, or by what means, I could not imagine; but for this, as I was laughed at by nurse, and some other women that were then present, so I was wondered at by others, who said, they never heard a child but myself ask that question; upon which, when I came to riper years, I made this observation, which afterwards a little comforted me, that, as I found myself in possession of this life, without knowing anything of the pangs and throes my mother suffered, yet, doubtless, they did not less press and afflict me than her, so I hope my soul shall pass to a better life than this without being sensible of the anguish and pains my body shall feel in death. (*Autobiography*, 15–16)

This passage contains the most basic intuition of Herbert's philosophy as developed in *De Veritate* and his later treatises. Like Descartes, Herbert derives a principle of self-certainty from his own ignorance and doubt about his origins. Unlike Descartes, however, he does not conceive of radical doubt in the form of stratagems of a *malin génie*, and therefore he does not achieve the melodrama of the Cartesian *cogito*. To the contrary, Herbert is evidently certain as to the "pangs and throes my mother suffered," even though he could not have been able to witness them.[25]

*De Veritate* is Herbert's attempt to discern or discover

a rational—and therefore a universally binding—account of truth and knowledge. The anxious and acrimonious social divisions created by the activities of manifold contending sects is what motivates this project, but the argument here is primarily metaphysical rather than strictly political. Herbert adopts a moderate position on the question of knowledge, rejecting both the dogmatic certainties of faith as well as the principled ignorance of skepticism:

> Now I hold neither that we can know everything, nor that we can know nothing; but I think there are some things which can be known. And they are those which are testified to by the presence of a faculty, though the faculty and the object are not necessarily in conformity with each other even when they are both present. For unless the intermediate conditions are favourable, each factor is confined to its own sphere. Accordingly I hold that truth, being a matter of conformity between objects and faculties, is highly conditional.[26]

There are two fundamental principles that make possible this moderate, fallible and limited capacity for knowledge. First, objects and states of affairs actually exist, or, as Herbert puts it, "everything remains constant with itself" (*De Veritate*, 88). Second, human beings possess basic faculties such that the perception of objects can be brought into conformity with the truth of objects, at least provisionally.

The doctrine of the faculties gives rise to the principle of the *Common Notions*, an idea central both to Herbert's overarching metaphysical beliefs and to his more specific historical consideration of religious difference. Unfortunately, this idea, though central, is not always clear and consistent. Herbert's discussion of this concept is vague with respect to both the nature of the Common Notions and their origins. Although the Common Notions are linked at one point to the idea of *Universal Consent*, Herbert is very far from adopting a consensus theory of truth. The commonness of Common Notions amounts to a confirmation of their truth, but it is not the underlying reason for their truth.

The universality of the Common Notions follows from

the basic conformity between objects and perception: "All truth according to this doctrine consists of conformity. And since all conformity consists of a relation, it follows that all instances of truth will be relations, or aptitudes realized in act, that is in perception" (*De Veritate*, 88). But if truth is a relation and therefore always and everywhere conditional, then it is not clear how the universality of the Common Notions emerges out of the manifold local interpretations of a diverse and changing world. At one point Herbert even concedes that "it is the nature of natural instinct to fulfil itself irrationally, that is to say without foresight" (*De Veritate*, 120). Nevertheless, Herbert maintained that the systematic elaboration of the Common Notions would lead to "the attainment of universal harmony" (*De Veritate*, 121).

Herbert's account of the origin or the derivation of the Common Notions is also somewhat unclear. At times the Common Notions are described as if they are in some way identical with the basic faculties, especially the faculty of *Natural Instinct*. This would imply that the Notions are themselves innate or "hard-wired." At other times the Common Notions seem to be the outcome of an interaction between the faculties, which are in fact "hard-wired," and the underlying regularities in metaphysical as well as physical realities: "I do not then call these notions common because they are revealed in every man, whether he will or no; they are termed common because they would be so but for the fact that we ourselves prevent them entering our minds" (*De Veritate*, 126–27). In any case, Herbert advances the Common Notions against all parochial accounts of truth, most of which are "hindered by prejudice" (*De Veritate*, 126).

The Common Notions themselves are a somewhat eclectic aggregation of very basic categories such as order, degree and change, combined with ethical precepts (the law of self-preservation) and metaphysical beliefs (there is a first cause and final purpose of the world). Despite what we would now construe as a lack of rigor, elegance and precision in the formulation of his basic doctrine, Herbert is very clear about the value and the preeminence of a universally binding truth disclosed by way of the Common Notions. Although this truth certainly exists, access to it is difficult and requires a disciplined overcoming of prejudice. This is expressed in Herbert's best known poetry, especially the sonnets on "Black Beauty" and "Black Itself."

For Herbert, truth is not openly manifested in the appearance of things, nor is it available by way of unexamined common opinion. In this sense truth is dark or hidden. Herbert's privileged metaphor for this understanding of truth is the optical condition of blackness, which is distinguished "above that common light" as constant and unvarying (Poems, 38).

> And like an object equal to the view,
> Art neither chang'd with day, nor hid with night;
> When all these colours which the world call bright,
> And which old Poetry do so persue,
> Are with the night so perished and gone,
> That of their being there remains no mark,
> Thou still abidest so intirely one,
> That we may know thy blackness is a spark
> Of light inaccessible, and alone
> Our darkness which can make us think it dark.[27]
>
> (*Poems*, 38)

Among other things, this poem may express Herbert's view of institutional religion. The forms of appearance of religion are "colours which the world call bright." These forms of appearance, together with the "old Poetry" of religious myth, liturgy and ritual, all belong to the specious light of common opinion, which is in the end subdued by Black, "wherein all colours are composed, / And unto which they all at last return" (*Poems*, 39).

The seductive and dazzling colors of common opinion are a hindrance to knowledge, as they obscure the truth of the Common Notions. Herbert's sharpest criticism, therefore, is directed against the doctrine of implicit faith or revelation:

> Anything that springs from the productive, so to say seductive seed of Faith will yield a plentiful crop. What pompous

charlatan can fail to impress his ragged flock with such ideas? Is there any fantastic cult which may not be proclaimed under such auspices? (*De Veritate,* 289)

Against the arguments of infallibility and the consequent rejection of human reason and judgment found in various church doctrines, Herbert advocates a form of universal religious belief based on a special set of religious common notions. These common notions are:

1. There is a supreme God (*De Veritate,* 291).
2. This sovereign deity ought to be Worshipped (*De Veritate,* 293).
3. The connection of Virtue with Piety, defined in this work as the right conformation of the faculties, is and always has been held to be, the most important part of religious practice (*De Veritate,* 296).
4. The minds of men have always been filled with horror for their wickedness. Their vices and crimes have been obvious to them. They must be expiated by repentance (*De Veritate,* 298).
5. There is a reward or Punishment after this life (*De Veritate,* 300).

Herbert supports this with evidence drawn from his study of both ancient religious belief and of contemporaneous non-Christian religions.

Although *De Veritate* was completed after his retirement from active engagement in politics and in diplomacy, Herbert was clearly a man of the world, and I would want to stress that his writings speak very forcefully to his own historical moment. Specifically, his doctrine of natural religion and of the theological *a priori* expressed in the idea of the religious Common Notions is clearly prompted by the incessant religious strife and by the massive derangement of European society that we know as the Thirty Years' War. He writes:

What, namely, shall the layman, encompassed by the terrors of divers churches militant throughout the world, decide as to the best religion? For there is no church that does not breathe threats, none almost that does not deny the possibility of salvation outside its own pale. (*De Religione,* 87)[28]

Given the omnipresence of violence and intimidation as the fundamental policy of every system of religious institutions, Herbert undertakes a critique of faith, "which the Wayfarer will not easily distinguish from any notorious credulity" (*De Religione*, 89). The criticism of faith, or "notorious incredulity," must, however, be reconciled with the most fundamental of the religious common notions—that is, with the assertion that a supreme God exists.

Herbert's conception of a theological *a priori*, derived from his study of non-European religions, emphasizes a group of common beliefs as the fundamental substratum of the many disparate cults found all over the world. These beliefs are accessible to reason, even when they are concealed by extreme differences in their typical forms of expression. No matter how bizarre the theology or how degraded the ritual practices of exotic religious cults may appear to outsiders, they nevertheless reflect an underlying commitment to a core of stable truths. Even the abominations practiced in the pagan sects reflect this deeper understructure of common belief, which in Herbert's analysis is universally inscribed in human rationality.

In this interpretation of religion, Herbert recognizes the binding character of sectarian belief in the way the cult sustains the feeling of collective identity. What is novel here, however, is the view that there is a wider sense of community, of general human interests, accessible through the principles inscribed in the theological *a priori*. This analysis leads inevitably to notions of inwardness, private religiosity and rational tolerance in official state policy toward matters of belief. It also leads to a flat rejection of the claim of any parochial tradition to sovereign authority over these matters. For Herbert, of course, the notion of tradition is explicitly linked to the institutional form of religion and in particular to the institution of the priesthood.

In his poetry and his writings on pedagogy, Herbert of Cherbury maps a shift of the media in which political authority is sustained, from the sphere of religious discipline to the sphere of literary culture and education. Herbert's ideas about the refusal of tradition lead to a consideration of a substantive curriculum organized around mathematics, philosophy and divinity, though this last category is construed philosophically in accordance with the principles of the theological *a priori*.[29] Although the authority of tradition is to be abandoned, some equivalent for the binding function of tradition within the parochial social life-world Herbert still inhabited remained a fundamental imperative in his world-consciousness. We recognize that functional equivalence today as something we like to call our "cultural tradition," though strictly speaking this purely secular manifestation of collective identity has little to do with the authoritative nature of tradition, at least in the sense intended by Edward Herbert. Within the urban and courtly coteries of seventeenth century London, the writing and circulation of poetry facilitated communication within the elite milieu without the risks of social violence that ensue from adherence to revealed religion. In the more developed variant worked out by Herbert of Cherbury, a broader secular culture—that includes scientific research as well as a universal hermeneutic—assumes the much larger task of providing for social continuity and collective identity. In a sense, this collapses the category of religion into the category of literature, and comparative literature at that.

The cultural policy implications of Herbert of Cherbury's ideas were not adequately grasped in the early seventeenth century, probably not even by Herbert himself. His valorization of reason, together with his repudiation of tradition as the primary source of cultural and social authority, anticipates the principles of contemporary orthodox pluralism. This is not, however, an extreme variant of pluralism or relativism, since the central principle of rational tolerance is founded on universally binding truths. What is envisioned here, I would suggest, is first of all the privatization of religion and religiosity (as opposed to its abolition), and second, a corresponding "sacralization" of culture as the basis of social discipline. This public policy did not, however, emerge out of any "emancipatory interests," since it is clear that Herbert's proposals were intended to conserve the position of traditional elites even after the collapse of traditional society.

Nevertheless, Herbert's writings remain important as an early analysis of the principles of universality and ecumenical tolerance as the most promising policy orientation toward chronic social violence.

# 2 • Propaganda and the Pulpit
## Robert Cecil, William Barlow
## and the Essex and Gunpowder Plots

*Thomas S. Nowak*

On 10 November 1605, William Barlow, Bishop of Rochester, mounted the outdoor pulpit at St. Paul's Cathedral in a state of nervous bewilderment, for he realized that it was only through the direct intervention of God that he now stood there before his captivated audience. Five days earlier, Guy Fawkes, an English Catholic and soldier of fortune, had planned to blow up Parliament with 36 barrels of gunpowder hidden in a rented cellar directly beneath the House of Lords (Williamson, 252.) Fawkes and his 12 co-conspirators had chosen 5 November because it was the first day of the new session of Parliament, and thus they could kill with one blow not only the combined members of both Houses, but also those attending the opening ceremonies: King James, his wife and eldest son, his counselors and secretaries, and the Bishops of England—including Barlow himself (185). Rumors about the plot must have run rampant throughout the streets of London over the next several days: but on the following Sunday, Barlow, acting upon government orders, delivered a sermon that gave the people their first detailed description of the plot and its aftermath, a description that is still accepted as being largely accurate by most historians and English men and women today.[1]

Paul's Cross (as the Cathedral's outdoor pulpit was generally known) was used by the government throughout its history as a means of spreading news and/or propaganda. Millar Maclure notes that when "the cross is first mentioned in surviving documents, it is rather a place of assembly for the hearing of proclamations that a preaching place." The earliest documented example of the Cross' political role is 1241 when Henry III consulted there with his subjects about a proposed visit to Gascony during a war in France.[2] Closer to the period of this study, Henry VIII used the Cross with various degrees of effectiveness in the establishment of his own national church, first with the goal of settling himself as this church's head, and secondly validating its new doctrines (Maclure, 20–25). During the Edwardian Reformation, attacks against the traditional rituals and beliefs ot Roman Catholicism continued, the hardest hit being the veneration of images and the worship of "idols" such as the Host (40–42). Queen Mary's counselors, unlike the counselors of her father and brother, failed to realize the political potential of the Cross during her five-year reign. Though sermons were preached that sought to restore the Church of Rome to England, Paul's Cross was primarily reserved for pageantry (49). In comparison with these earlier periods, Elizabeth's reign represented an era of political and religious stability. This allowed crises or controversies that arose in either the government or the church to be handled at the Cross as they appeared. Maclure points out that these Elizabethan sermons possess "a singular preoccupation with what in our time is called *security*, with the theme of unity and the power and happiness which attend and justify it" (86). One such call for unity, delivered during a time of national crisis, first brought William Barlow, Elizabeth's chaplain and favorite preacher, to the public's attention.

Barlow delivered two sermons on the character of Robert Devereux, Earl of Essex, national hero and traitor, under two very different sets of circumstances. The first sermon, preached before a large and enthusiastic audience at Paul's Cross despite resistance from the Crown, praised the earl upon his triumphant return following his capture of Cadiz, Spain in 1596. While this oration is no longer extant, its excessive praise is attested to both by reports of the crowd's boisterous response and Elizabeth's increased disfavor toward the Earl of Essex. The sermon itself was ordered by John Whitgift, Essex's tutor at Trinity College, Cambridge, and Archbishop of Canterbury, whose plan for a national celebration had been confined to the London area by the queen and her advisers, including Essex's chief rival, Robert Cecil, Elizabeth's new Secretary of State. Perhaps more daring than this praise, however, is Barlow's supposed criticism of Essex's detractors.[3] While Cecil's name presumably would not have been mentioned, many in Barlow's audience must have heard rumors of the rivalry between the young hero and the "hunchbacked dwarf," as many in London saw Cecil; and they must have given the anonymous target of these criticisms a name.

Five years later, however, Cecil was virtually in complete control of the government, while Essex's head, to use Barlow's words, "was seuered from his bodie by the axe at three stroakes" on 25, February 1601.[4] Despite his failed attempt to seize Whitehall and the queen, Essex retained his popularity even after his death, as evidenced by the narrow escape of Derrick, his executioner, from the hands of an angry mob soon after the event, as well as by the publication of several ballads and pamphlets apologizing to various degrees for Essex's actions (Lacey, 3, 318). Cecil, who had been accused by Essex of supporting the Spanish Infanta's right to succeed Elizabeth and who was directly blamed by many for the earl's death (306–11), now found himself in the difficult position of having to justify to the populace the earl's execution.[5] For this thankless task, Cecil turned to the man who five years earlier had defied the government in his public praise of Essex, namely William Barlow.

To say that Barlow was simply a mouthpiece for the official government position would not be an overstatement, for

Cecil had issued to Barlow a thorough set of instructions—a virtual sermon outline—which the ambitious young preacher followed to the tee. Barlow, as Elizabeth's chaplain and one of her favorite preachers, was quickly coming to learn the benefits of royal preferment! In order to appreciate how much the final product was Cecil's own, it would be best to reproduce his letter in full:

> I leave all the things which I have delivered you by my Lord's direction to be carried and applied as you like, only the Lords desire that when you touch the practice and purpose of coming to Court with a power, you move them to consider how perilous a thing it was to have put a lady, a Queen, in that fright she must have been in: for when it was appointed that Sir Christ. Blount with one company should seize the gate, another company should possess the hall with Sir John Davies, and a third should master the guard by seizing the halberts in the guard chamber, and Sir Ch. Danvers master the presence chamber with another company, how can it be imagined but some resistance would be made? Blood once drawn, more would have followed, which would be no small horror to the Queen's nature. Neither can it be expected that these three commanders, Blount, Davies, and Ch. Danvers, whereof the first two are proved to be Papists, and the third that way affected, would have cared much to commit any insolence rather than be frustrated in their designs. That this was true the Earl penitently confessed, also the Earl of Southampton, Sir Ch. Danvers, and Sir Ferd. Gorges (all men yet untried), confess it.
>
> Yet the Earl ever protested that when he entered into the purpose, and sent the articles to be considered of at Drury House, he ever resolved to have all things done with as little blood as could be; and for the Queen's own person, would never have suffered it to receive any harm.
>
> In anywise remember to name the particulars of his obstinate speeches to Mr. Dove, which my Lord of London can deliver you. Remember also precisely to declare it, so as it may be clearly conceived how great suit the Earl made that he might die privately in the Tower, and how much he even to yourself expressed his thankfulness for it, wherein also you may not forget how himself was possessed with an opinion that he should have had of the people a great

acclamation. If you can bring it in well, it will be very fit
to remember that his purpose of taking the Tower was only
to have been a bridle to the city, if happily the city should
have misliked his other attempt.[6]

Cecil was not simply acting overcautiously in his issuance
of such detailed instructions, for he knew from past experience that while the pulpit was a powerful weapon for the
broadcasting of government propaganda, it could easily misfire
if not handled carefully. Such was the case immediately
following Essex's arrest, as testified to by a contemporary
letter by Vincent Hussey. Before the trial began, the Star
Chamber had ordered all of the churches in London to publicly
"decry the Earl as a hypocrite, Papist, and confederate with
the Pope and King of Spain, to make him King and bring
in idolatry." Some preachers had taken these exaggerations
of his crime and amplified them "from malice of desire to
please . . . beyond all probability," while other preachers "it
is rumored . . . will rise and deliver him out of the Tower".[7]
The content of these sermons made the Star Chamber realize
that while much of the public supported the Crown's position, there was more than enough support for the earl to
be a matter of much concern. Obviously, the government's
strategy misfired because it depended upon the cooperation
and talents of every preacher in the country. This failure
did make the government's officials realize, however, that
in order to keep any future sympathy to a minimum, they
would have to reduce the charges against Essex to a more
realistic level.

If Essex was a threat during his imprisonment because
of the risk he represented as a potential rallying point for
the disaffected men of both extremes, Catholic and Puritan,
how much more dangerous would he prove to be as a martyr?
Cecil had no intention to find out, and he immediately set
to work to head off any upsurge of public sympathy, or
worse, before it could begin. Learning from the mistake of
the previous two weeks, Cecil turned to only one man to
explain and excuse the Crown's actions the Sunday after
the earl's execution. Barlow was the perfect man for this

task, for he had attended Essex during his final days, and was present at his semiprivate execution in the Tower. Such firsthand information, shaped and controlled by Cecil's precise instructions and preached just once before a large crowd at Paul's Cross, would help to decrease the chances of wild rumors running free through the city. Even the fact that Barlow once praised Essex from the selfsame pulpit could be made to work in Cecil's favor, for if one of the earl's admirers could see the danger in allowing him to live, why not his other supporters as well?

The art of sermon writing and its ability to synthesize politics and religion into a cohesive whole (or at least appearing to do so) did not reach its full culmination until the reign of King James. Barlow's sermon is stylistically primitive in that it is so obviously broken down into two distinct, sequential halves: the sermon proper and a propagandistic speech. Barlow himself, in his preface, "To the Reader," seems to realize the inherent contradictions of such an endeavor:

> Yet, I confesse, that the addressing my selfe to this sermon (containing in it matter rather of state then diuinitie, and beeing... subiect to offence one way, eyther to them of authoritie if I should renounce this dutie, or the auditorie if I should speak of vncertaintie) was, as the Apostle speaketh... with much fear and trembling. (*A Sermon Preached*, A3)

For three days, Barlow investigated every detail of the plot in order to keep himself "from the controlment either of ill tongues, or mine owne conscience." That Barlow did not escape "the malignitie of the meany" is a historical fact (A3v), for he himself tells us of the many rumors spread about him after the delivery of his sermon, ranging from the mild (that his sermon had angered Queen and Council) to the ironic (that he was himself imprisoned in the Tower for speaking treason) to the extreme (that he immediately went insane for having lied in the pulpit). As for the state of his conscience, perhaps the fact that he felt it necessary to write this 14-page preface to excuse his excuse says a thing or two about that. Whether or not it was a sense of guilt and embarrassment that led him to pry carefully into temporal affairs, however, the final result is a sermon that loses its credibility because it loses sight of God.

The sermon proper—the tripartite division of a short biblical text, typical of the style of the metaphysical preachers—takes up only the first quarter of Barlow's total oration. Unsurprisingly, his theme for this section of the sermon is the importance of giving one's total obedience to one's monarch; and his proof for saying that this is a virtue highly valued by God is Mark 12.17, "Give to Caesar the things of Caesar." The first third of the sermon is an introduction that sets the historical context of this text, the attempt of the Pharisees and Herodians to trick Jesus into speaking treason and/or heresy. Barlow proves through citations to other books of the Bible that the sin of the Pharisees here is pride, the foremost of the seven deadly sins. This introduction ends with one of the favorite arguments of the future Gunpowder sermons, that God and kings "have interchangeably borrowed names," thus implicitly linking Jesus and Elizabeth together as one (B3).[8] While Essex is never explicitly mentioned here either, Barlow is clearly preparing us for the focus of the second half of his sermon: the fall of the earl through his excessive pride. When Barlow quotes Isaiah (8.9–10) to describe the Pharisees, he intends for his auditory to envision Essex and his followers, and thus hopes to offset immediately any sympathy that they might hold: "Gird you, and you shall be broke in peeces: gather counsell together, and it shall be brought to naught" (B2v).

Adopting one of the more common methods for text division, Barlow treats the words of his chosen text in the order in which they appear. The first division focuses on the word "give," citing the Bible 13 times in the space of 45 lines, as well as Lactantius and Aquinas, in order to demonstrate that good Christians should freely give alms to those below them "and obedience unto your superior reverently" (B3v). The second division, the longest of the three, focuses on Caesar, who is "the Lords annointed" regardless of whether he is a friend or foe of the Lord (B5).

This idea that monarchs must be obeyed even if they are corrupt is another argument the Gunpowder preachers will later pick up on and develop more fully. It is also in this section, ten pages into the sermon, that Essex is mentioned for the first time. Barlow reminds his audience of the controversial and illegal book, *A Conference on the Next Succession to the Crown of England* (1595), whose author, the English Jesuit Robert Parsons, dedicated his work to Essex, most likely in the hope that, by depicting the earl as a future kingmaker, he could create a rift between the queen and her favorite (Lacey, 127). Barlow blames this book for planting in Essex's heart "the originall poyson" that caused him to believe that he had the right "to rise agaynst his soueraigne" (B5v). Once again the Gunpowder sermons are foreshadowed, for in both plots the preachers see the Jesuits as the original instigators, turning native English citizens against the throne.

Barlow's third division, the shortest of the three at only 43 lines, returns for the most part to the general nature of the first division, alluding to Essex and his followers only briefly as "some of late" toward the end. This section primarily concentrates on what is owed by all subjects to their monarch, regardless of that monarch's abilities or virtues:

> ... the crowne exacteth of us reuerence: the scepter, obedience: and the sword, feare ... and sithence theis require large maintenance, 1.Reg.4. their expence must be supplied, and because they lie open manifold daungers, with our prayers they must be assisted. (B7)

If Essex had just neglected these last two duties (subsidies and prayers), he would not have dared to attack the queen. Since he neglected his three most important duties, however (honor, obedience, and fear), he not only betrayed queen and country, but also himself since he pitted his will against God's. It is with this argument that Barlow leaves his religious explication behind and embarks upon Cecil's secular path.

The second half of this sermon, the propagandistic speech, is simply a fleshing out of Cecil's instructions. Only once does Barlow's voice rise above Cecil's. This comes right away in what Barlow call a "short preface personal," in which he attempts to defend himself from accusations of being an ambitious government puppet, "leaving the great man that is dead, and now cleaving to others, and closing with them for preferments" (B7v). Realizing that memories of his Cadiz sermon would only serve to strengthen such accusations, rather than trying to hide the fact, Barlow raises it himself by saying that he was one of the earl's most loyal followers despite being "not either a penny the richer or a steppe the higher for him" (B8v). Barlow goes on to admit that he would prefer not to give this sermon, but the Bible compels him to obedience, and therefore he must preach since he was ordered to do so by his superiors. By saying this, he connects the two halves of his sermon together, but also offers himself as an example to be contrasted against the disloyal earl.

Not only does the matter of Barlow's sermon come from Cecil's instructions, but some of its art does as well. The most famous characteristic of the metaphysical preaching style is the farfetched conceit. In this particular sermon, Barlow compares the public's false conception of Essex's rebellion to a mushroom (the entire lifespan of which is only one night)[9] and his pride to fire (which can be either beneficial to a house or destructive, depending upon how it is used); but his most developed conceit is borrowed straight from Cecil's instructions. According to these instructions, Barlow was first to mention how Essex had hoped for an enthusiastic welcome from the people, but then to mention that because he did not trust them, he intended to take the Tower of London and use is as a bridle to control the city.[10] Barlow follows Cecil to the letter, beginning with Essex's contempt for the people: "Thus he accompted your loue at the best to be but vanitie . . . an *Aeqiptian* reede, which eyther breaketh & fayleth him that leaneth on it or pearceth his hand to his hurt" (D6v). Barlow then develops Cecil's metaphor, putting it directly into Essex's mouth for added emphasis. According to Barlow, when asked why he wanted to take the Tower, Essex

answered, that he meant it should haue beene a bridle, to

*your citie*, marke that worde, *a bridle* hath raines and a bit: so that if you had made an head for him agaynst the Queene (which I hope you would not) he would haue giuen you the raines, you should haue gone on without restraint to haue beene rebels to your prince and country: but if you had vnited your force against him as good subiects (and as I am fully perswaded you would) they are his owne wordes, if *happely the Citie should haue misliked his other attempt*, then you should taste of the Bit. (D7)

Four years later Barlow would establish the motif of "the destruction that might have been" for the Gunpowder sermons. Here, he finishes his horse metaphor (making use of remarkably homely language) by likewise graphically describing what might have been, "They call it the playeng of the Bit in the horse mouth: but I beleeve the playing of the Ordinance from the Tower would haue fetcht both your houses downe, and your *bloud* out" (D7v). Obviously, the function of this conceit was to quench any sympathy the people still held for the earl. Despite this picture of him as an insensitive, egotistic aristocrat (at one point Barlow likens him to Plutarch's Coriolanus [Ciiiv]),[11] Barlow was not entirely successful in his endeavor to turn the people against the now dead earl, as we have already seen from the scathing rumors about Barlow that began to circulate immediately following his delivery of the sermon.

Many more characteristics typical of the metaphysical style can be found throughout this sermon. For example, Barlow employs "unnatural" natural history when he uses "the Nabis in Egipt . . . a beast shaped of many beasts" to describe Essex's rebellion, "the compound of all the famous rebellions eyther in Gods booke, or our owne land." Following this exemplum, Barlow proceeds to list a series of biblical rebellions (six in all, from *"Abners* discontment" to *"Hamans* pride and ambition"), as well as the rebellion "of *Henrie* Duke of Lancaster, against *Richard* the second," in order to show that no previous rebellion was as dangerous and malicious as this present one (D5–DSv).[12] Such historical narrations would later become one of the favorite tools of the Gunpowder preachers in general, who used the worsening of events over time to suggest both the approach of Armageddon and the special favor conferred upon the English Church by God. In fact, Barlow uses one of the favorite historical examples of the Gunpowder preachers— the assassination of Henry III of France by Friar Clement— earlier in the sermon to show how Essex, like Clement, sinfully used the Bible to justify his crimes: "Let Papists lay these grounds, and make these proofes, I am sory that any, who caries the name of a Protestant, should argue thus" (C5v).

Finally, as far as the facts that were presented to the congregation at Paul's Cross about the uprising are concerned, they need not overly trouble us, for despite his self-proclaimed investigation into the matter, Barlow, for the most part, simply publicly reiterates the facts privately given to him by Cecil. Naturally, Barlow never mentions this source in either his sermon or his written introduction to it, for if its official inspiration was made generally known (though, of course, it must have been suspected by many), the sermon would lose what little credibility it managed to have. By concealing the fact that these are not his words, Barlow hopes to present himself as a loyal and outraged subject, rather than as the tool of propaganda that he really was. Nevertheless, Barlow was not free to choose; and the last 16 pages of his sermon (a third of the total text) are dedicated to the events of three weeks before. Following the order established by Cecil, he begins with the queen's fright, virtually quoting Cecil verbatim:

> But resistance beeing made, as it is not possible but there would, there must needes be bloud shed: now thinke you what an horror would this haue beene to her gratious nature, to haue seene bloud running in her chambers? (Dv-D2)

Barlow then proceeds to discuss the roles assigned to Essex's commanders and their Papist alignment, and concludes with Essex's plans for taking the Tower, all the while borrowing direct quotes from Cecil's instructions.

We can detect Barlow's uneasiness, anxiety and lack of conviction in almost every line of his introduction and sermon. As a result, it fails on the political, religious and aesthetic levels mainly because it fails to integrate these three levels into one cohesive whole. The best of the Gunpowder sermons, such as those of Lancelot Andrewes, correct this mistake by keeping God, king and style in proper perspective. On the other hand, many of the Gunpowder preachers continued to fall into the same trap as Barlow. For example, John Donne, who detested Barlow for his "extreme flatteries," is just as guilty as Barlow is for his placing of praise and propaganda foremost in his Gunpowder sermon of 1622 (qtd. in Maclure, 180). What makes this Essex sermon a greater failure that even the worst of the Gunpowder sermons, however, is this lack of conviction. The preacher here is truly trapped between Scylla and Charybdis, for Barlow had to please both his audience and superiors, a task made more difficult by the fact that the interest of these two groups tended toward two very different directions in this particular situation. To quote Maclure, this text is unparalleled as a historical document because it conveys "with great vividness an atmosphere of tension, fear, and wild rumor" (86). That it was a failure in its time as a piece of propaganda we have already seen. As far as pleasing his superiors goes, Barlow was perhaps too successful here, for according to the diarist John Manningham, Elizabeth never received him again because he reminded her too much of Essex.[13]

After Elizabeth's death, however, Barlow's star began to rise once more. In 1604 King James summoned him to be a participant in the Hampton Court Conference, which was convened as an attempt to reconcile the various factions within the English Church. The conference itself, most likely held against the advice of Cecil, was a complete failure and arguably marks the point of no-return on the road to the English Civil War. The only tangible result of this three-day meeting was James's acceptance of the Puritan suggestion that a new English translation of the Bible be prepared; all other matters were deferred to a committee.[14] But for Barlow, the conference was a personal success. He was chosen by Whitgift to answer the Puritan reports of this parley, "some partiall, some vntrue, some slanderous" (*The Summe and Substance*, A4). The servile preface of his report deserves brief quotation, since it foreshadows the tumid flattery not only of Barlow's own Gunpowder sermons but of the sermons in general of what has been called the "worldly, courtly, talented place-hunting *dilettanti*, the ornamental betrayers of the Church, the Bishops of King James":[15]

> the onelie wrong, therein, is to his excellent Maiestie, a syllable of whose admirable speeches, it was pitty to loose, his words as they were vttered by him, being as *Salomon* speaketh, *Like Apples of gold, with pictures of siluer*. (*The Summe and Substance*, E4)

Such praise did not go unrewarded in a royal court in which the king "did not choose men for his jobs, but bestowed jobs on his men" (Trevor-Roper, 573). Within months of publishing this report, Barlow was consecrated Bishop of Rochester and became one of 47 scholars appointed for the translation of the Bible (Davies, 155).

Barlow occupied his new see in January 1605. As we have seen, shortly after midnight on 5 November of that same year, Sir Thomas Knyvet, a member of the King's Privy Council, was either "despatched expressly to look for gunpowder" or "discovered them (the 36 barrels) only by a piece of luck" in the cellar rented by the conspirators.[16] According to the official government account of the plot, Fawkes freely confessed his guilt to Knyvet, "declaring also unto him, That, if he had happened to be within the house when he tooke him, as he was immediately before . . . hee would not have failled to have blowen him vp, house and all."[17] King James recounted the facts of the plot, focusing primarily upon his own personal escape, in a speech delivered before Parliament on the Saturday following Fawkes's arrest. Drawing upon James's speech for information, and again having Cecil provide the "official inspiration," it was once more Barlow who was given the task of setting forth before the common people the details of a failed rebellion.

Cecil had outlined the earlier Essex sermon because he

wanted to make sure Barlow would quell the public's emotional reaction before it had a chance to grow. In 1605, however, Cecil's aim was the exact opposite, for any emotion aroused by the plot's failure would undoubtedly be to the advantage of the king and his government. That Cecil used Barlow's sermon for this purpose is clear from its emotional intensity. Some critics and historians, however, might argue that Cecil was doing more than merely taking advantage of a situation; rather, they would argue that he had created the situtation himself. While most of England, historians and the general populace alike, has come to accept Barlow's government account, a small but vocal minority, from the days following the event down to modern times, has argued that the Gunpowder Plot was really a conspiracy designed and engineered by Cecil himself, with the intention of ridding England of the taint of Catholicism forever.[18] Hurstfield rejects the notion put forward by several critics that Shakespeare's *The Winter's Tale*, written about five years after the plot's failure, is actually an indictment against the government, the play's title being a reference to Thomas Winter's confession of his role in the plot (107). Margaret Hotine, however, points out that the play was actually performed before James and his court on Gunpowder Day, 1611, following the annual religious celebration; and that the choice of this play may very well have been intended as a criticism of the king.[19] On the other hand, Hurstfield does acknowledge that Ben Jonson's *Catiline His Conspiracy* is, in truth, a defense of Cecil (107), and perhaps even himself (Durst, 85), though this is not really surprising since Johnson most likely assisted Cecil in his published defense of the execution of the traitors.[20] Almost since that November midnight, then, critics and historians have argued back and forth, defending and attacking Cecil, citing various pieces of evidence, or lack thereof, to support their point of view. Yet not one of these critics has done more with Barlow's sermon—the ultimate, articulate expression of the government's point of view—than simply to mention it briefly in passing.

This neglect is indeed surprising when we consider the fact that it was Cecil who once again acted as the "official inspiration" for Barlow's sermon. Unfortunately, Cecil's instructions no longer survive; and, of course, only the most intrepid postmodernist critic would try to analyze a text that does not exist. Nevertheless, from what we know of Cecil's and Barlow's personalities, and by using Barlow's Essex sermon as a model, it seems reasonable to assume that much of this sermon is Cecil's, with bits and pieces borrowed from James's and the Lord Chancellor's speeches delivered before Parliament on the preceding day. Therefore, if Cecil was responsible for instigating the Gunpowder Plot, we would expect this sermon to be vehement in its attack against Roman Catholicism. This is not the case, however. Cecil possessed no great love for the English Catholic community in general, or for the extremists, especially the Jesuits (Hurstfield, 113–14). In this sermon, however, Catholicism itself is not condemned, and only the Jesuits are harangued against in its concluding paragraph. If Cecil were seeking to destroy, or even simply discredit, Catholicism in England, would he not have wanted to add fuel to the fire of hatred that was already beginning to burn? But in fact, he never seized upon this rather fortunate opportunity.[21]

When we compare this first Gunpowder sermon to the more than 35 surviving Gunpowder Day sermons that were delivered in commemoration of this event over the next 50 years, we are struck by just how mild it is in its attacks. Here, the villain is Guy Fawkes, "the true name of a false *traytor*" (D). Only briefly are his co-conspirators, the "false-hearted rebels," mentioned (E2), and even then Barlow insists that these men only "pretend the *Catholike Cause*" and "make *Religion* the *stawking-horse* for Treasons" (E3v). Toward the end of this sermon, Barlow talks about the various Catholic scholars, primarily Jesuits, who make "this practice of murthering princes . . . a conclusion of positiue Diuinitie" (E3); but this is merely a list of names and factions completely devoid of any rhetorical punch or feelings of emotion. Overall, this attitude reflects that of King James in his own speech, in which he insists that the plot was not a Catholic conspiracy at all, but the work of a few lone fanatics. This thanksgiving for the nation's survival, however, was quickly replaced with a thanksgiving for the destruction of its enemies. The subsequent Gunpowder sermons make slight use of Fawkes, preferring to blame the whole affair on the Jesuits and, later still, on the Pope. Quite surprisingly, the weaker Catholicism became in England during the seventeenth century, the stronger the attacks against it grew. Rather quickly, this allegedly Jesuit-led plot came to be seen by the English government and church as an international conspiracy directed by Satan himself.

The surviving evidence suggests that this anti-Catholic propaganda was never "officially inspired" by the government at all. In fact, Gunpowder Day was originally set aside, beginning in 1606, for the praise of James and his divine attributes, an idea first developed by both James's speech and Barlow's sermon:

> an vniuersall Scholer, acute in arguing, subtle in distinguishing, Logiclal in discussing, plentifull in inuenting, powerfull in perswading, admirable in discoursing . . . a perfect Textuar, a sound Expositor, a faithfull Christian, and a constant Professor, or affectuall, for Regeneration, an assiduous prayer, a chast husband, of sweet carriage, of humble deportment, of mortified lusts, of sanctified life . . . an vpright arbitrator in cases of Iustice, a louing father to his subiects, a carefull guardian of his kingdomes, a wise manager of his State, an especial fauourer of this Citty, an absolute Monarch both for Regiment & iudgment. (E2v–E3)

Borrowing directly from the king's own speech on his own miraculous survival, Barlow argues that even if all of England's political and religious leaders had been destroyed in the explosion, 5 November would still be a day for rejoicing if the king alone had escaped, "for that euen in the very *person* of the *King*, there are many liues" (D3v). Barlow is quick to point out, however, that even though James is fully aware of his personal greatness, the deliverance of "the best part of his people . . . did more *Comfort* him then his *Personall escape*" (D4). In short, Barlow here is setting his sovereign up, in this sovereign's presence, as something of a Christ figure, as the Good Shepherd who cares more for the safety of his flock than for his own.

This deification of the living might strike us as odd, but it is an idea which runs throughout the Gunpowder sermons. Even when there is no longer a monarchy left in England, this practice continues with Parliament itself occupying the top earthly link in the Great Chain of Being. That Barlow believed in such a hierarchy of order is made evident by this sermon, which implies that the Gunpowder Plot was an inconceivable sin because it threatened the very fabric of the universe; that is, it threatened to disrupt the Great Chain of Being. The death of the king would directly lead to the overthrow of God's church upon the earth because it would break humanity's primary link to heaven. This particular sermon is primarily directed toward James: but it ends with a message aimed at a larger audience, a message intended to preserve this chain:

> I shall desire you to ioyn with me in hearty prayer vnto Almighty God for the continuance of our good King, our State, and our Religion amongst vs, giuing him thankes for his wonderfull mercie, in preseruing vs from this terrible blow (as they called it) from this desperate and damnable attempt, saying *O Eternal God and our most mighty Protector.* (E3v–E4)

With these closing words, Barlow conveyed to the people of London the same sentiments that James conveyed to Parliament the day before, that the people should give thanks that God's lieutenant still reigned upon the earth, and that they should offer up prayer that he might continue to do so.

As mentioned above, such praises continue even throughout the Commonwealth period; but, after Gunpowder Day was established as a national holiday in 1606 and was put into the hands of the people and their preachers, the focus of the sermons shifted from pro-government to anti-Catholic propaganda, from the King to the Jesuits. The question, of course, becomes "Why?" For one answer, we must turn once again to the Essex rebellion. During Essex's imprisonment, the sermons ordered by the government, but not supervised by them, were inflated, in many cases, to the point of ridiculousness. Once the Gunpowder Plot was put into the hands of the people and their preachers, this subject too was greatly exaggerated, perhaps for hope of preferment or maybe just the attention of the auditory. But this occasion was also the perfect opportunity for the preachers to give to the English people the message they wanted to hear—a message proven to be true by the plot's failure—that they were God's chosen people.[22]

Thus, in a very real sense, the people themselves co-wrote their own sermons. Nevertheless, Barlow's sermon, derived from material provided by both Cecil and James, served as a model (in terms of content, if not style) for the Gunpowder preachers of the next 50 years. While it does not preach anti-Catholicism, its inflammatory rhetoric was adopted by more zealous speakers, who saw to it that England's burning fear of the Whore of Babylon would not quickly cool down. Perhaps Barlow's most important contribution to this future prejudice was his establishment of the proper themes for a Gunpowder sermon: the "inhumane crueltie" of the conspirators, the "beastlike" manner of their planned kill, "the multitude of the slain," and finally the sheer physical destruction of *"the Hall of Iudgement, the Courtes of Records,* the *Collegiate Church, the Cittie of Westminster,* yea, *White-hall,* the *Kinges House"* (C3). In his Essex sermon, Barlow attempted to persuade his auditory by vividly describing to them the destruction that might have been. This rhetorical strategy failed because the listeners did not believe that there was any real threat to begin with. In this sermon Barlow includes two catalogues of the bloodshed and physical carnage that was narrowly avoided, with the intention of horrifying the people into thanksgiving. Here he succeeds perhaps all too well—for this, more than any other strategy or motif of his, was picked up by his successors. The anger raised by these images of what almost came to pass quickly translated into religious prejudice; and beginning with the first anniversary celebration of the plot's failure, and progressing steadily from there, the papacy, the Jesuits and the Catholic Church as a whole came to be substituted for Guy Fawkes and his coconspirators. Though Barlow had intended to paint a fairly accurate picture of the Gunpowder Plot, the means he chose—or was assigned by Cecil—to do so indirectly gave birth to the popular legends and misconceptions of Guy Fawkes Day.

In terms of propaganda, this first sermon was the one that was the most directly controlled by the monarchy and its agents; and though many of the future Gunpowder sermons were not "officially inspired" by the government, their primary purpose was the legitimization of the current power structure. From its beginnings, the Church of England allowed itself to be subverted to the uses of the Crown, and nowhere is the government's use of religion for its own ends made clearer than in Barlow's Essex sermon and in the sermons preached every year on the fifth of November. For the next five decades, this celebration presented English government officials with the perfect opportunity for the spreading of propaganda, for the nature of this holiday provided them with both willing spokesmen and an audience all too eager to hear the virtues of this government lauded and praised.

# 3 • The Triumph of London
## Lord Mayor's Day Pageants and the Rise of the City

*Raymond D. Tumbleson*

. . . . that vast metropolis,
The fountain of my country's destiny
And of the destiny of earth itself,
That great emporium . . . .[1]

L ondon's first recorded Lord Mayor's Day pageant occurred in 1535, its last in 1701.[2] With its origins in the
medieval Midsummer Show, the festival was already the
principal civic event of the city by the earlier date; by the
later it had become a vestigial localizing anachronism in a
national and international metropolis. London, with a population of only 50,000 under Henry VIII, grew to 160–180,000
by 1600, and continued to increase in the seventeenth century
at a rate much beyond that of the country overall, while
such regional centers as York, Bristol and Norwich remained
relatively static in population, none over 20–30,000.[3] It was
in the heyday of the elaborate Lord Mayor's Day pageant,
then, that London advanced beyond its medieval status of

first among equals, the principal city of the realm, to another order of magnitude, to being *the City*, no adjective needed. An example of conspicuous consumption on a municipal scale, the pageant asserted the importance of the city in the awkward adolescence of its economic explosion from local to global center. By 1701, there was no longer a need to enact symbolic Triumphs of London because London had triumphed.

The class of great merchants from which the Lord Mayor was chosen, recognized as the masters of the city, put on spectacles to symbolize their dominance. These extravaganzas functioned not only to impress the generosity and legitimacy of their rule upon their social infereiors, as Theodore B. Leinwand proposes, but also to advance a claim to what was virtually an alternative sovereignty.[4] Thomas Middleton asserts at the opening of *The Triumphs of Truth*, his first Lord Mayor's Day pageant in 1613, "that there is no subject upon earth received into the place of his government with the like state and magnificence as is the Lord Mayor of the city of London."[5] He repeats the vaunt, with some variation in the wording, in the first sentences of his last two pageants, *The Triumphs of Integrity*, 1623, and *The Triumphs of Health and Prosperity*, 1626. David Bergeron has argued that *The Triumphs of Truth* may be likened to a stage comedy in its moral design, but civic pageantry is closer to the masque in its political purpose as an enactment of dominance, and Middleton's subsequent pageants display an awareness that his new genre differs from plays for the stage.[6] Further, whereas the structure of *The Triumphs of Truth* is an anomaly even among Middleton's own Lord Mayor's Day pageants, the purpose of these foremost city spectacles remains as true to itself as Polonius could ask. The pageants emerged into prominence when London was beginning to become the national metropolis, and they ceased, in Raymond Williams's formulation, once city had conquered country, once mercantile imperialism and the cash nexus had absorbed the traditional economy and polity. The pageants of Middleton and Elkanah Settle reflect, respectively, the ideological posture of the city at the peak of the pre-Civil War political struggle and after its final victory in 1688.

Power and its means of legitimation have become a contentious subject in studies of English Renaissance theater. Stephen Greenblatt has suggested that power perpetuated itself in the Renaissance by creating a demonized opposition, as accusations of atheism indirectly upheld orthodoxy, and more generally by provoking and then releasing anxiety, as when James I followed a set of grisly public executions with pardons announced upon the scaffold, winning vast applause.[7] In contrast to such ceremonies of affirmation as those ritually theatricalized pardons, Franco Moretti and Jonathan Dollimore see tragedy as subversive of the social order. If, as Moretti claims, "the historical 'task' effectively accomplished by [tragedy] was precisely the destruction of the fundamental paradigm of dominant culture," and if, as Dollimore argues, such a work as *The Revenger's Tragedy* subverts authority by inverting the relation of masque and antimasque in courtly entertainments, the question remains of just what the paradigm and authority are.[8] As Albert Tricomi observes, Middleton's *A Game of Chess*, with its adversarial metaphor for politics, exposed the Crown's pretense of ruling impartially from atop a stable order when it was simply one of multiple factions competing for power.[9] The court and the country have long been conventional terms for the principal opposites—the "two warring cultures"[10]—but the foremost stronghold of resistance to the court throughout the seventeenth century—by means political, financial, military and literary—was London.[11] Nor did King and Parliament alone possess authority and a cultural paradigm. Every year the ruling elite of the city celebrated its power and wealth with a pageant on the day of the inauguration of the Lord Mayor. Like the royal masques, these pageants provided a performative affirmation of authority, but the authority affirmed was in covert competition with that of the Crown.

Middleton, whom Ben Jonson called "a base fellow" (Heinemann 171), held the office of City Chronologer for the last years of his life, and throughout his career was identified with the city. Susan Wells calls Jonson, Middleton

and Marston the three "most accomplished" practitioners
of city comedy, but William Hemminge's satire, "Elegy on
Randolph's Finger" (1630–32), suggests a difference between
the relations of Jonson and Middleton with the commercial
classes:[12]

> They quaked at Jonson as by him they pass
> Because of Tribulation Wholesome and Ananias,
> But Middleton they seemed much too adore
> For's learned exercise 'gainst Gundomore[13]

Jonson wrote occasionally for the city, but principally for
the court; his masques fill 400 pages. Middleton's one masque,
on the other hand, was *The Inner Temple Masque*; the 1603
*Magnificent Entertainment: Given to King James*, to which
he contributed, was a welcome by the city to the new
monarch; and the lone "entertainment" he wrote for performance in Whitehall to honor the installation of Charles
as Prince of Wales in 1616 was *Civitatis Amor. The Cities
Love (Works, 269)*. When he wrote a piece for a royal audience,
then, he wrote not directly for the court but for the city
to address the court. Middleton's fame for *A Game of Chess*,
the "learned exercise 'gainst Gundomore" and the biggest
hit of the Jacobean stage, resembles that of Settle for *The
Female Prelate*, an anti-Catholic tragedy of the Exclusion
Crisis, although Settle also engaged in open political
pamphleteering.[14] Middleton, however, enjoyed no such lapse
in the censorship as coincided with the Exclusion Crisis,
and Charles I had greater powers than Charles II to restrict
and punish authors and their patrons, so we cannot be certain
whether the performance of *A Game of Chess* was the result
of catching the Master of the Revels napping or royal
Machiavellianism. Censorhip necessarily creates uncertainty
of meaning.[15] Nonetheless, if writers had to be circumspect
in their criticisms, they remained free to praise, and whom
they praised and for what can supply a perspective not found
elsewhere.

After the indefatigable Anthony Munday, who had at least
partial responsibility for 15 pageants, Middleton was the
next most prolific writer of Jacobean Lord Mayor's Day

pageants, producing seven: *The Triumphs of Truth*, 1613; *The Triumphs of Honor and Industry*, 1617; *The Triumphs of Love and Antiquity*, 1619; *The Sun in Aries*, 1621; *The Triumphs of Honor and Virtue*, 1622; *The Triumphs of Integrity*, 1623; and *The Triumphs of Health and Prosperity*, 1626. All but the first are about the same length, occupying 18 pages the spacious nineteenth century Bullen edition, except the last takes up only 15. Of the 18 or 15 pages, the first six, being largely or entirely blank, could be compressed into one. Thus the 40 pages of *The Triumphs of Truth* are not only twice but almost three times as long as any of the rest. This first of Middleton's pageants also possesses a structure vastly different from his other works in the same genre, but hardly unusual among masques and plays. The later pageants simply progress through a series of set pieces, describing an emblematic scene, then giving the speech recited there in honor of the new mayor by Expectation (*Love and Antiquity*, 316), the Queen of Merchandise (*Honor and Virtue*, 358), or whatever the presiding figure in that display, and moving on to the next scene. There is no interaction and no opposition.

It is unsurprising that a playwright's first pageant should have much reminiscent of the playhouse about it. *The Triumphs of Truth*, unlike Middleton's later pageants, provides an Error with one long and two short speeches, a sidekick Envy, who has two lines, and the ongoing activity of their both being "chased before" the mayor in his processional (*Truth*, 250). After Envy says his two lines, "Learn now to scorn thy inferiors, those most[16] love thee, / And wish to eat their hearts that sit above thee," Zeal directly addresses Error and Envy, crying "Bold furies, back! or with this scourge of fire, / Whence sparkles out religious chaste desire, / I'll whip you down to darkness" (*Truth*, 244–45). It is tempting to read such lines satirically, particularly when one recalls that Middleton wrote the not particularly naive *A Chaste Maid in Cheapside* at almost the same time. Yet such a reading would at once place the speech at odds with the rest of the pageant, with the very purpose of the pageant, and require the supposition that Middleton was covertly laughing in the faces of influential men for and to whom he was to continue to write paeans until the year before his death.

If intentional satire becomes an untenable hypothesis, an inadvertant bleeding-over from his customary form of composition is more plausible. The transition from satire to panegyric can be awkward. Every ringing affirmation suggests that a denial is being outshouted, and an oligarchy of merchant princes could hardly avoid generating resentment among those they ruled. Envy is quickly hushed up, but its bare appearance, and the necessity that it be silenced—as Duke Vincentio silences Lucio in *Measure for Measure*—reminds those present of something that sits awkwardly with full-throttle praise. A dialoguic structure cannot help but introduce uncertainties and ambiguities. Playing the part of Satan in the wilderness, Error tempts the new Lord Mayor to abuse his trust:

> Great power this day
> Is given unto thy hand; make use on't, lord,
> And let thy will and appetite sway the sword; ...
> The worth of every office to a hair,
> And who bids most, and how the markets are,
> Let them ["Gluttony and Sloth"] alone to smell; and, for a need,
> They'll bring thee in bribes for measure and light bread;
> Keep thy eye winking and they hand wide ope,
> Then thou shalt know what wealth is, and the scope
> Of rich authority; ho, 'tis sweet and dear!
> Make use of time then, thou'st but one poor year,
> And that will quickly slide, then be not nice:
> Both power and profit cleaves to my advice;
> And What's he locks his ear from those sweet charms,
> Or runs not to meet gain with wide-stretch'd arms?
>
> (*Truth*, 242–43)

For Error to appear to tempt the new Mayor implicitly admits that, unless merchants equal Christ in virtue, they may at times succumb. Despite all his subsequent chastisement, Error has revealed—in a way that cannot be entirely expunged—the fallibility and potential for corruption of the officeholder and his class, since he and they necessarily achieve their positions through "power and profit." Thus David Bergeron's argument that *The Triumphs of Truth* has the same moral design as a comedy may be recast to say instead that *The Triumphs of Truth*, borrowing much of its structure from comedy—the form Middleton was accustomed to using—in the process inadvertently borrows in part the self-doubting, self-destabilizing dynamic of the stage. He never again introduces dialogue or humor into his pageants; he had learned that the inaugural ceremony of the Lord Mayor was not a stage, and was not a fitting place to give even devalued speech to the excluded. Comedy would compromise the dignity of the event. Captives do not get lines in triumphs. A pair of zanies "chased before" the Lord Mayor would depreciate his authority and release the subversive energies of popular carnival into an occasion intended to reinscribe hierarchy.[17]

Middleton's subsequent pageants display his mastery of this lesson, and the frequency of his selection to write them shows the appreciation of his patrons. After *The Triumphs of Truth* in 1613, he did not compose another pageant until *The Triumphs of Honor and Industry* in 1617; but thereafter, having demonstrated he understood the form, he got most of the commissions until his death. His period of favor from 1617 to 1623—authoring the pageant in 1617, 1619, 1621, 1622 and 1623—was perhaps broken by *A Game of Chess*: even if that play did have court backing, the support would have had to be surreptitious, or the satire would have lost the aura of sensational daring that made the show the hit of its generation. *The Triumphs of Honor and Industry* makes no attempt to connect its several symbolic tableaux with action, and all speeches are serious and directed to the Lord mayor and audience. As to content, these speeches exemplify what Oliver Goldsmith, at the zenith of England's first colonial empire a century and a half later, called "The wealth of climes, where savage nations roam, Pillag'd from slaves, to purchase slaves at home."[18] "The first invention" shows

A company of Indians, attired according to the true nature of their country, seeming for the most part naked, are set at work in an Island of growing spices; some planting nutmeg-trees, some other spice-trees of all kinds; some gathering the fruits, some making up bags of pepper, every one severally employed. These Indians are all active youths, who, ceasing in their labours, dance about the trees, both to give content to themselves and the spectators.

After this show of dancing Indians in the Island, follows triumphantly a rich personage presenting India, the seat of merchandise. This India sits on the top of an illustrious chariot; on the one side of her sits Traffic or Merchandise, on the other side Industry . . . (*Honor and Industry*, 297–98)

While no image so openly coercive as an overseer is shown, the Indians do not merely work but are "set to work." Further, although India sits at the top and center of the chariot, the figure that gives the speech for this tableau is Industry, a speech whose theme is praise of Industry itself: "Behold this ball of gold, upon which stands / A golden Cupid, wrought with curious hands; / The mighty power of Industry it shows" (*Honor and Industry*, 299). The Indians labor, dance to display their contentedness, and remain mute, while voice is reserved for those who have set them to work. The difference between non-Europeans, who are only sources of "Traffic or Merchandise," and Europeans, who have individuality and the empowerment of speech, is underlined by the next display, the "Pageant of Several Nations." Here a Frenchman and a Spaniard salute the new Lord Mayor and the Society of Grocers in their respective tongues, with translations supplied as well (*Honor and Industry*, 300–01). France and Spain were, of course the foremost European powers, as well as major trading partners with England. Power is a precondition of speech; no Error or Envy here requires silencing.

One peageant differs suggestively from the others. The 1619 *Triumphs of Love and Antiquity* celebrates "the noble Fraternity of Skinners" (*Love and Antiquity*, 313), a less internationally oriented company than the Grocers, and Sir William Cockayne of the Cockayne project,, whom Heinemann calls the only "creature of the Crown" among the ten London merchants to whom Middleton dedicated works (259). This pageant features no colonial trade, but is instead remarkable for what follows the customary recitation, a brief one in this case, of past Lord Mayor of the same fraternity as the incoming. "[I]n the Parliament of Honour," on the "mount of royalty," and at length, Antiquity celebrates the fact that "Seven kings, five queens, only one prince alone, Eight dukes, two earls, Plantagenets twenty-one" have been "of this fraternity made free, Brothers and sisters of this Company" (*Love and Antiquity*, 323, 324). Afterward, three and a half pages go to listing every one of the royal "brothers and sisters," more than of any other company. A polemical nuance may be speculatively inferred from the fact that Middleton's next pageant, the 1621 *Sun in Aries* (his only title that does not begin with "The Triumphs of . . .") starts, unlike any of his others, by rejoicing that "Pisces being the last of the signs, and the wane of the Sun's glory, how fitly and disiredly the Sun enters into Aries, for the comfort and refreshing of the creatures, and may be properly called the spring-time of right and justice" (*Sun in Aries*, 341). Whereas Middleton's other pageants all open with an exclamation at the wonder and the glory of the ceremony itself, this begins with rejoicing at a new season, which could be read as criticism of the old, of the antiquarianism of his own previous pageant. A more solid evidence that *The Triumphs of Love and Antiquity* differs in its object of praise from the rest of his pageants lies in what it does and does not contain. It does contain the long list of "Plantagenets twent-one"; it does not contain a reference to overseas adventures. Nor, unlike *The Triumphs of Integrity*, does it declare that "tis the noblest spendour upon earth/For man to add a glory to his birth," better "Than to be nobly born and there stand fix'd" (*Integrity*, 387). When employed by a royalist, Middleton could pass for a Royalist.

Two years later, in 1621, he returned to his customary imperialist orientation. Middleton wrote *The Sun in Aries* for the Company of Drapers, whose traditional patron or representative was Jason, because of the Golden Fleece. Jason fetched the Fleece from Colchis, a barbarian (non-Greek) kingdom across the Black Sea, and was politically able to repudiate his wife because she was a foreigner, according to Seneca's *Medea* which, being in Latin, was more available to the Renaissance than Euripides. The epithalamium for his new wife that the Chorus sings—in Seneca's *Medea*, unlike Euripides', the wedding does take place—expresses pleasure that at last he is getting a proper Greek wife, not an outlander. In The *Sun in Aries* Jason makes the first speech: "I am he, / To all adveturous voyages a free And Bountiful well-wisher, by my name / Hight Jason, first adventurer for fame" (*Sun in Aries*, 340–41). Honor does not reside in idle state with kings, queens and dukes, but is a prize sought abroad, and by trade. The 1626 *Triumphs of Health and Prosperity*, again for the Drapers, recycles the use of Jason but only as the type for "Sir Francis Drake, England's true Jason . . . Never returning to his country's eye Without the golden fleece of victory" (*Health and Prosperity*, 406). Both *Sun in Aries* and *Health and Prosperity* celebrate the imperial wealth of London and construct it as the theological seat of British power, the true inheritor of the classical imperialism of Greece and Rome. Its merchants rule the seas and foreign lands, where as the power of the Court is confined to England.

The 1622 *Triumphs of Honor and Virtue*, like *Honor and Industry* written for the Grocers, returns to "the Continent of India" for its first scene (*Honor and Virtue*, 357). This scene presents

> a black personage representing India, called, for her odours and riches, the Queen of Merchandise, challenging the most eminent seat, advanceth herself upon a bed of spices, attended by Indians in antique habits: commerce, adventure and traffic, three habited like merchants, presenting to her view a bright figure, bearing the inscription of Knowledge, a sun appearing above the trees in brightest splendour and glory. (*Honor and Virtue*, 358)

The presentation of the "Queen of Merchandise," symbolizing the commodification of women, expresses the

commodification of colonial peoples. In the posture of the
exotic Queen of the East whose archetype is the Cleopatra
of legend (not that of history), she submissively presents
herself as sexual object and colonial subject, and hence doubly
other. Unlike "India, the seat of merchandise" in *The Triumphs of Honor* and Industry, she is permitted to speak,
but only to delegitimize her own claims in favor of those
of European adventurers.

> Draw near: this black is but my native dye,
> But view me with an intellectual eye,
> As wise men shoot their beams forth, then you'll find
> A change in the complexion of the mind:
> I'm beauteous in my blackness
> I that command (being prosperously possest)
> The riches and the sweetness of the east,
> To that fam'd mountain Taurus spreading forth
> My balmy arm, whose height does kiss the north,
> And in the Sea Eoum [sic] lave this hand,
> Account my blessings not in those to stand,
> Though they be large and fruitful, but confess
> All wealth consists in Chirstian holiness.
> To such celestial knoledge I was led,
> By English merchants first enlightened.
> (*Honor and Virtue*, 358–59)

The fantasy is the same as that which Greenblatt finds in
Thomas Harriot's 1588 *A Brief and True Account of the
New Found Land of Virginia*: heathen natives will be so
swept away by Christianity that they will enrich Europeans
for no other reward than that of being converted.[19] Not only
soldiers "desire . . . to live by the sweat of other mens brows":[20]
a small trader can only grow to a great merchant by capi-
talizing on the labor of others. In practice, colonial peoples
quickly tired of so one-sided an arragement, but Middleton's
pageants after *The Triumphs of Truth* permit only a single
point of view, that of London's merchant elite, whoever the
putative speaker.[21] His deliberate monocentrism, so in
contrast with his theatrical writings, affirms the right of that
elite to rule; his text silences or co-opts alternative voices.[22]

In later decades, this propagandistic fixedness of purpose

persisted in the last Lord Mayor's Day pageants, but altered circumstances altered content. The Civil War crippled royal independence, and the Glorious Revolution all but ended it. In the place of a Stuart Crown attempting to emulate Continental absolutism, in King William the people at last had a monarch who, like the Lord Protector, would fight for English trading interests and had no indefeasible hereditary right to reign. The monarchy had been tamed. With the end of the necessity for a strong symbolic assertion of the power and dignity of the city, the end of the pageants was approaching. In the few years before inertia permitted changes in forms to catch up with changes in power relations, however, they continued, but in a lighter vein, eased of their previous politico-metaphysical urgency.[23]

The official City Poet of London (as Middleton had been City Chronologer), Shaftesbury's chief propagandist during the Exclusion Crisis, and the former master of ceremonies of London's Pope-burnings in 1679 and 1680, Elkanah Settle wrote all the pageants in their last decade of existence, from 1691 to 1701.[24] The 1698 pageant, *Glory's Resurrection: Being the Triumphs of London Revived*, was the first pageant after the custom had been allowed to lapse for the two preceding years, and the only Lord Mayor's Day pageant Settle wrote that was not entitled *The Triumphs of London*. *Glory's Resurrection* has four pages of dedications, six of text and five of pictures. As his *Empress of Morocco* was the first English tragedy to be published with illustrations (the "sculptures" that provoked John Dryden's indignation), so here Settle is embellishing all he can to conceal that he is commemorating a dying mode of communal performance. The dedications laud the Goldsmiths for having, "after a three-Years Cessation, reviv'd the Customary *Splendor* of the *City* on this Solemn Occasion," and praise the mayor because "*Charity* and *Hospitality*, those two Illustrious Ornaments of Magistracy, You Lordship has resolved to recal from their late *Banishment*."[25] There is no further mention, however, of any charity or hospitality other than holding the pageant, and no invocation of illustrious and generous previous mayors. Settle's expression, "recal from their late *Banishment*," and his governing metaphor of resurrection echo the rhetoric of Caroline providentialist panergyric following the Restoration.[26] In the place of neglected or forgotten civic traditions, he redefines the city as supplanting the country by rewriting the royalist myth of national redemption into a teleology of municipal victory.

In *Glory's Resurrection*, the actual text to be spoken is vanishingly slight, 54 lines in heroic couplets, broken into four speeches of 11 to 20 lines each, plus a 24-line "Song" at the end which has no apparent place in the pageant and which may well have been added afterward to pad out an exceedingly thin volume. Two of the speeches and the song place primary emphasis on *"Britain's* Dread Caesar" (Glory's, 6) and little more than append the mayor: "So Rules Great WILLIAM: So, my Lord, shall You" (Glory's, 2). The Third Pageant, however, "A Triumphant CHARIOT of Gold," efficiently compacts its historical and political logic into a small space:

> ASTRAEA [Justice] thus Salutes His Lordship.
>
> Justice of old by long Oppression driven,
> Left the Tyrannick World and flew to Heav'n.
> But when Great NASSAW, *Albion's* Scepter bore,
> Our Laws and Rights sent kindly to restore,
> She visited the *Albion* World once more.
> Thus whilst our Caesar yields a Trust so large,
> As proud *Augusta* to Your Guardian Charge.
> As He from Heav'n His Sovereign Justice drew;
> He's Heav'ns Vicegerent [sic], his Vicegerent, You.
> *Astraea* then must here her Pow'r resign,
> Her brightest Glories in Your Hand shall shine.
> You'll best, my Lord, my Righteous Ballance hold,
> No Poise so even as in the Scales of Gold.
>
> (*Glory's*, 4)

Under the Stuarts, that is, municipal liberties and oligarchic privileges were invaded, but after the Glorious Revolution and the coming of William III, the "natural rulers"—those of London among the rest—were able to seize uncontested local supremacy in their respective districts. Lords Mayor

did not presume to call themselves viceregents under James
I. The closing pun does not observe the most sober decorum,
but neither does the exchange between St. Dunstan and the
Devil, the only dialogue in the volume, in The Second
Pageant, "The GOLDSMITHS Laboratory":

> St. Dunstan.   The Triumphs of this Day, deserv'd so well,
>                When Farn shall in Recorded Story tell,
>                Those Oracles of Truth—
> Devil.         Can You speak Truth?
> St. Dunstan.   Peace, snarling Devil! Thus I'll stop your
>                Mouth.
> [Catches him by the Nose]
>
> *(Glory's, 3)*

Farce does not come amiss in *Glory's Resurrection* because
it has no metaphysical claims to make. Nothing is threatened by the subversions of dialogue—a dialogue in which
the Devil only gets four words because a festival in the
streets is no longer imbued with meaning. Also, a saint
could hardly be invoked with serious reverence only a decade
after the expulsion of James II, so the Devil's role is to
disrupt the disruptive, to preempt audience suspicion of any
spokesman with a miter and crosier, as the illustration
portrays St. Dunstan. Whereas Middleton used a satiric humor
in *The Triumphs of Truth* that proved too disruptive, too
dangerous to the solemnities of hierarchy, Settle's nose-
tweaking slapstick threatens nobody. Settle praises the mayor,
the Goldsmiths, the city, King William—everyone he
should—but no sense of London as a community and distinct entity remains. Lords Mayor of past centuries are not
recalled; the mayor is not reminded to look after the poor
as part of his duty; London is no longer a place apart but
an integral part of the kingdom it has done so much to
remake in its own image. All that is left to do as the public
world recedes into the private is to get rich and cheer on
the Crown in Parliament, for City, Crown and Parliament
have become united. By the time Settle comes to write
them, the ideological work of the pageants has already been
accomplished—by the upheavals of the seventeenth century,

by such proto-revolutionary authors as Middleton, and by the advent of an emphatically Protestant king with an aggressive foreign and mercantile policy.

Thomas Middleton wrote Lord Mayor's Day pageants when they were at their peak of magnificence and significance, when they asserted to both Crown and crowd the right of the merchant elite to rule the city. He articulated the legitimation the merchants required. Next to Middleton the author of cynical comedies and subversive tragedies stands Middleton the apologist for emergent bourgeois imperialist ideology. However he undercut the royal mystifications of masques and aristocratic power in his theater work, the evidence of his pageants indicates that he was not implacably hostile to all authority. Once those he had hymned dominated the nation, the sort of poetry he had supplied them as a symbolic reinforcement of their position became archaic, rooted as it was in the very precapitalist system they had overthrown. Once mercantile interests felt secure in their power, the pageants became obsolete because their historical moment at the transition between the medieval and the modern was over, because the City had consummated its hostile takeover of the Crown. It is fitting that in the last Lord Mayor's Day pageant ever performed, Mercury says:

> Let Schoolmen in their Academies sit,
> And fancy their Learn'd Heads claim all the Wit.
> All vain Mistake. Search where true Learning lies:
> The MERCHANT is the *Witty* and the *Wise*
> *Philosophers*, who Nature's Depths explore,
> Seek but for Airy Treasure; they, no more
> But view the Mines. The MERCHANT digs the *Oar*.
> Let Book-learn'd Heads survey the Golden Strand,
> Like cold *Platonick Suitors* distant stand.
> To warmer Joys does the brisk MERCHANT press;
> They but read Worlds, He pushes to possess.[27]

Subversive ambiguities collapse with what they have been undermining; in the new world where money justifies itself, the merchant need no longer disguise his acquisitiveness with a doctrine subtler than "dig[ging] the *Oar*" and push[ing] to possess  the "Golden Strand." If wit and wisdom lie in wealth, wealth does not need poetic confirmation. The two Middletons do not stand independent of each other; to subvert one order is to construct another. The apparently contradictory sensibilities of the cynic and the panegyrist illuminate both one another and the treacheries of history. In Middleton's Lord Mayor's Day pageants, by muting every voice but that of power, the word ultimately conspires to silence itself.

# 4 • Bringing Forth Wonders
## Temporal and Divine Power in *The Tempest*

*Heather Campbell*

I n James I's entry into London at his accession, which
followed exactly the same route as had Queen Elizabeth's
and the young King Edward's, the addition of seven elaborately decorated arches transformed the procession into a
triumphal entry, a victory parade, with all the implications
of imperial power provided by its Roman origins. The triumph differs from the royal entry or progress primarily in
that the authority it celebrates is absolute: Jonathan Goldberg
describes these arches as bearing "a strong meaning, since
they announce the basic architectural element of classical
style and situate James's entrance in the context of the
absolutist revival of classicism" (33–34). A similar difference
exists between the theater proper and the masque. Masque,
which Jonathan Dollimore accurately describes as "an ideological legitimation of the power structure" (27), recuperates
the potentially subversive energies of the theater and draws
them into the service of the king.[1] Like the triumph, the
Jacobean court masque celebrated both the resolution of

chaos into universal harmony and the agent of that resolution—the triumphator, or monarch. Ideologically linked with both the masque and the triumph is the royal wedding, similarly a vehicle for the expression of temporal power, as well as for its consolidation, and often graced with a masque as a major element in the celebration.

There is an obvious structural relationship among the triumph, the masque and the wedding procession that supports the statement each of them makes about the nature of the power they express. Alastair Fowler notes, for example, that the triumphal emphasis on the center is also fundamental to the shape and purpose of the masque. When the triumphator is placed in the center of the procession, he is placed in synchrony with other mystical centers—the Tree of Knowledge, the Temple of Solomon, the Sun (27–32). This positioning was particularly significant in the Stuart court masque which, as Jonson and Jones developed it, became an increasingly extravagant affirmation of the centrality of the king's position in the universal order. The wedding procession also is clearly similar in structure to the triumphal entry, with the central position accorded to the bride, emphasizing her role as locus for the consolidation of power and its promised continuance. At court weddings, moreover, the masque included in the celebrations idealized marriage in just these terms.

In this context, marriage figures as a symbol of, as well as an essential element in, the universal harmony in which power descended from the deity through the monarch and the male. Dekker described James's entry into London in terms of a wedding (Nichols, 374–75), and his metaphor was by no means randomly chosen. James himself was fond of using images drawn from marriage to illustrate his perception of the relationship between monarch and realm, as in his 1603 speech to Parliament concerning the union of Scotland and England:

> What God hath conioyned, let no man separate. I am the Husband, and all the whole Isle is my lawfull Wife; I am the Head, and it is my Body; I am the Shepherd, and it is my flocke. (McIlwain, 272)

Here James commands the marriage metaphor to endorse the doubling of his realm and his position as divinely appointed ruler, God's vicegerent on earth. His juxtaposition of the marriage service and the body politic, and his presentation of himself as the Shepherd, direct attention away from the companionate context of marriage and toward the Christian concept of earthly marriage as patterned after and signifying the union of Christ and the Church. The series of nouns in parallel—husband/head/shepherd; wife/body/flock—emphasizes the patriarchal foundation and the divine significance of the absolutist monarchy.

Marriage was also a way of disciplining what male society saw as the inherently disorderly—and therefore dangerous—energies of women. Katherine Usher Henderson and Barbara F. McManus note that Renaissance women were considered to be "possessed of a powerful, potentially disruptive sexuality requiring control through rigid social institutions and carefully nurtured inhibitions within the woman herself" (55). Among the aristocracy, moreover, since women were also the vessels through which wealth and power were established and consolidated, chastity was emphasized for young women for practical as well as moral and religious reasons: a virgin bride ensured legitimate heirs. Marriage thus provided a way of containing women's essential unruliness, their rebelliousness, and most particularly their proclivity for sexual excess.[2]

In *The Tempest*, masque, triumph and betrothal function in a complex network of relationships with one another. Prospero carefully and ruthlessly manipulates the other characters in preparation for his triumphal reentry into Milan. He orchestrates a victory procession to celebrate his resumption of power; he also demonstrates an assumption of divine authority which, for the Stuart court, was by no means incompatible with worldly victory. His vehicle for achieving this is a masque of his own invention, in which his captives, appropriately though unwittingly, take part. Prospero's own role is an intensely complicated one: he is the dramatist, the inventor of the spectacle, raised by the apparently miraculous nature of the illusion to theurgist; he also, however, occupies the sovereign center. The drama he creates is ostensibly for the instruction of Alonso and the Neapolitan nobles, but the triumphal procession, which is its real purpose, is his own. Miranda's marriage is crucial at once to his resumption of temporal authority and to his achievement of "immortality"—his progeny as kings of Naples. Thus both marriage and the masque work together to repress all the elements that threaten the order Prospero represents and that his final triumph celebrates. Despite his apparent success, however, the play ultimately declines to endorse the absolutist values Prospero enforces. In *The Tempest*, then, the chief elements of the Jacobean courtly aesthetic, triumph and masque, combine with a representation of state marriage to present a power structure that is precariously maintained, morally suspect, and substantially less effective than it appears on the surface.

It is fitting that the "accident most strange" (1.2.178)[3] by which bountiful Fortune brings Prospero's enemies within his grasp itself stems from a marriage, that of Alonso's daughter. The introduction of Claribel in this way provides a clear statement of the assumptions about marriage that underpin Prospero's treatment of Miranda. As he laments the loss of his son, Alonso faces criticism from Sebastian for marrying his daughter to a Tunisian Prince. Sebastian reminds him that he was "kneel'd to and importun'd otherwise, / By all of us; and the fair soul herself / Weigh'd between loathness and obedience, at / Which end o' th' beam should bow" (2.1.124–27). Faced with the choice between a marriage she loathes and disobedience to her father, Claribel has properly chosen obedience and the dreaded marriage. Her situation is wrenching in human terms, but Sebastian's criticism is, in fact, at least as concerned with the political decision as with Claribel's unhappiness:

> Sir, you may thank yourself for this great loss,
> That would not bless our Europe with your daughter,
> But rather loose her to an African;
> Where she, at least, is banish'd from your eye,
> Who hath cause to wet the grief on 't.
>
> (2.1.119–23)

Sebastian's harsh judgment here is that Alonso deserves his present suffering for disposing of his daughter in a politically inappropriate union.

The absent Claribel provides an example for Miranda, a pattern of the proper conduct expected of a marriageable princess. In his manipulation of Miranda, Prospero displays no greater concern for his daughter's happiness than did Alonso: from the beginning his movements are deliberate, politically motivated and self-regarding. In his careful orchestration of the events of the afternoon, he ensures that Miranda's first sight of Ferdinand occurs immediately on the heels of the encounter with Caliban. Her response to the contrast is predictable and clearly according to plan:

> *Mir.* I might call him
> A thing divine; for nothing natural
> I ever saw so noble.
> *Pros.* [Aside] It goes on, I see,
> As my soul prompts it.
>
> (1.2.420–22)

Even Miranda's rebellion is contrived: Prospero's attack on Ferdinand and his subsequent punishment of him are a ruse prompted, he says, by his desire to throw difficulties in their way "lest too light winning / Make the prize light" (1.2.454–55). While Miranda's comforting of Ferdinand in his enslavement appears as disobedience, in fact this entire scene is presided over by Prospero. Thus Miranda's behavior is given implicit licence as part of Prospero's design. Her spontaneous rebellion in defending Ferdinand from Prospero's (apparent) anger and the accusation of treachery is repressed harshly and immediately by her father in the language of the body politic, designed to remind Miranda of her proper place in the social and familial hierarchy: "What, I say— / My foot my tutor?" (1.2.471–72).

In this context, the chastity Prospero emphasizes so heavily figures (in his eyes) as a civilizing force: its role here is to support the established order, for chastity alone can assure the desired alliance and protect the purity of line that is to be Prospero's route to immortality, his Neapolitan posterity. Prospero establishes the crucial link between chastity and lineage early in the play when he explains to Miranda their presence on the island; he ackowledges ironically that he is assured of Miranda's own legitimacy because "Thy mother was a piece of virtue, and / She said thou wast my daughter" (1.2.56–57). Stephen Orgel suggests, rightly in my opinion, that the judgment implied in Prospero's mild joke is actually fundamental to his assumptions about women:

> Prospero's wife is identified as Miranda's mother, in a context implying that though she was virtuous, women as a class are not, and that were it not for her word, Miranda's legitimacy would be in doubt. The legitimacy of Prospero's heir, that is, derives from her mother's word. But that word is all that is required of her in the play. Once he is assured of it, Prospero turns his attention to himself and his succession. ("Prospero's Wife," 217–18)

Indeed, much of the early seventeenth century woman-debate centered on the need to keep wives chaste and the difficulties of doing so. That his succession depends for its legitimacy on the potentially licentious female is a matter that clearly proccupies Prospero in his manipulation of the next generation. His admonition to Ferdinand not to "break her virgin-knot before / All sanctimonious ceremonies may / With full and holy rite be minister'd" (4.1.15–17) shifts the responsibility for chaste courtship from Miranda to Ferdinand, where it is presumably safer, although not necessarily absolutely safe. Prospero's warning to "be more abstemious, / Or else, good night your vow" (4.1.53–54), similarly directed to Ferdinand since no vow has been required of Miranda, acknowledges Ferdinand's own potential as a seducer while still giving Miranda no credit for the ability to protect her own chastity.

The relationship between chastity and lineage is also central to Prospero's treatment of Caliban. Prospero reminds the rebellious slave that he cared for him in his own cell until the attempted rape of Miranda, for which he was banished. Caliban, energetically unrepentant, articulates precisely the danger that concerns Prospero: "oh ho, oh ho! Would 't had been done! / Thou didst prevent me; I had peopled else / This isle with Calibans" (1.2.351–53). It is Miranda who responds to him, although for many years the speech was reassigned to Prospero as inappropriate to Miranda's character. She redefines the reasons for Caliban's banishment in more comprehensive terms:

> Abhorred slave,
> Which any print of goodness will not take,
> Being capable of all ill! I pitied thee,
> Took pains to make thee speak, taught thee each hour
> One thing or other: when thou didst not, savage,
> Know thine own meaning, but wouldst gabble like
> A thing most brutish, I endow'd thy purposes
> With words that made them known.But thy vile race,
> Though thou didst learn, had that in't which good natures
> Could not abide to be with; therefore wast thou
> Deservedly confin'd into this rock,
> Who hadst deserv'd more than a prison.
>
> (1.2.353–64)

Miranda perceives Caliban's transgression in terms of the more general issue of failure to accept the superiority of civility, of which failure the attempted sexual violation is a symptom. For her, too, chastity is an essential element in civilization. It is perhaps not surprising that the lines have so frequently been given to Prospero, for here Miranda does indeed energetically defend the order her father represents. To take the lines away from her, however, is to undermine this portrayal of the degree to which she has been absorbed by her father's discourse.

Miranda herself, as a result of her childhood isolated from the world, has clearly absorbed her father's opinions regarding the rules and priorities that prevail in society and govern her position in it. Even in the exhilaration of meeting and falling in love with Ferdinand, she acknowledges that her own choice is secondary to her father's: "This / Is the third man that e'er I saw; the first / That e'er I sighed for: pity move my father / To be inclin'd my way!" (1.2.447–50). In fact, as her name suggests, she is his creation. "Miranda," the gerundive form of *mirare*, means both "(one) to be wondered at, a wonder" and "(one) who wonders." Like the storm, Miranda herself figures as a product of Prospero's theurgy. In addition, *mirare* is the root of "mirror," indicating Miranda's role as reflector of Prospero's grandeur.

As Prospero's creation, Miranda is the only woman present and active on the island, and she has been entirely assimilated by his discourse. Women who might challenge his order are represented in the play, but they are significantly contained in various ways, since absolute authority depends in large part on the strict repression of all potentially rebellious groups. The most dangerous of the women, from Prospero's point of view, is Sycorax who, though absent, still looms in his imagination as a threatening figure. Sycorax is a prime example of the unruly woman: according to Prospero, she was ugly, envious, disobedient, licentious, fertile, malevolent and enraged. Prospero, of course, never saw her: she was already dead when he came to the island. But he describes her in vivid terms: "the foul witch Sycorax, who with age and envy / Was grown ito a hoop" (1.2.258–59). The descriptions of Sycorax's character and appearance, then, derive either from Prospero's imagination, or from Ariel's report (the obvious source) or both. The one thing we do know to be the truth, since we learn it from Caliban as well as Prospero, is that she was a witch, and this, for an early seventeenth century audience, would be enough to characterize her in precisely the terms Prospero uses.[4]

For the Jacobean court, the power of witchcraft was perceived as directly antithetical to the power of the king to work miracles of healing and to maintain order. In this play, the witch Sycorax, though safely banished by death, still preoccupies Prospero as a threatening power. She is, in fact, doubly removed from civilization, having been first banished from Algiers for "mischiefs manifold, and sorceries terrible / To enter human hearing" (1.2.264–65). Still, Prospero is at pains to remind Ariel that his magic is stronger than hers was:

Thou best know'st
What torment I did find thee in; thy groans
Did make wolves howl, and penetrate the breasts
Of ever-angry bears: it was a torment
To lay upon the damn'd, which Sycorax
Could not again undo: it was mine Art,
When I arriv'd and heard thee, that made gape
The pine and let thee out.

(1.2.286–93)

In fact, though, her career has been a pattern of his: banished from her homeland, she assumed rulership of the island, taking Ariel as her slave and punishing his disobedience. She remains a distinct presence on the island, regularly invoked by Caliban, as we might expect, but also by Prospero, who more than once addresses Caliban in terms of his mother: "Thou poisonous slave, got by the devil himself / Upon thy wicked dam" (1.2.321–22); "Hag-seed, hence!" (1.2.367). Clearly, for Prospero, the shadow of Sycorax, with her dark, dangerous, female magic, remains as a threatening reminder of the need to maintain his own authority with rigid determination.

Sycorax is, of course, ultimately powerless because she is only a memory. An alternative way of containing the idea of the unruly woman in this play is to consign her to the realm of bawdy jokes, and this is achieved in parallel and complementary ways by Gonzalo, who belongs to the aristocracy, and Stephano, who represents the servant class. In effect, Gonzalo makes a joke in the opening scene that provides a frame of reference for Stephano's bawdy song in the second act.

As the ship goes down in act 1, scene 1, Gonzalo—who is praised by Prospero as wise and honorable—remarks to Antonio that he would guarantee the Boatswain against drowning, "though the ship were no stronger than a nutshell, and as leaky as an unstanched wench" (1.1.46–48). It is an unpleasant joke, and exclusive on the two counts of class and gender. In addressing himself to Antonio and speaking of the Boatswain in his presence in the third person,

Gonzalo exploits the separateness of an aristocratic elite. Here he clearly seeks to reestablish hierarchical power, which has been dramatically and effectively challenged:

> *Gon.* Good, yet remember whom thou hast aboard.
> *Boats.* None that I love more than myself. You are a coun-sellor; if you can command these elements to silence, and work the peace of the present, we will not hand a rope more: use your authority: if you cannot, give thanks you have lived so long, and make yourself ready in the cabin for the mischance of the hour, if it so hap.
>
> (1.1.15–26)

Gonzalo's authority cannot, of course, command the elements, and he is reduced to bringing in Sebastian and Antonio as reinforcements, seeking refuge in exclusivity.

The informal designation of the ship as female was common enough and still persists in the English idiom. The wench in this case is leaky because "unstanched," generally read as a reference to menstruation. In his edition of the play, however, Orgel offers an alternative reading, that "unstanched can mean unsatisfied, and leaky may therefore imply sexual arousal" (1.1.47–48n.). Thus, Gonzalo's joke can just as readily be read as referring to the perception, described by Natalie Zemon Davis, that a woman's womb "was like a hungry animal; when not amply fed by sexual intercourse or reproduction, it was likely to wander about her body, overpowering her speech and senses" (124) and making her a very unsafe vessel indeed. Here, then, Gonzalo links two potential threats to order—libidinous women and rebellious servants—and seeks to repress them through the comradeship he shares with Antonio.

The use of the unruly woman as the target of a joke is echoed and extended in the subplot by Stephano in his drunken song:

> *The master, the swabber, the boatswain, and I,*
> *The gunner, and his mate,*
> *Loved Moll, and Meg, and Marian, and Margery,*
> *But none of us cared for Kate:*

For she had a tongue with a tang,
Would cry to a sailor, Go hang!
She loved not the savour of tar nor of pitch
Yet a tailor might scratch her where'er she did itch.
Then to sea, boys, and let her go hang!

(2.2.47–55)

Here the contrast between acceptable and unacceptable female conduct is made clear. The women preferred by the sailors are those who are appropriately silent and anonymous. Even their names merge: they are bonded by a common initial letter, and are all derivatives of Mary or Margaret. In addition, they are characterized by soft consonant sounds and open vowels, so that they sound gentle and compliant. Kate's name announces her distinctiveness: the hard consonants and clipped vowel sounds, combined with the name's emphatic placement at the end of the quatrain, express harshness. The sailors dislike her because she has a sharp tongue and the effrontery to refuse them her favors. Moreover, her admonition to the sailors to "go hang" clearly suggests deflation of phallic power. The tailor, whom she prefers, is an appropriate partner for her. Tailors were conventionally thin, weedy, and feeble—the aptly named Robin Starveling in *A Midsummer Night's Dream* is a case in point—good candidates for the henpecked husbands of dominant wives (Orgel 2.2.54n.). "Tailor," however, was also current idiom for male genitals, implying that Kate is not embracing chastity: she is usurping the male prerogative of choice.

Stephano's song is a longer and more elaborate exercise than Gonzalo's single line, but the assumptions about women expressed in them are precisely the same. Both make women the targets of jokes between men, and both emphasize the potentially dangerous, disruptive nature of female sexuality. Gonzalo uses the sexually aroused woman as a simile for a ship about to capsize and probably drown the king, and Stephano dismisses the sexually independent woman as not worthy of male attention. Both seek refuge in male camaraderie. Clearly, the need to repress unruly women is not confined to the upper classes.

In Prospero's betrothal masque, questions of gender and power are brought together with dramatic effect. The vision Prospero conjures is one of idealized civility, and the spectacle itself is strongly reminiscent of Jonson's *Hymenae* in its presentation of Juno and Iris and its emphasis on universal harmony. Thus Prospero is obliquely associated with royal power through the exploitation of the audience's knowledge of the occasion for which *Hymenae* was devised— the dynastic wedding of Frances Howard and the Earl of Essex.

Iris, the rainbow, is herself a firmly established emblem of harmony, of benign Providence, the covenant after the storm. Her presentation of Ceres emphasizes the earth goddess's role as patron of agriculture, the civilizing of nature. The scene she paints is of nature carefully ordered and governed. It is also both pure—the chaste nymphs are cold and the bachelors rejected—and contained—its coastline is "sterile and rocky-hard" (4.1.69). The forces of erotic love are explicitly banished: Cupid is reduced from rebellious and dangerous youth to innocent and playful childhood, and Venus's "dove-drawn" entry into the world of the betrothed is aborted.

The introduction of chariots, with their specifically triumphal associations, is significant here. Venus, in her dove-drawn chariot, clearly represents a triumph of love, fittingly disarmed by the stronger power of the vow of chastity. The other chariot belongs to Juno, who enters the play as an apparent anomaly: both powerful and female. She is present in her capacity as symbol of union and patroness of marriage, and as a queen, which Miranda is to become. Unlike Miranda's, though, her royal authority is her own, and is emphasized as such: she is invoked by Iris as "the queen o' th' sky" (4.1.70) and "Highest queen of state/Great Juno" (4.1.101–02), and she occupies the central position in the masque. Between the blessing of the betrothal and the dance of the reapers, however, the moment at which, in a court masque, the masquers would take to the floor with the other courtiers and the allegory of the spectacle would collapse into the reality of the court, the masque is interrupted by Ferdinand and Prospero in such a way as to draw attention to its fictive nature: "*Fer:* May I be bold / To think these spirits? *Pros:* Spirits, which by mine Art / I have from their confines call'd to enact / My present fancies" (4.1.119–22). By the early seventeenth century, "fancies" as a diminutive form of "fantasies" already carried overtones of the frivolous. Here, then, the spectacle, in which all the principals are women and which presents female monarchical power, collapses into the "reality" of Prospero's world. Prospero invalidates the powerful potential of Juno by reminding Ferdinand that she is simply "some vanity of [his] Art" (4.1.41) not even a serious demonstration of power but a trifle, an airy nothing. In presenting a powerful woman as the goddess of marriage, then neutralizing her power by reducing her to a momentary trifle of illusion, Prospero doubly represses that power.

The use of illusion here complements that in the first act, in which the Boatswain challenges the nobles to calm the storm if they can, and if not to accept that their status in the face of death is no higher than his own. In the second scene, it is made immediately clear that there is, in fact, a nobleman who can and does control the weather: the roaring of the winds and the rebellion of the Boatswain are both discovered to have been orchestrated and produced and therefore licenced by Prospero. The source and nature of Prospero's power are called into question in this context. The Boatswain's challenge to Gonzalo clearly evokes the episode in the Gospels in which Christ stills the storm (Matthew 8.23–27; Mark 4.35–41; Luke 8.22–25), so that a familiar question is present in the minds of the audience as they discover this element of Prospero's power: "What manner of man is this, that even the winds and the sea obey him!" (Matthew 8.27). Superficially, the association adds a divine dimension to Prospero's art. However, the power of Christ *stills* the storm; it does not *raise* it. Orpheus, too, as a type of Christ, uses his art to calm the natural world, not to engender turbulence within it. The power to raise tempests is a very different matter: more than one contemporary scholar had specifically linked the power to control the weather with witchcraft. In his 1608 *Discourse of The Damned Art of Witchcraft*, for example, Calvinist William Perkins includes the raising of storms, winds and weather in his catalog of the powers of Satan, and Shakespeare himself invests witches with the ability to disrupt the weather in Macbeth: "Though his bark cannot be lost, / Yet it shall be tempest-toss'd" (1.3.24–25). Thus, the nature of Prospero's power is rendered suspect from the moment it is revealed: the art by which he raises the storm may be regarded as more closely linked with the powers of Sycorax than with those of Christ or Orpheus.

The explicit relationship between masque and triumph established in the processions of Venus and Juno is central to the play as a whole. *The Tempest* is a combination of masque and triumph proper: Prospero's purpose in the invention of the spectacle is to effect his own triumphal reentry into the world and to establish his immortality. The notion of the eternal, or immortal, as indivisibly associated with royal power is fundamental to the assumptions behind the Stuart courtly aesthetic: the central position of the monarch at any courtly celebration specifically symbolized the monarch's role as divine surrogate. Ultimately, the monarch at the center of this masque is not Alonso, King of Naples, but Prospero himself. The masque is both for and about him, as well as created and directed by him, and he is the royal spectator in that he is the only one who sees the whole thing. Prospero, however, is not a king at all, but merely a duke: his claim to royalty depends entirely on the success of his plan to marry his daughter to the son of the King of Naples. He is seeking a version of immortality, in that his issue will reign as kings of Naples, and he is ironically willing to sacrifice a significant degree of immediate temporal power to achieve it: when Miranda marries Ferdinand, Milan will automatically become once again subordinate to Naples, since Prospero has no son.[5] The overriding irony is that the notion of eternity Prospero pursues is demonstrably false; it is by definition temporal.

The element missing from the betrothal masque, but

superficially present in the main action, is the antimasque. The purpose of the antimasque was to provide comedy, and to define by contrast the ideals of the main masque: antimasque offers a gross inversion of the action of the masque proper. As Dollimore points out,

> Working in terms of the principle of contrariety, virtue (masque proper) is defined, initially, in terms of its opposite (antimasque). As James I put it: 'since the Devill is the very contrarie opposite of God, there can be no better way to know God, than by contrarie' (quoted in Clarke, "Witchcraft and Kingship," 175). As masque proper displaced the inversion of antimasque it was typically the royal figure who was shown to be responsible for accomplishing this, restoring order and equilibrium analogically with God or even more directly as His delegate (27).

In this play, however, the apparently antimasque action defines the assumptions of the main masque, not by inversion, but by similitude. The relationship of the subplot to the main action is not, in fact, that of antimasque to masque proper: rather, the subplot offers a combination of burlesque and parody, subversive elements that are never part of the court masque. Linda Hutcheon defines parody as "imitation with critical ironic distance, whose irony can cut both ways" (37). Burlesque, a branch of parody with application beyond the specifically literary, employs "incongruous imitation and deflationary treatment of serious themes for satiric purposes" (Preminger, 88). Here, the satire is directed both at the masque itself and at the political structure it seeks to authorize.

The action of the subplot invites the audience to expect antimasque by including the "low" characters—Stephano, Trinculo and Caliban—and by replicating elements of masque structure, but it offers burlesque and parody instead. The ugly and deformed, half-human Caliban, for example, figures in the play as the traditional wild-man of both the antimasque and the triumphal procession. Trinculo describes him in terms of the aboriginal peoples frequently brought back to England by travelers, to be exhibited for money: "there would this monster make a man: any strange beast there makes a man: when they will not give a doit to relieve a lame beggar, they will lay out ten to see a dead Indian" (2.2.30–34). Sebastian and Antonio, however, express the same initial reaction to their first sight of Caliban:

> *Seb.* What things are these, my lord Antonio?
> Will money buy 'em?
> *Ant.* Very like; one of them
> Is a plain fish, and, no doubt, marketable.
>
> (5.1.264–66)

Thus the noble characters are drawn into the low action, rather than transcending it, and become subject to criticism in the same terms.

The clumsy antics of the clowns, choreographed by Ariel's interventions, may be seen as a kind of dance of the antimasquers, culminating, as they do, with an ugly mockery of the betrothal:

> *Cal:* . . . she as far surpasses Sycorax
> As great'st doth least.
> *Ste.* Is she so brave a lass?
> *Cal.* Ay, lord; she will become thy bed, I warrant,
> And bring thee forth brave brood.
>
> (3.2.100–03)

The language, however, offers a parody, not an inversion, of the barter imagery Prospero uses in offering Miranda to Ferdinand:

> *Pros.* O Ferdinand,
> Do not smile at me that I boast her off,
> For thou wilt find she will outstrip all praise,
> And make it halt behind her.
> *Fer.* I do believe it
> Against an oracle.
> *Pros.* Then, as my gift, and thine own acquisition
> Worthily purchased, take my daughter.
>
> (4.1.8–14)

Moreover, Caliban's perception of Miranda's function as the vessel through which a dynasty is to be established is essentially the same as Prospero's.

All the elements of the subplot define the main action not by contrariety but by imitation, or repetition. The raucous caterwauling of the inebriates provides a striking contrast to Ariel's ethereal balladry, but the music punctuates the action of the subplot in precisely the same way as Ariel's music figures in the main action. Caliban's absurd devotion to Stephano mockingly elaborates the theme of the improper use of temporal (and particularly colonial) authority, and the somewhat more sinister, but ineffectual, attempt on Prospero's life obviously mimics Sebastian and Antonio's attempt on Alonso and Gonzalo. There is no fundamental difference, however, merely distance, between the plot against Prospero and the one against Alonso and Gonzalo. Stephano's bawdy rhyme expresses the same assumptions about women as Gonzalo's joke. And Sycorax's career up to her death has been a pattern of Prospero's.

The low characters pretending to be kings are patently foolish, but only because they are not in fact aristocrats. The power structure depicted in the subplot is far from being the chaos generally depicted in antimasque. It is a precise imitation of the order prevailing in the main action, and requires the audience to regard the actual aristocrats—including Prospero—from the critical distance provided by this burlesque version of events and relationships. Thus, in inviting the audience to expect antimasque and offering instead burlesque and parody, the play undercuts not only the power structure it delineates but also the art form that legitimates it.

Nor, in fact, is order truly restored, as a masque audience would expect. Prospero's declared intention is to seek the penitence of those who have wronged him. Alonso begs his pardon readily, but Antonio, whom Prospero regards as the principal traitor, remains silent throughout the denouement: there is no expression of repentance from him. Prospero demands his dukedom and articulates his knowledge of the plot against Alonso: the knowledge gives him power, but there is no sign of reconciliation between the brothers and no resolution of Antonio and Sebastian's rebellion.

Prospero's role as inventor and theurgist sets him apart from the other characters, for he is both inside the action, experiencing it, and outside, controlling it. This is a significantly different role from that of the royal spectator, who experienced the masque first as audience and then as participant, but who did not control the action, and who might therefore be obliquely instructed by it. Alonso has clearly learned something of significance, but Prospero, as inventor, needs to function as his own guide. This element of his role is defined in the long soliloquy before he meets with the nobles, in which he reflects on his decision to abandon his magic and return to Milan. It is in this context also that he appears to accept from Ariel, his partner in invention, a lesson in mercy. In the final scene, though, there is little indication that Prospero has learned anything at all from the spectacle. Mercy is significantly absent from his "forgiveness" of Antonio, and his plan to return to Milan and retire once again to his study suggests little understanding of his original failure as a ruler.

The vision of harmony, fundamental to the form and purpose of the masque, is significantly absent here. In the aftermath of the disrupted betrothal masque, Prospero draws a conventional parallel between the play and the world: "Our revels now are ended. These our actors, / As I foretold you, were all spirits, and / Are melted into air, into thin air" (4.1.148–50). The word "revels" is distinctively associated with the court masque: it most often refers to the dance at the end in which the masquers join the courtiers, intended as an affirmation that all was right with the world. Prospero interrupts the revels here to deal with Caliban's conspiracy—itself a pattern both of the events in Milan 12 years earlier and of the aborted attempt on Alonso's life—and advises Ferdinand that the world itself is no more substantial than a masque. Thus the real world is collapsed into the illusory world of the spectacle, and not the other way around, as was the case in the Stuart court drama. Most particularly, Prospero never figures as the divine delegate, restoring order out of chaos.

The symbolic action of the long last scene is based more

firmly on the orchestration of a triumphal procession than on the masque. The fourth act closes with Prospero's claim of victory: "At this hour / Lies at my mercy all mine enemies" (4.1.263–64), and the final act begins with an elaboration of the image. He bids a formal farewell to the "rough magic" of the dramatist, which has been the agent of his victory, and at the same time calls for the "solemn air" (5.1.58) that is appropriate for a triumphal procession. The music is raised by Prospero himself, not by Ariel, who now figures as the Master of Ceremonies to the triumph, and leads in Prospero's first group of captives. The Italian nobles enter in order of rank; Prospero disposes them in his circle and begins to enumerate the wrongs he has suffered at their hands, and the reasons for their captivity. Then he dons his ceremonial robes in preparation for resuming his position in the world. Thus, when the nobles awake, Prospero stands before them ceremonially robed and centrally positioned, instantly recognizable as the Duke of Milan.

It is against the backdrop of this representation of victory that Prospero presents the culmination of his labors, the union of Ferdinand and Miranda, as a tableau in the triumphal procession and as an apparent miracle of resurrection. Gonzalo describes the essence of the moment and its significance to Prospero in an image that draws together the Christian sense of miracle with the implications of triumph:

> Look down, you gods,
> And on this couple drop a blessed crown!
> For it is you that have chalk'd forth the way
> Which brought us hither . . .
> Was Milan thrust from Milan, that his issue
> Should become Kings of Naples? O, rejoice
> Beyond a common joy! and set it down
> With gold on lasting pillars.
>
> (5.1.201–08)

The apparently rhetorical question Gonzalo asks here demands an answer, and the superficial response is affirmative. Gonzalo invokes Providence and the possibility of a divine plan in operation. Prospero is emphatically not Providence;

still, his implacable purpose from the beginning has been to establish his progeny as kings of Naples. The tableau he presents is the vision of his triumph, with the chess game as an appropriate metaphor: he has indeed used his queen to bring the Neapolitan king into check. Thus, in his final triumph, Prospero presents himself as both theurgist and monarch: his victory is apparently established; his dukedom resumed; his brother, if not penitent, is within his power; and his temporal continuance is assured in the union of his daughter and the next king of Naples. It is an ending that, like the play as a whole, looks both happier and more successful than it actually is.

In the play's shift from masque to triumph, and most particularly in the avoidance of the revels, the values of the Stuart court are inscribed but not endorsed. Despite his superficial victory and apparent power, Prospero is far from the idealized Christian monarch a masque audience would expect: every level of his triumph is called into question. His equivocation about the loss of his daughter places him in the quasi-divine position of being apparently able to resurrect the dead, but the audience remembers his claim earlier in the same scene that "graves at [his] command/ Have wak'd their sleepers, op'd and let 'em forth / By [his] so potent Art" (5.1.48–50). This is necromancy, the reverse of the divine power of resurrection. Moreover, his lie is also a cruel manipulation, one of many, which makes Alonso agree to the marriage before it is formally negotiated: "O heavens, that they were living both in Naples, / The king and queen there!" (5.1.149–50). Prospero invokes the divine power of mercy, but his forgiveness of Antonio is expressed, at best, equivocally, and it is indivisible from temporal power: "For you, most wicked sir, whom to call brother / Would even infect my mouth, I do forgive / Thy rankest fault— all of them—and require / My dukedom of thee" (5.1.130– 32). Moreover, his power in this instance depends as much on secret knowledge as on moral rectitude. Caliban finally perceives him as a god and promises, in Christian language, to "seek for grace" (5.1.295); but Caliban remains a thing of darkness and the son of the powerful Sycorax, and Prospero must ultimately acknowledge him as his own. Indeed, as he describes it, Sycorax's power to "control the moon . . ." (5.1.270) is not much different from, only somewhat less than, his own power, with which he has "bedimm'd / The noontide sun" (5.1.41), so that the implication of witchcraft remains to taint Prospero's power even in his final moment of victory.

In fact, he is returning to a world not necessarily less troubled than when he left, nor necessarily improved by his return. He has won back his dukedom and arranged the marriage of his daughter to the Neapolitan heir, but his methods have been selfish, ruthless and manipulative. And in rendering Milan thus subordinate to Naples once again, he has traded much of his newfound temporal power for a severely limited—because wholly temporal—version of immortality. Nor does the future promise harmony: in the tableau of resurrection, Prospero's final act of theurgy, Miranda acknowledges cheating as a way of political life in the world she is about to enter:

> *Mir.* Sweet lord, you play me false.
> *Fer.* No, my dearest love,
> I would not for the world.
> *Mir.* Yes, for a score of kingdoms you should wrangle,
> And I would call it fair play.
>
> (5.1.172–75)

Without the final affirmation of universal harmony to validate it, Prospero's power figures as (at best) worldly, harshly repressive and narcissistic, rather than absolute by divine decree, and his victory is essentially an empty one.

# 5 • The Politics of Disguise
## Drama and Political Theory in the Early Seventeenth Century

*Douglas F. Rutledge*

The populous globe of this our English ile
Seemde to moove backward, at the funerall pile
Of her dead female Majestie; all states,
From Nobles downe to spirits of meaner fates,
Moovde opposite to Nature and to Peace,
As if these men had bin th' Antipodes.
But see, the vertue of a Regall eye,
Th' attractive wonder of man's Majestie,
Our globe is drawne in a right line agen,
And now appeare new faces, and new men.
The elements, Earth, Water, Ayre, and Fire,
Which ever clipt a naturall desire
To combat each with other . . .
See at the peacefull presence of their King,
How quietly they movde without their sting;
Earth not devouring, Fire not defacing,
Water not drowning, and the Ayre not chasing;
But proping the queint fabrick that heere stands,
Without the violence of their wrathfull hands . . .

And then so rich an Empyre, whose fayre brest
Contaynes four Kingdomes, by your entrance blest;
By Brute divided, but by you alone
All are againe united and made one . . .
. . . in the name
Of this glad Citie, whither no Prince ever came,
More lov'd, more long'd for, lowely I intreate,
You'ld be to her as gracious as y'are great.
So with reverberate shoutes our globe shall ring,
The musick's close being thus: "God save our King."[1]

T his is how Thomas Middleton helped London celebrate the coronation of King James I. It was his contribution to the city's *Magnificent Entertainment*. Here he evokes a common theme, but one that is important to the understanding of both culture and political theory in England during the early seventeenth century. It suggests that social chaos is evoked at the passing of one monarch and can only be settled when a new monarch comes to the throne. Middleton's evocation of social chaos is horrible. Every Englishman has decided to oppose nature and peace. This opposition is represented by the inversion of cultural and physical order that Middleton imagines occurring at the antipodes, where everything is upside down. But this inversion is righted by the new monarch, who is able to prevent the elements from doing battle. James brings them together in a new physical order, just as he brings kingdoms together in a new political order for the first time since the mythical Brutus divided them.

King James himself also believed that social chaos occurs when monarchs replace one another.[2] For James, the concept is represented by a phrase that repeats itself throughout his political writings: "unsettled kingdoms." When kingdoms are peaceful, kings should rule within the law. "So as every just King in a setled kingdom," James argues in his 1609 speech to Parliament, "is bound to observe that paction made to his people by his Lawes . . ."[3] However, in James's political mythology, there was a time before the first king offered the civilizing force of law, when places were unsettled.

For example, when King Fergus appeared, Scotland was chaotic; he settled it with the raw exercise of royal power (McIlwain, 62–63). James suggests that when one monarch replaces another, the kingdom momentarily returns to this premonarchical chaos, and when it does the king regains the power of a king in his "first originall" (Speech of 1609, McIlwain, 308; Rutledge, *Measure for Measure*, 422–23). In the *Basilikon Doron*, he explains to his son Henry that the kingdoms of England, Scotland and Ireland will become unsettled when he dies, and that Henry must settle them with strict and unmitigated justice. Once they are settled, however, Henry must mix justice with mercy; otherwise, he will become a tyrant (McIlwain, 20). James envisions history, then, as a divinely controlled process of exchanging monarchs. God replaces good kings with tyrants when people are excessively licentious. He will reinstate a good king once the tyrant has settled the kingdom. In other words, both God and his king manipulate history in a circular process that releases and represses social chaos in pursuit of political harmony (*Measure for Measure*, 422–23).

The political model that describes social disorder being released each time one monarch replaces another resembles the ceremonial movement that occurs in rituals of status elevation. According to Victor Turner, rituals of status elevation and inversion, such as certain coronation ceremonies and the festival of misrule, move from structure to antistructure to renewed social structure.[4] This is achieved as ritual passengers move from rituals of separation from social status into liminality—a ritual time and space in which license is enjoyed—and finally to reincorporation into the social hierarchy.[5] During liminality, office seekers often assume a disguise that denies their social status, whereas those of low social status become more powerful. When the liminal period ends, all return to their former status. Liminality is often marked by a return to precreation chaos.[6] In other words, the unleashing of social chaos is a structural aspect of the elevation to high office.

The political potency of ritual forms has been emphasized by many experts. James Boon has argued recently that ritual "plays with structure and questions moral standards" (65). Certainly, ceremonial and carnival inversion can challenge the social hierarchy. As Bakhtin explains, "this is why festive folk laughter presents an element of victory not only over supernatural awe, over the sacred, over death; it also means the defeat of power, of earthly kings, of the earthly upper classes, of all that oppresses or restricts."[7] According to many experts, the process of disguise and social inversion involved in rituals of transition actually has the power either to criticize or praise the monarch and the principle of monarchy. Natalie Zemon Davis argues that rituals of inversion and other forms of carnival release "can both reinforce and suggest alternatives to the existing social order."[8] Turner agrees. According to him, such rituals release hostility toward authority normally held in check by the existing order, but the degree to which the ritual undermines or reinforces that order depends on the relative strength of the existing social hierarchy.[9] In other words, the politics of disguise releases pent-up hostility that might otherwise continue to foment. At least temporarily, it releases free speech. Rulers try to mitigate the release of chaotic hostility and reinforce social order, but to do that they have to have heard the hostile voices, voices that in turn suggest alternatives to the power that represses them.

If rituals evoke moments of inversion and chaos in between periods of social structure, the theater, too, can become a place of disguise and inversion in between times of authorized and hierarchical social activity.[10] A group of plays that appeared between 1603–1605 (during which time James assumed the throne, and when, after the plague abated, London celebrated his coronation) profoundly resemble rituals of status elevation and inversion. These plays include Middleton's *The Phoenix* and Marston's *The Fawn* and *The Malcontent*. At the beginning of each play, a duke or prince either lowers or has lowered his social status to assume a disguise, whereas at the end of the play he accepts a most powerful social position. In every case, this process of exchanging offices moderates a release of social chaos. Leonard Tennenhouse has considered the implications of the appearance of these plays when England was changing monarchs and concludes that "it is . . . likely that dramas were staged to remain constant to their purpose of authorizing the monarch in the face of a new political challenge."[11] Tennenhouse is certainly correct to be wary of isolated causes or single influences; however, he overstates his case. This form is more prevelant and more politically powerful than he suggests.[12] Similar forms were employed at the change of monarchs in 1553 in *Respublica*, the dramatic celebration of Mary's coronation, and can be found in works of several dramatists Tennenhouse considers.[13] Middleton wrote *Honourable Entertainments for the City of London* and contributed to *The Magnificent Entertainment*. John Marston has been associated with rituals of inversion through the Inns of Court.[14]

It is a profound coincidence that the plays Tennenhouse mentions appeared so close to the time when James was undergoing his own ritual of status elevation. As we have witnessed, rituals of status inversion and elevation contain an element of orchestrated chaos as an aspect of transition into renewed social order. In rituals of transition, subjects become kings, and kings can learn the art of rule by becoming subjects. Disguise becomes a method for Lords of Misrule to encourage chaos, but monarchs can also employ disguise to limit chaotic release and to encourage the restoration of a renewed social order, an order that should incorporate the popular complaints that will have found voice during these moments of release (*The Ritual Process*, 185).

*The Phoenix*, *The Fawn* and *The Malcontent* are plays that operate very much like ritual. They imitate the absence of a monarch through the ritual of disguise to free the repressed speech that criticizes authority. They release the chaos and discontent in the manner of rituals of transition, so the new monarch can emerge to limit chaos and renew social order. Like Middleton's celebration of James's coronation, these plays imply that James is responsible for overcoming the chaos encouraged by England's moment of transition. However, they also suggest that James either contributes to the chaos he is being called upon to restructure, or that he fails to hear the voices that the moment of transition has released.

Middleton's *The Phoenix*, for example, operates like a ritual of status elevation for both the character within the play and the king who watched it.[15] During his progress from Edinburgh to London, and during London's celebration of his coronation, James received dozens of encomiums referring to him as a Phoenix.[16] The very predictability of the word *Phoenix* being associated with transition into high office is important here because that is the central concern of the play. As he would during the ritual process, a Prince, who will soon be Duke, assumes a disguise that denies his high social position until he can reveal himself and prove himself worthy of promotion. The plot structure itself becomes an initiation into high office.

*The Phoenix* opens with the old Duke telling us that he must soon die because he has ruled exactly the number of years Elizabeth was on the throne. The old Duke is not an allegorical representation of the queen. Nevertheless, the play seems to be announcing its interest in the transition between Elizabeth and James.

Ostensibly, the Phoenix travels because traveling should make him ready to rule.[17] Yet, as he might in a ritual of status inversion or elevation, the Phoenix wants to transform his travels into a process that will invert his status, that will make him low, so he can be made high:

> *Phoenix:* For, should I bear the fashion of a prince,
> I should then win more flattery than profit;
> And I should give 'em time and warning then
> To hide their actions from me: if I appear a sun,
> They'll run into the shade with their ill deeds,
> And so prevent me.
>
> (1.1.65–70)

According to the ethos of the play, the flattery the Phoenix would receive if he represented himself would make him unworthy of rule, whereas the truth he gains in disguise will prepare him for high office. He procures this truth because (as in rituals of inversion) his disguise allows subjects openly to say what they feel. Only by reducing his status can the Prince release this hostility and learn about those who threaten his promotion. Only by becoming a subject can he become worthy of being king and insure that his kingdom is worthy of benign rule. This is the politics of disguise and the logic of rituals of status elevation.

These rituals of status inversion and elevation, which release pent-up hostility toward the social order and prepare the new monarch to rule, can help restore harmony between the ruler and the ruled, a harmony that can diminish over time (*The Ritual Process*, 177–78). Clearly, the Phoenix is thinking of the plot he designs for himself in a similar fashion, since he believes disguise itself can dissipate the disagreement between ruler and ruled that has accumulated during the last reign:

> *Phoenix*: So much have the complaints and suits of men seven, nay, seventeen years neglected, still interposed by coin and great enemies, prevailed with my pity that I cannot otherwise think but there are infectious dealing in most offices, and foul mysteries throughout all professions. And therefore I nothing doubt but to find travel enough within myself, and experience, I fear, too much. Nor will I be curious to fit my body to the humblest form and bearing, so the labor may be fruitful: for how can abuses that keep low come to the right view of a prince unless his looks lie level with them, which else will be longest hid from him, he shall be the last man sees 'em.
>
> (1.1.106–77)

Middleton may well have been warning James about vices, like bribery and flattery, that would be all too pervasive in his new court. However, the logic the Phoenix adopts to discover them—the logic of a prince becoming a subject so he can gain the wisdom of a good king—is profoundly similar to rituals of status inversion and elevation. Moreover, the wisdom he gains should help those on the lower end of the social scale and therefore restore harmony between the ruler and the ruled.

Each of the villains the Phoenix meets while in disguise threatens a principle of social order and so threatens to unsettle the kingdom. The Captain, for example, undermines the social order by inverting the value of social institutions and, like all his fellow villains, by pretending to be what he is not. The institution he most continually challenges is the family. The first time we meet Castiza, the Captain chastises her for referring to him by the title her social relationship would confer on him:

> *Castiza*: Captain, my husband.
> *Captain*: 'Slife, call me husband again and I'll play the captain and beat you.
>
> (1.2.68–70)

The Captain wants to free himself from marriage, but he cannot find the fault with his wife that would justify divorce, so he sells her for 500 crowns. This bizarre act leads the Phoenix to praise marriage, and as he does, he outlines the threat to the social order the Captain represents (2.2.161–70). If the Captain's disregard for marriage were to become legally and socially acceptable, we all, according to the Phoenix, would become bastards, and our desires would become as disordered as those of beasts.

Through his disguise, then, the Phoenix is able to observe this release of disorder, and by revealing himself, stop it. He reestablishes marital value and therefore social hierarchy and identity. In this sense, the Prince operates like James's principle of the king as lex *loquens* (McIlwain, 309). The Prince enters this scene of social chaos in disguise. When he reveals himself he becomes a speaking law, so his very presence brings order out of chaos. Just as King Fergus once settled barbaric Scotland, King James struggled to settle the Highlands, and James would have his son Henry settle his new kingdoms, so the Phoenix settles his version of social chaos by exposing the undisguised power of his social position.

The question of identity is important to this episode. The Captain is one of many characters who threaten social order by maintaining a difference between their social facade and their true characters. Like the role of husband, the social facade he displays as Captain is continually referred to as questionable. In reference to the sexual desires the word

*captain* often arouses, he himself acknowledges the difference between the social appearance of his title and the reality
of his person:

> Why didst thou marry me?
> You think, as most of your insatiate widows,
> That captains can do wonders, when 'las,
> The name does often prove the better man.

(1.2.86–89)

When he declares that he intends to sell her, Castiza agrees
that there is a difference between the title and the man,
social sign and signifier:

> Oh, then, show pity to that noble title,
> Which else you do usurp. You're no true captain
> To let your enemies lead you foul Disdain
> And everlasting Scandal oh, believe it!
> The money you receive for my good name
> Will not be half enough to pay your shame.

(2.2.28–33)

Neither socially, sexually nor ethically is the Captain's
character worth his title. Nevertheless, the title gives him
power: it gives him a wife and credit to sell. This means
he can undermine both marriage and the system of social
hierarchy that marriage reinforces.

The Prince also refers to the Captain as counterfeit. The
context in which he does underlines the logic behind the
politics of disguise. The Phoenix and Fidelio temporarily
invert their social status, so the Prince can become Duke
and Fidelio can rescue his mother. However, a similar, though
unlimited, disguise makes the captain villainous:

> *Phoenix*: Fear not me, Fidelio; become you that invisible
> rope-maker, the scrivener, that binds a man as he walks,
> yet all his joints at liberty, as well as I'll fit that common
> folly of gentry, the easy-affecting venturer, and no doubt our
> purpose will arrive most happily.
> *Fidelio*: Chaste duty, my lord, works powerfully in me; and
> rather than the poor lady my mother should fall upon the
> common side of rumor to beggar her name, I would not only
> undergo all habits, offices, disguis'd professions, though e'en

opposite to the temper my blood holds, but, in the stainless
quarrel of her reputation, alter my shape forever.

(2.1.1–12)

Fidelio is willing to become something less than he is to
prevent the reputation of his mother from being slandered.
The Phoenix, however, suggests that it is impossible for
Fidelio actually to become less because his essence determines his character and that cannot be reduced: "thou hast
a noble touch." The Phoenix and Fidelio can exercise the
logic of rituals of status elevation: they can become less in
order to become more and expose evil, but the Captain is
*essentially* less. Nothing he can do, even with the tools of
nascent capitalism in the process of marrying or venturing
for capital, can make him better. He has the essence of a
diminished character. "*Phoenix*: Captain? Off with that noble
title, thou becom'st it vilely; I never saw the name fit worse"
(2.2.323–24). Like the fool during a ritual of inversion, or
like an actor, the Captain can pretend to be something more
than he is, but he must finally be exposed and returned to
his low position in the social order.

The Captain is only one of many characters who erode
England's social hierarchy by misusing titles. For example,
Falso undermines the judicial, linguistic and familial systems by being both judge and thief: "I can take my ease,
sit in my chair, look in your faces now, and rob you; make
you bring your money by authority, put off your hat, and
thank me for robbing of you." (3.1.61–65). We see Falso
undermining the judicial system by taking bribes and condemning the thief, his servant, to confinement within his
own home. Falso's language also threatens the social system.
Not only is he able rhetorically to make a hero out of someone
who has looted the church vestry, but he also tries to make
uncles into husbands:

> *Falso*: And what's a husband, is not a stranger at first? And
> will you lie with a stranger before you lie with your own
> uncle? Take heed what ye do, Niece, I counsel you for the
> best: strangers are drunken fellows, I can tell you; they will
> come home late o'nights, beat their wives, and get nothing

but girls! Look to't, if you marry, your stubbornness is your dowry.[18]

(2.3.60–66)

If Falso undermines the family structure by using language, his daughter does much the same thing. She begins by telling the Knight she can commit adultery with him anywhere; she then tells her father that the Knight is her brother-in-law, and she concludes by confusing the sexual identity of husband and brother-in-law (2.3.11–20). Social hierarchy is eviscerated when people can change social roles and alter the language of family. When the Prince becomes less and subjects become more, the social structure diminishes into chaos. The Jeweller's Wife helped create the world in which, according to the Phoenix, we are all bastards and our desires are bestial.

The Knight not only contributes to the deterioration of the familial structure, but to that of the social hierarchy as well; for just as the Captain bears a title that fails to reflect his worth, so the Knight lacks the essence of knighthood. This is perhaps best demonstrated in an interchange between Falso and the Knight:

> *Falso:* Why, this is but the second time of your coming, kinsman; visit me oft'ner. Daughter, I charge you bring this gentleman along with you: gentleman I cry ye mercy, sir, I call you gentleman still, I forget you're but a knight; you must pardon me, sir.
> *Knight:* For your worship's kindness; worship—I cry you mercy, sir, I call you worshipful still, I forget you're but a justice.
>
> (2.3.1–8)

The point is that neither man is worth his social position.[19] The Justice is able to steal, to defraud his niece of her inheritance, and to free thieves in the act of condemning them because he has a social identity of which he is unworthy. The Knight sells himself to the Jeweller's Wife, thereby undermining the family. She is willing to buy, because she wrongly thinks he has influence at court. Moreover, the Knight receives credit from others who think him worthy of it because of his social position, but they are clearly wrong. The language of family and of social structure is being destroyed. The question is whether the new Duke will be able to make the social language coherent again by returning those who release social chaos through the use of counterfeit titles to their appropriately low position in the social hierarchy.

Given the extent to which the process of assuming an undeserved identity is shown to undermine social and familial order, the criticism of the Knight becomes a serious satirical glance at James I. The Knight clearly represents one of those hundreds of knights James created during his progress to London or shortly after his coronation (Stone, 74). Middleton's play, like his speech in *The Magnificent Entertainment*, wants to celebrate James's ability as a new monarch to bring order out of chaos. Simultaneously, however, *The Phoenix* exercises its own license to suggest that James has been contributing to the very social chaos he is being called upon to restructure.

In that regard, this play offers another serious challenge to James's political theories:

> *Phoenix*: That king stands sur'st who by his virtues rises
> More than by birth or blood; that prince is rare
> Who strives in youth to save his age from care . . .
> *Fidelio*: Thou wonder of all princes, precedent, and glory,
> True phoenix, made of an unusual strain!
> Who labors to reform is fit to reign.
> How can that king be safe that studies not
> The profit of his people?
>
> (1.1.130–39)

The suggestion that a king's virtue is more important than his blood would be antithetical to James's belief that God chooses monarchs. God chooses them by birth, and the degree to which they are either good kings or tyrants would depend on how much God wanted to restrain the licentiousness of his people.

Fidelio continues this challenge to Jacobean absolutism when he suggests that only a king who labors to reform is fit to reign. In James's political theory, reform cannot be seen as a prerequisite to rule. That is a matter between God and his kings. The next implication, that kings cannot feel safe if they do not work toward reform and study the profit of their people, suggests that this dynamic might not strictly belong to the power and judgment of God and king, but that people might *justifiably* revolt if their interests are not considered. This clearly would be threatening to James's position.

While rituals normally reinforce the social order, Peter Burke argues that "there might be a 'switching' of codes, from the language of ritual to the language of rebellion."[20] Such switching nearly seems to have occurred within this play. Margot Heinemann argues that Middleton was a radical Puritan throughout most of his career, but she asserts that *The Phoenix* does not reflect this.[21] However, the position the Phoenix and Fidelio outline here could be considered radical in relationship to Jacobean absolutism. The politics of disguise is becoming threatening.

James is further challenged by the theme of deserving, as opposed to inheriting, social position. The importance of this theme becomes evident if we compare the play's attitudes toward Proditor and Fidelio. Proditor is noble by birth but not by virtue. His name, after all, means traitor. Phoenix is led to ask of him, "Why should this fellow be a lord by birth, / Being by blood a knave" (2.2.235–36)? The other nobles we meet waste their time and estates on gambling and dissolute living (5.1.89–97). By contrast, Fidelio lacks Proditor's power, but he has the essence of nobility: "the noble touch." On one hand, the play questions James's gift of so many knighthoods, which has diminished the value of this social position. On the other, it questions the value of inherited office, since merit and birth do not always conjoin. It is worth noting that James could claim the throne by right of birth, but two acts of Parliament made his assuming the throne illegal.[22]

James is also powerfully, if subtly, challenged by the play's exposure of legal disease in the person of Tangle. If characters like Proditor, the Knight and the Captain threaten

social hierarchy by failing to make their interiors and their
social positions equivalent, Tangle threatens the entire legal
if not linguistic system by making the result of legal action
different from the intent of the law—and the law, according
to James, is equivalent to the voice of the king.[23] Tangle
changes occurrences into legal jargon, not because he is
concerned with questions of facts, law or legal processes.
Often he translates concepts into Latin simply to impress
and ultimately to confuse. Part of Tangle's purpose seems
to be to invert the entire social order by confusing people
and pulling them into the legal system. At 1.4.111–46, Tangle
so confuses the social order with legal argument that he
inverts it, turning beggars into gentlemen and fellows into
knaves, as he vexes the community.

Tangle's cure fits a series of disease metaphors which
imply that the community's lack of morality is responsible
for disease and that the monarch is responsible for the
morality of his subjects. In the same way that the Phoenix
has to cut into his subject's world—hitherto kept secret from
him by his social position—to scourge his subjects' licentiousness and settle his duchy, so Quieto must cut into
Tangle to purge him of the excesses that make him live
up to his name:

> *Phoenix*: Oh, do you sluice the vein now?
> *Quieto*: Yes, my honor'd lord. . . .
> *Quieto*: The balsam of a temperate brain
> I pour into this thirsty vein, [*pours fluid from bottle.*]
> And with this blessed oil of quiet,
> Which is so cheap that few men buy it,
> Thy stormy temples I allay: [*rubs fluid on* Tangle's *fore-
> head.*] . . .
> Therefore no more this combat choose,
> Where he that wins does always lose . . .
> *Tangle*: Hail, sacred patience! I begin to feel
> I have a conscience now; truth in my words,
> Compassion in my heart, and, above all,
> In my blood peace's music. Use me how you can,
> You shall find me an honest, quiet man. . . .

*Phoenix:*We both admire the workman and his piece.
Thus, when all hearts are tun'd to honor's strings,
There is no music to the choir of kings.

(5.1.304–47)

The disease from which Quieto cures Tangle becomes a
metaphor for the moral disease of various subjects the Phoenix
must cure.[24] We have heard the old Duke of Ferrara note
the disease of too much pity (1.1.9–10) and the Phoenix
speak of the diseases that develop from lax enforcement of
the law (1.1.109). Within the imagistic pattern of the play,
moral disease is often described as the plague. For example,
just after the Phoenix and Fidelio expose the Captain, he
describes himself as being punished by a divine plague
(2.2.309–11). He soon recognizes himself as both an object
and a source of the plague: "Well, I'm yet glad, I've liberty
and these; / The land has plagu'd me, and I'll plague the
seas" (2.2.336–37). By getting rid of the Captain, the Phoenix
relieves his land of a source of the disease. Later (5.1.227–
29) the Phoenix implies that the carnal sins of the Jeweller's
Wife are spreading the plague and that her exposure might
help stem its spread. This theme suggests that the plague
is a divine punishment for the moral laxness of the citizens
of Ferrara. This laxness, the disease of pity, can become
acute as the old reign ends. For example, Lawrence Stone
asserts that, "Despite all Elizabeth's efforts . . . moral standards at court deteriorated during her later years" (665).
Therefore, it becomes the responsibility of the new ruler to
purge the duchy of its immorality in order to settle the
kingdom and placate the God who punishes it with the
plague that never leaves the city.

An outbreak of the plague may have postponed the
performance of this play by several months, not in a fictional
city, but in the English one that was preparing to receive
its new king. As James moved toward his new court, London
was tormented by the plague, which killed at least 30,000
people there and closed the theaters from March 1603 until
April 1604.[25] Even the city's celebration of James's coronation,
*The Magnificent Entertainment*, had to be postponed until

the rages of the plague subsided (*Elizabethan Stage*, 1: 349).
*The Phoenix* suggests that the plague London suffers from
is a metaphor for a moral disease James has the responsibility to cure through justice and reform. It implies that
James has contributed to London's moral disease by promoting people to knighthood who are unworthy. It also suggests
that if James proves incapable of reform, he is himself
unworthy of monarchy. *The Phoenix* achieves all this with
a plot that is remarkably similar to rituals of status elevation
and the structure with which James I imagines God managing history in the *Basilikon Doron* and the *Trew Law of
Free Monarchies.*

   Written very close to the time *The Phoenix* was composed, Marston's *Malcontent* is even more clearly concerned
with rituals of status elevation and inversion, for it contains
a ritual of status elevation within itself:

> *Mendoza*: And, Celso, prithee, let it be thy care tonight
> To have some pretty show, to solemnize
> Our high installment—some music, masquery . . . .
> *Celso*: Of what shape, sweet lord?
> *Mendoza*: Why, shape? Why, any quick-done fiction,
> As some brave spirits of the Genoan dukes
> To come out of Elysium, forsooth,
> Led in by Mercury, to gratulate
> Our happy fortune . . .[26]

The real answer to Celso's question is that the pretty show
to solemnize installment to high office should be shaped
like rituals of status elevation. They should be structured
through the process of a ruler assuming a disguise and later
revealing himself. This shape involves the exchange of offices
that prepares subjects to be ruled and monarchs to rule.
Through Malevole's trickery, Mendoza's masque is given
this shape, and so is the larger play.

   Pietro unknowingly begins to describe this process of
inversion when he first offers his impression of Malevole:

> *Pietro*: This Malevole is one of the most prodigious affec-
> tions that ever convers'd with nature: a man, or rather a
> monster, more discontent than Lucifer when he was thrust

out of the presence. His appetite is unsatiable as the grave,
as far from any content as from heaven. His highest delight
is to procure others' vexation, and therein he thinks he truly
serves heaven . . .

(1.2.16–28)

Pietro speaks more wisely than he realizes. In some respects,
Malevole is like Lucifer, who lost the struggle for rule and
was thrust from God's presence. As Altofronto, Malevole
did rule, but when he lost a political struggle, he was thrust
from the presence chamber. Although this discontent, as
Pietro suggests, makes him vex others, Pietro correctly implies
that Malevole serves heaven through this process. Like God's
exchange of good king for tyrant in James's political theory,
and the exchange of competent king for fool in rituals of
status elevation, Marston's exchange purges people of their
licentiousness and prepares the Duke to rule so a new
harmony can be achieved. By making Pietro and his court
perceive those weaknesses, which the flattery of others
palliates, Marston brings them closer to God, and therefore
makes them more capable of being ruled by a good king.

We are told that Altofronto and the people he ruled needed
to learn how to fulfill their roles in the social order:

> Behold forever-banish'd Altofront,
> This Genoa's last year's duke. O truly noble!
> I wanted those old instruments of state,
> Dissemblance and suspect. I could not time it, Celso;
> My throne stood like a point in middest of a circle,
> To all of equal nearness; bore with none;
> Reign'd all alike; so slept in fearless virtue,
> Suspectless, too suspectless; till the crowd,
> Still lickerous of untried novelties,
> Impatient with severer government,
> Made strong with Florence, banish'd Altofront.

(1.4.7–17)

Both ruler and ruled must learn the lessons that can only
be taught through the politics of disguise. The process of
exchange forces the central character to integrate both
extremes of his personality to make a good ruler. The idealistic

Altofronto must learn some of the cynical suspicion of Malevole, and Malevole must integrate the noble virtue of Altofronto. He must learn to hear the legitimate needs of his subjects and to distinguish them from licentious desires. This is one of the goals of the play and of the politics of disguise. The other is that the corrupt and licentious court should become worthy of a good ruler by being punished with a bad one. All of this occurs through a process of disguise and revelation that resembles rituals of status inversion and elevation.

Learning how to rule is achieved during ritual by a release from high social position. Just as the fool enjoys a psychological release when he is elevated to the ruler's status, so the ruler experiences release when he is freed from the responsibility of rule. Ironically, as we have seen, when released from power, the ruler also discovers the concerns of his subjects and the ways to govern them. When Malevole describes his experience with disguise, he describes both the release and the revelation in a similar fashion:

> Well, this disguise doth yet afford me that
> Which kings do seldom hear, or great men use—
> Free speech; and though my state's usurp'd,
> Yet this affected strain gives me a tongue
> As fetterless as is an emperor's.
> I may speak foolishly, ay, knavishly,
> Always carelessly, yet no one thinks it fashion
> To poise my breath; for he that laughs and strikes
> Is lightly felt, or seldom struck again.
>
> (1.3.158–66)

Just as fools become monarchs during rituals of status inversion and elevation, so Altofronto, as Malevole, has become a fool—or at least assumed the right of speaking foolishly—and fools, unlike great men, can speak freely. However, the benefit of inversion is even greater than this. Malevole points out that not only do great men seldom use free speech, they seldom hear it. Now the flatterers who surround the king are unable to influence Malevole. Only by having the ear of a subject will Malevole hear the truths that offer the right to rule once again. This is an aspect of the politics of disguise.

The shape of *The Malcontent* reveals itself most profoundly when Pietro becomes the second duke to assume a disguise. Shortly after he dons the monk's cowl, which denies his political authority, he wishes that authority returned to Altofronto (at 4.5.119–28). Immediately after Pietro's disquisition, Malevole undisguises himself to become Altofronto. The fool, who has been imitating a monarch, covers his disguise and reveals that he is not a king. Simultaneously, the monarch sheds the fool's disguise to reassume the monarchy and restore order. This is the shape of rituals of status inversion and elevation. As if to make certain we have gotten the point, Malevole soon describes the process of disguise in terms that resemble a description of such rituals:

> O God, how loathsome this toying is to me! That a Duke should be forc'd to fool it! Well, "*Stultorum plena sunt omnia*": better play the fool lord than be the fool lord.
>
> (5.3.41–44)

As in rituals of status inversion and elevation, the Duke must temporarily imitate a fool. Of course, even while he is playing the fool, the Duke remains essentially a duke, whereas the fool must remain a fool. Although Pietro develops toward the end of the process of exchange, he remains lower than, more foolish than, and essentially a subject of Altofronto.

As we have noted, rituals of status inversion and elevation move from structure to antistructure to renewed social structure. Since Altofronto has already been removed from the throne to become Malevole, the play opens in a period of antistructure. Bilioso responds to that atmosphere by declaring, "Fore God, I think the world be turn'd upside down too" (3.1.121). Bilioso contributes extensively to the atmosphere of inversion. As Altofronto fulfills half the equation of inversion by acting the fool and assuming a disguise that denies his status, Bilioso wishes to fulfill the other half by dressing his fool as if he were an aristocrat:

> *Bilioso*: . . .Passarello, my fool, shall go along with me; marry,

he shall be in velvet.
*Biancha*: A fool in velvet?
*Bilioso*: Ay, 'tis common for your fool to wear satin; I'll have
mine in velvet.
*Biancha*: What will you wear, then, my lord?
(3.1.59–64)

This is a "world most vile, when thy loose vanities, / Taught
by this fool, do make the fool seem wise" (1.8.53–54). This
world will lose its vanities only when the fool and the tyrant
lose power, to be replaced by Altofronto.

It is appropriate that Altofronto replace Mendoza in a
masque, a masque designed as part of a ritual of status
elevation, because a masque, like ritual, demands that rulers
undergo a process of disguise and revelation. The masque
begins as Mendoza's celebration of high status and ends as
Altofronto's. It resembles Aurelia's dance. As Aurelia struggles to ignore the announcement of her husband's death,
she is offered the opportunity to dance the *Passa regis*. This
dance of kings is a metaphor for the masque, the play, and
for rituals of status inversion and elevation. During the ritual,
the dance, and the play itself, rulers continually change places.
During the masque, Duke Altofronto disguises himself as
a subject and reveals himself to be a ruler. He transforms
Mendoza's "quick done fiction," intended to celebrate the
tyrant's enthronement, into a ritual of status elevation that
celebrates his own return to high office.

*The Malcontent's* relationship to James's elevation to the
English monarchy is interesting. Finkelpearl's helpful definition of the word *malcontent* as a "prime source of danger
to the kingdom" (184) relates to certain documents contemporary with this play. For example, Sir John Harrington sent
his new king a gift, and attached to it the following poem:

Come, Tryumph; enter Church, Court, Citty, Towne;
Here James the Sixt, now James the First, proclaymed:
See how all harts ar heald, that erst were maymed,
The Peere is pleasd, the Knight, the Clarck, the Clowne.
The mark, at which *the Malecontent* had aymed,
Is mist, Succession stablisht in the Crowne,

Joy, Protestant; Papist, be now reclaymed;
Leave, Puritan, your supercillious frowne,
  Joyn voice, hart, hand, all discord be disclaymed.
Be all one flock, by one great sheppard guided:
  No forren wolf can force a fould so fenced,
God for his house a Steward hath provided,
  Right to dispose what erst was wrong dispenced.
  But with a loyall love and long praepenced,
With all, yet more than all, rejoyce do I,
To conster James Primus, et non VI.

(Nichols 1: 49, my emphasis)

This poem reveals that, during a short period surrounding James's coronation, it was at least possible to use the word *malcontent* to refer to groups that either opposed the succession or justified overthrowing the king. Within the play, Malevole suggests that he is a similar kind of malcontent:

*Malevole*: . . . I mean to turn pure Rochelle churchman, I.
*Mendoza*: Thou churchman! Why, why?
*Malevole*: Because I'll live lazily, rail upon authority, deny kings' supremacy in things indifferent, and be a pope in mine own parish.

(2.5.117–122)

This is certainly the pose of the Puritan who expresses frowning discontent with authority. It is often difficult to tell the difference between Malevole and Altofronto, so it is difficult to tell how seriously to take some of Malevole's ironic salvos. Nevertheless, the politics of neither is congruent with James's, which is perhaps why the censor found the original version of *The Malcontent* challenging to the king (Finkelpearl, 192–93). So both the play's main character and the play itself resemble, to some extent, this dangerous kind of malcontent.

The play earns the title of Malcontent by satirizing the king. One personality trait of a bad king, according to the play, is a weakness for flattery. This is one of James's attributes that became obvious to his subjects shortly after he arrived in London;[27] it and a lack of honor are the subjects of the play's slurs against Scots:

*Bilioso*: 'Fore God . . . I am in wondrous credit, lady.
*Biancha*: See the use of flattery; I did ever counsel you to
flatter greatness, and you have profited well. Any man that
will do so shall be sure to be like your Scotch barnacle, now
a block, instantly a worm, and presently a great goose: this
it is to rot and putrefy in the bosom of greatness.

(3.1.44–49)

The barnacle, a tree native to Scotland, hosts a white shell,
which, in turn, hosts larvae. The important image is that
of a parasite clinging to something strong and noble, and
while it clings, it rots. In Biancha's narration, its right to
cling is earned only by its ability to flatter, and the nation
from which this rotting, flattering parasite hails is Scotland.

Not only Scotland, but St. Andrew, her patron saint, and
the name of James become the butt of another joke told
by Biancha and the woman of ill repute, Maquerelle:

*Biancha*: And is not Signior St. Andrew [Jaques] a gallant
fellow now?
*Maquerelle*: By my maidenhead, la, honor and he agrees as
well together as a satin suit and woolen stockings.

(5.5.23–25)

Suggesting that someone called St. Andrew was antithetical
to honor in 1603–1604, when the English theater was replete
with anti-Scottish jokes, could by itself be a challenging
reference to James. The original quarto, however, referred
not simply to St. Andrew, but to St. Andrew Jaques, and
Jaques is the French equivalent of James (Finkelpearl, 192–
93). The passage associates the patron saint of Scotland with
James, and then suggests that neither agrees with honor. The
censor found this reference too suggestive and perhaps too
inflammatory, so it was struck. The question for the censor
and for the rest of its audience is, does this play of changing
monarchs teach us the difference between a good king and
a bad one, and then challenge James's claim to the title of
good king?

Altofronto's concluding political vision is by no means
democratic, but in some respects it is closer to the views
of the Puritans, the Rochelle churchmen that Malevole

ironically invokes, than it is to those expressed in the *Basilikon Doron* and *The Trew Law of Free Monarchy*:[28]

> For such thou art, since birth doth ne'er enroll
> A man among monarchs, but a glorious soul.
> O, I have seen strange accidents of state!
> The flatterer, like ivy, clip the oak
> And waste it to the heart; lust so confirm'd
> That the black act of sin itself not sham'd
> To be term'd courtship.
> O, they that are as great as be their sins,
> Let them remember that th' inconstant people
> Love many princes merely for their faces
> And outward shows; and they do covet more
> To have a sight of these than of their virtues.
> Yet thus much let the great ones still conceive:
> When they observe not heaven's impos'd conditions,
> They are no kings, but forfeit their commissions.
>
> (5.6.130–44)

The concluding couplet here is a little ambiguous and more than a little threatening. James certainly believed that kings were answerable to God and that God would punish kings who did not rule according to his divine will. However, especially considering the earlier separation of birth from monarchy, one could read these lines as implying that kings rule according to commission or contract, and once that contract is violated, they are no longer kings. Like ordinary citizens, they could now be tried and executed. Altofronto would not entrust "that beast with many heads" (3.3.4), as Celso refers to the population of ordinary citizens, to judge that a king has forfeited his divine commission. But would he, like Calvin, allow certain magistrates to make such a decision (502–04),[29] or would he entrust the decision to a process of judicial review, as Buchanan does (60-63)? Within the play, Malevole drives Duke Pietro to reform himself and to decide to relinquish his rule. This would have been in keeping with James's political philosophy (McIlwain, 61). The concluding couplet of Altofronto's speech, however, might suggest that at least certain people can judge the king and that their response is absolute. After all, the speech is part of a dramatic event that has taught us how to judge. We have been shown the qualities of a good king, a foolish king and a tyrant, and we have been told that when a king stops being a good—when he stops ruling within heaven's imposed conditions—he is no longer a king. The play has taught us to make a judgment that, according to James, it is illegal for a subject to make. Even to consider the difference between a good king and a tyrant is to violate the *arcana imperii*, the divine mystery of monarchy.[30] But this play, like rituals of status inversion and elevation, has brought the monarch low enough to be judged, and it has raised the audience high enough to make a judgment. As it did for Malevole, disguise seems to have offered this play an unheard of degree of free speech.

Free speech is also one of the central concerns of *The Fawn*, and in it speaking freely is linked with rituals of inversion (Finkelpearl, 227ff).[31] Considering that Jonson, Chapman, and perhaps Marston himself were imprisoned for the political implications of *Eastward Ho*, and that the censor had demanded changes in *The Malcontent*, one can understand why Marston might want to offer a disclaimer in his prologue to anyone who finds political implications in the *Fawn*. The prologue promises to respect social structure. It promises not to satirize specific public or private persons; it will "let others dare the rope."[32] However, the fool, Dondolo, tells us that his satire has a broader political license:

> I warrant thee, old lad, 'tis the privilege of poor fools to talk before an intelligencer. Marry, if I could fool myself into a lordship, as I know some to ha' fool'd themselves out of a lordship . . . I should talk treason though I ne'er open'd my lips.
>
> (4.1.222–27)

The fool can speak before a spy with license, but if, in the way of rituals of inversion, the social order were to invert itself and the fool were to gain a lordship, he would immediately be guilty of treason, because he has always spoken freely. One wonders whether the structure of the prologue or the license of the fool is to be more respected.[33] The fool has something in common with Hercules. Hercules is taken for a spy a second time here, and rightly so. He is Cupid's spy, who will put many members of the court into the ship of fools, but he is taken for the kind of spy who would prevent free speech: the duke's spy. Ironically, however, as Cupid's spy, he will end by challenging the prologue and encouraging free speech.

One of the primary themes of the play sides with the fool's freedom, not with the restraint of the prologue:

> Most spotless kingdom,
> And men, O happy born under good stars,
> Where what is honest you may freely think,
> Speak what you think, and write what you do speak,
> Not bound to servile soothings.
>
> (1.2.319–23)

This is Hercules, who will expose the Duke of Urbin's court through a speech that is anything but free; fawning or flattery is the most restrained kind of speech because its speaker says exactly what his or her auditor wants to hear. While the prologue was similarly restrained, Hercules is here speaking something like the fool's treason because he is openly criticizing the kind of kingdom that would send Jonson, Chapman and Marston to jail for *Eastward Ho* and would censor *The Malcontent*.

Significantly, by the time he says this, Hercules has undergone something similar to a ritual of separation. Just before they part, Duke Hercules's brother, Renaldo, must ask his sovereign for the license to speak freely: "My prince and brother, let my blood and love challenge / the freedom of one question" (1.1.5–6). This is a culturally appropriate thing to say, but it also means that people do not have license to say what they want to the Duke of Ferrara. Hercules has something to learn by separating from his high status:

> Ye proud, severer, stateful complements,
> The secret arts of rule, I put you off;
> Nor ever shall those manacles of form
> Once more lock up the appetite of blood.

'Tis now an age of man, whilst we all strict
Have liv'd in awe of carriage regular
Apted unto my place, nor hath my life
Once tasted of exorbitant affects,
Wild longings, or the least of disrank'd shapes.
But we must once be wild, 'tis ancient truth.
O fortunate, whose madness falls in youth!

(1.1.37–47)

Hercules puts off the secret arts of rule, just as he will put on a disguise that denies his power. He separates himself from social restraints because he wants to move into something wild.[34] He wishes a temporal space in which he can release his inherent wildness before it is restrained again by returning to social structure. During that release, he will learn the significance of free speech. This is the shape of the play, and it is the shape of rituals of status inversion and elevation.

The liminal portion of the ritual, between temporal spaces of social structure, allows for the release of free speech both within and without the play. The play speaks freely, if treasonably, outside itself by the very act of demanding a license to speak freely and by satirizing flattery—a vice for which, as we have noted, the Jacobean court quickly became famous. Within the play, excessive flattery itself releases a kind of free speech that forces those in power to reexamine themselves. The question is whether or not free speech will have a similar effect on those in power *outside* the play, and whether or not—both in and outside the play—the allowance of free speech will remain after the return to social structure.

Within the liminal section, Hercules learns the value of free speech through inversion. Of course, he can only do this by playing a subject in the court of a fool, for if he were recognized as a duke, no one would speak openly to him. Significantly, the scene in which Hercules learns the value of free speech is set off by his being taken as a spy for Duke Gonzago, a spy who would report and therefore restrict free speech. When Herod sees Hercules enter, he responds by saying, "Now the jail deliver me, an intelligencer!

Be good to me ye cloisters of bondage" (1.2.202–04). Hercules is in turn afraid that Herod and Nymphadoro will inform on him if he speaks his mind, but Herod reassures him (at 1.2.246–50). This may be a comic world, but it also seems to be a dangerous one; people openly worry about being punished if they say what they believe. In this context, Herod and Nymphadoro explain how unnatural they believe the proposed marriage to be between Duke Gonzago's 15-year-old daughter and the 65-year-old Duke Hercules. They can tell him this—and more importantly, he can hear this—because his status has been reduced. In this diminished state, Hercules learns an important truth about himself and about the principle of free speech:

> I think a prince
> Whose tender sufferance never felt a gust
> Of bolder breathings, but still liv'd gently fann'd
> With the soft gales of his own flatters' lips,
> Shall never know his own complexion.
> . . . I now repent
> Severe indictions to some sharp styles;
> Freeness, so't grow not to licentiousness,
> Is grateful to just states.
>
> (1.2.306–19)

Ironically, after various declarations that Hercules, Herod and Nymphadoro can speak freely in each other's presence, Hercules agrees to spy on the Duke and Dulcimel for them: "I'll be your intelligencer, your very heart, and if need be work to most desperate ends" (1.2.286–87). Of course, he does spy on the court, but not in the way he suggests to Herod and Nymphadoro. Now that he has learned the value of free speech, he will actively promote it. He only spies on and exposes the degree to which all are foolish and subject to flattery. Not until Hercules presides at Cupid's court will Nymphadoro realize to what extent his friend has acted as a spy: "Shame o' Folly, will Fawn now turn an informer? Does he laugh at me" (5.1.234–35)? By the time he has insight enough to ask those questions, Nymphadoro realizes to his cost that the answer is obviously yes.

Moreover, through this inversion, the theater itself is taking more license than the prologue implies, for it clearly suggests that the Jacobean court and James himself would improve if free speech were possible and flattery repressed. As a number of critics have pointed out, Duke Gonzago resembles James I in many general ways.[35] Gonzago, for instance, is proud of himself as a philosopher and as a wise king. He suggests that he speaks briefly and plainly, when in fact the opposite is true. In a speech remarkably similar to a passage in the *Basilikon Doron* (McIlwain, 19–20; also see 277, 288), Gonzago also praises Cupid's legal vision:

> Since multitude of laws are signs of either much tyranny in the prince or much rebellious disobedience in the subject, we rather think it fit to study how to have our old laws thoroughly executed, than to have new statutes cumbrously invented.
>
> (5.1.172–76)

In addition to this general satiric portrait, the play contains a specific challenge to one of the basic tenets of Jacobean absolutism: the premise that kings receive special grace from God and are therefore in a privileged position to make executive decisions.[36] Duke Gonzago gives voice to exactly this principle (4.1.580–85). If he were simply human, Gonzago admits, he would be simply foolish, but as heaven interferes, he believes he has the wisdom that God confers on his monarchs. Yet every act Gonzago accomplishes and thinks is wise, the play argues is simply foolish. Every time Gonzago attempts to prevent the union of Tiberio and Dulcimel, every time he consults Granuffo, the silent lord whom Gonzago regards as intelligent, and every time Gonzago cites Cicero or Pliny for no apparent reason, the play ironically lets us know that the Duke is simply foolish. Only flatterers speak to Gonzago until the conclusion of the play, but outside his presence, Herod offers the unflattering, but popular opinion of his duke:

> By this night I'll speak broadly first and thou wilt, man. Our Duke of Urbin is a man very happily mad, for he thinks

himself right perfectly wise, and most demonstratively learned;

(1.2.252–55)

That this duke, who clearly belongs on the ship of fools, should believe that he receives the special grace and share of wisdom that God grants monarchs, undercuts the principle of monarchical grace itself. That Gonzago should so remarkably resemble James I undercuts James's claims to eloquence and wisdom. Like Dondolo, the play is exercising the license of free speech to the extent that it is becoming treasonous.

The distance between the political silence the prologue promises and the treasonous free speech Dondolo engages in makes the point of the play ambiguous.[37] Indeed, the play seems to operate in a fashion similar to Dulcimel's plan to trick her father into conveying her messages to Tiberio:

> let my wise, aged, learned, intelligent father... forbid all interviews, all speeches, all tokens, all messages, all (as he thinks) human means. I will speak to the prince, court the prince that he shall understand me. Nay, I will so stalk on the blind side of my all-knowing father's wit that, do what his wisdom can, he shall be my only mediator, my only messenger, my only honorable spokesman.
>
> (3.1.236–46)

Dulcimel is among the most politically suppressed people in this play. As the daughter of the Duke, she has a degree of power and privilege, yet because she is a woman, she has very few rights. And if her father were to have his way, she would become a powerless and, more important, a voiceless element in a political marriage. She defies that repression, however, and gains the license of free speech through ambiguity and the inflation of her father's ego. As long as he thinks what she says reflects his high position in the patriarchal hierarchy, he will interpret the text she offers accordingly. However, because the text she offers is ambiguous, she uses it to overthrow his authority as father and even as duke. The most important question the text of the larger play asks is: to what extent is it operating like Dulcimel's text? To what extent does it also speak to the blind side of a monarch's wit?

The play's central satirist, in fact, suggests that court reform should occur in a similarly indirect, yet dramatic fashion:

> O mighty flattery,
> Thou easiest, common'st, and most grateful venom
> That poisons courts and all societies,
> How grateful dost thou make me? . . .
> Free speech gains foes, base fawnings steal the heart.
> Swell, you impostum'd members, till you burst,
> Since 'tis in vain to hinder; on I'll thrust,
> And when in shame you fall, I'll laugh from hence,
> And cry, "So end all desperate impudence."
> Another's court shall show me where and how
> Vice may be cur'd. . . .
>
> (2.1.554–66)[38]

This passage is interesting not only because it sums up a number of themes we have been examining—such as the physical and psychological damage that flattery offers, as opposed to the curative powers of free speech—but also because of the reflective, almost fictional, way the cure is to take place. Another's court will show Hercules how his can be cured. Afterwards, he will reenact the cure in his own court. According to much seventeenth century theory, this is the way drama should operate.[39] The rulers of one court come to the theater to observe another, and the reform the logic of the drama implies is to be enacted by the rulers when they leave the theater. This brings us back to the prologue. There, the play claimed to be satirizing no public or private persons, but here it tells us how it is to be interpreted, and who but the obvious ruler of the obvious court could be expected to respond to the fictional Court of Urbin in the way that Hercules outlines here? Marston, like Dulcimel, seems to be speaking to the blind side of a monarch's wit, but the text would ultimately become more effective if the monarch's wit were a little less blind.

The fictional duke does, in fact, become a little less blind.

As the play moves from liminality and antistructure back to renewed social structure, Gonzago is made to recognize his foolishness:

> Death o' discretion! if I should prove a fool now. Am not I an ass, think you, ha? I will have them both bound together, and sent to the Duke of Ferrara presently.
>
> (5.1.443–45)

Hercules undergoes something profoundly resembling a ritual of reincorporation when he changes himself back from the Fawn that Duke Gonzago knows throughout the play to Hercules, the Duke of Ferrara, whom he knew before the play began. When that happens, Gonzago must acknowledge the embarrassing truth that only he has been foolish enough to wish his 15-year-old daughter married to the 65-year-old duke. When he recognizes this, Duke Gonzago grows: "By the Lord, I am ashamed of myself, that's the plain troth. But I know now wherefore this parliament was. What a slumber have I been in" (5.1.452–54). The process of disguise and the satire of inversion have awakened Duke Gonzago, as they earlier awakened Duke Hercules. Free speech has achieved something within the fictional court, but presumably it had little effect on the court outside the play. Both inside and outside the fiction, this play, like a ritual of inversion, has raised subjects high enough to judge monarchs and has brought monarchs low enough to be judged.

# 6 • Angels, Alchemists and Exchange
## Commercial Ideology in Court and City Comedy, 1596-1610

*Catherine Gimelli Martin*

G old fever, privateering and profiteering were conspicuous features of the period that closed the sixteenth and
began the seventeenth centuries. A joint stock company
proposing to explore the Guianas literally "promised gold
mountains" and "filled the minds of [the] company so full
of vain expectations and golden hopes, that their insatiable
and covetous minds, being wholly set thereon, could not
be satisfied with anything but only gold."[1] Since L.C.
Knights's seminal study of the theatrical representation of
the outright avarice and covert chicanery encouraged by the
new commercialism (the Guiana Company, for instance,
yielded not a penny to its investors), most critics have agreed
that the drama of the period engaged in a wholesale rejection
of the new men and their new methods. Either because
of their innate traditionalism, their need for aristocratic
patronage, or some combination of the two, the premiere

playwrights of the period are generally regarded as adopting the hostile attitudes of the governing class toward trade. Thus, although capitalism could not simply be ignored as a factor in the contemporary scene, the stage of Jonson and Shakespeare could—and according to Knights, *did*—become a vehicle for exorcising its influence:

> . . . company-promoting, "projecting" and industrial enter-prise certainly formed an important part of the world which Jonson and his fellows observe, and the world which gave them their knowledge of human nature. It is equally obvious that the standards of judgment that they brought to bear were nor formed in that new world of industrial enterprise. They belonged to an older world which was still "normal," a world of small communities in which, a recent economic historian has remarked, "human problems can be truly perceived, which in larger social structures must more or less necessarily be sacrificed." (Knights, 7)

Although Knights's "recent economic historian" is no longer recent, and although subsequent critics, particularly the new historicists, have frequently been concerned to establish rather than (as Knights was) to refute a Marxist interpretation of Elizabethan and Jacobean drama, the view that these plays embody—or, in Stephen Greenblatt's phrase, "circulate"— a traditionalist commercial ideology has proven remarkably persistent.[2] Thus despite the fact that, in *Shakespearean Negotiations*, Greenblatt denies that the stage is part of a "single coherent, totalizing system," for him its ultimate design is hierarchical, regardless of whether this is

> . . . the design of the human patriarchs—the fathers and rulers who unceasingly watched over the errant courses of their subjects—or the overarching design of the divine patriarch. The theater then would confirm the structure of human experience as proclaimed by those on top and would urge us to reconfirm this structure in our pleasure. (17)

Yet in spite of the obvious prestige accorded this and related views, a *comparative* approach to the comic negotiations typical of the late Elizabethan and early Jacobean stage reveals an ethos of exchange potentially far more subversive of the established order than that which Knights ascribes to Jonson or Greenblatt to Shakespeare. While this subversive under-current does not represent an *established* bourgeois ideology, it does seem to indicate the first stirrings of an incipient one.[3] In both playwrights this takes the form not of a coherent doctrine but of a subtle strategy favorable to exchange, a set of attitudes that rewards rather than punishes the re-distribution of accumulated, insulated wealth. Thus, beneath Shakepeare's superficial orthodoxy, the antihierarchical impulse lurking in Jonson's dramatic sleight-of-hand is more subtly but just as insistently present.

One promising recent approach to uncovering the common source of these covert, perhaps subliminal, but certainly subversive strategies is to compare the practices common to both the market and theater economies of proto-capitalist England. Commenting on their shared interests and objectives (although not openly contesting the received views discussed above, and even echoing Knights's insistence on Jonson's deep "revulsion toward the acquisitive urge"), Jean-Christophe Agnew argues that the financial as well as representational economies of the theater inevitably encouraged attitudes favoring liquidity over stability and exchange value over use value. As he observes,

> Conservative lessons abounded in Renaissance drama, to be sure, and the defenders of the stage never hesitated to point out these homilies. But, as their opponents were equally quick to note, these were messages that the medium itself resisted, subverted, and at times openly contradicted. Despite its many ties to the court, the seventeenth century stage was in some measure constitutionally disposed to enact the representational crisis of authority occasioned by England's increasingly boundless market; it was by that same measure constitutionally incapable of providing all but the most ambiguous answers to the problematic of exchange that the market had brought with it. The Renaissance stage was an experimental, not a propitiatory, institution. (110)

Yet while these observations encourage a more ambiguous understanding of the relationship between theater and commerce, the same weighty tradition that seems to restrain even Agnew's partial reassessment of the social conservatism of the early modern theater can also encourage a neoconservative evaluation of his findings. Such an evaluation, in fact, continues to dominate current criticism, where the subversive undercurrents of the stage are usually regarded as always already contained. Evidence of the strength of the neoconservative view thus becomes especially obvious when a skillful Marxist reading of *The Merchant of Venice* offers conclusions that resonate agreeably (if ironically) with those advanced by Knights and Greenblatt. After tracing many of the antiabsolutist implications of the comedy, Walter Cohen concludes his essay not only by positing that these must have been invisible to the playwright, but also that, even if they were not, "stage performances also rationalized and contained such implications, not only by the specific resolution of the plot, but also by the channeling of anarchic instincts that is an inherent part of attendance at a play" (783). Thus in the early modern theater, the presence of competing ideologies *or* "analogies between the state and the theater are profoundly misleading," because "In England as elsewhere in Europe, absolutism served the interests of the neofeudal aristocracy against those of all other classes, in the epoch of western Europe's transition from feudalism to capitalism" (783).

However, Cohen's assessment, like the Greenblatt model it closely resembles, proves profoundly misleading on a number of verifiable accounts. The first and most obvious of these is that, as Cohen earlier admits, the project of the centralized absolutist state is at best partial and subject to contestation in Shakespeare's and Jonson's England.[4] Two parallel and even more damaging objections to the containment theory should also be noted: 1) that the English theater in every way *contrasts* with that of the truly neofeudal states of continental Europe, where it remained a tame and largely ceremonial or "propitiatory" medium; and 2) that far from regarding it as a medium of containment, its enemies and even some of its friends held the English theater accountable for the civil turmoils that directly followed upon its classic period, and which for a considerable time shut it down altogether. One might even argue that the theater never regained anything like its former social and intellectual vigor until the monarchy had finally *ceased* to threaten the values of the English bourgeoisie, and the tables were finally turned. In any case, even if these indications of the potential subversiveness of the theater can be explained away in a variety of ways, none of these effectively supports the hypothesis that its interests lay wholly or even largely in upholding the tenets of a quasi- or neofeudal political ideology. On the contrary, as Agnew's evidence consistently shows, the antitheatrical Puritan reaction itself derives from the fact that the stage only too clearly exposed and even exalted—in ways that a reforming party could not—the moral contradictions at the root of the bourgeois quest for social power and authority. These contradictions were neither the property nor the tool of one clearly identifiable "ruling class," but were central to the ideological and class conflicts of the period as a whole.[5]

While far more light needs to be shed on how and why Puritan interests were allied with some aristocratic values and opposed to others, Agnew's work *can* be used to support at least a partial revision of the received view. If by the time of David Hume's *History of England* and Adam Smith's *Wealth of Nations* it had been clearly established that the rise of commerce and the corresponding loss of power of the feudal lords "benefitted not only the newly rising merchants and manufacturers but the sovereign as well,"[6] it remains unclear exactly who these newly rising merchants and manufacturers were in the period under consideration, *and* how far they themselves either conceived or manipulated the potential alliance of their interests with the sovereign's. This already obscure picture is further complicated by the problematic nature of ideology itself, which, on the stage fully as much as in courts of law, tends to appeal "less to formal rationality" than to the traditions "of the ancient realm." Therefore, as David Little explains (171), although in the field of law "there is clear evidence of tension between the more or less pure traditionalism of the lawyers and the patrimonial tradition of the Tudors and Stuarts,"

At the same time, the "pure traditionalism" of the lawyers turns out to be a strange, incoherent mixture of ancient precedent and original innovation. As Weber said, "What is actually new is. . . claimed to have always been in force." Although the lawyers assumed they were but reinstituting the old order, as a matter of fact they helped to introduce a set of economic and social patterns that undermined the ancient realm and paved the way for rational capitalism. *Thus, in the name of the old order a distinctly new order was being prepared, an order that conformed as little with the designs of the Tudors and Stuarts as with the prescriptions of medieval England.* (171–72; italics supplied)

Finally, then, what *is* clear about the age of Jonson and Shakespeare is that the "middle ranks of men" were composed of a loose amalgam of struggling artisans and entrepreneurs whose ideas were in flux, but whose fortunes generally followed the commercial interests, both literal and figurative, of the cities.[7] For this reason, as Bacon in his defense "Of Usury" was perhaps the first to realize, the struggle over the limits and the legitimacy of exchange was not simply a struggle over religious or political authority, but a more complex and confusing "class conflict between the mercantile and the agrarian interests."[8] Because "agrarian interests" could include a wide spectrum of classes—from peasant and yeoman to petty squire and major landholder—the term obviously spans a number of traditional economic categories. The complexity of the situation is particularly reflected in *The Merchant of Venice* where, as Cohen observes,

> . . . the hostility between Antonio, the open-handed Christian merchant, and Shylock, the tight-fisted Jewish usurer, represents not the conflict between declining feudalism and rising capitalism, but its opposite. It may be seen as a special instance of the struggle, widespread in Europe, between Jewish quasi-feudal fiscalism and native bourgeois mercantilism, in which the indigenous forces usually prevailed. Both the characterization and the outcome of *The Merchant of Venice* mark Antonio as the harbinger of modern capitalism. (771)

So the mercantile Antonio is the harbinger of capitalism and the death knell of a traditional, largely agrarian set of values and practices, and as such, he is the exponent of an ethos that Cohen finds chiefly favoring the "neofeudal aristocracy." But the play also suggests that an explicitly nonagrarian, lower-class version of this ethos also serves the interests of characters like Shakespeare's Launcelot Gobbo or Jonson's Face in ways that subvert the authority and change the meaning of aristocratic values. In this context, it becomes obvious that Launcelot "the clown" is no rustic, but an unscrupulous lower-order wit who plainly advances his own proto-bourgeois material interests in complete disregard for traditional moral or spiritual values. While Marc Shell has usefully commented upon the thinly veiled anti-Semitism implicit in Launcelot's greeting of the elder Gobbo (68), a scene that parodies Jacob's deception of his blind father and displacement of his elder brother Esau, the parallel and obviously purposeful implications of its economic parody are even more pointed. The scene exposes the salient aspect of the Jacob story that Shylock's account necessarily censored, an aspect that is used not only to expand and Christianize the appeal of Jewish opportunism, but also to mock the traditional Christian constraints against it. Thus, the scene essentially constitutes a comic vindication of free market manipulation. Here, Launcelot not only gets away with laughing at the devil himself (2.2.24), but he also considerably deflates the pieties of Antonio-like Christians whose conversion of the Jews will (from his perspective) too much increase the price of pork (3.5.19–23). Nevertheless, as Launcelot clearly understands, his interests lie in taking advantage of the opportunities of advancement present in Antonio's party just as much as Antonio's own interests lie in increasing prices. *Neither* can benefit, except by fraud, from the close accounting and restrictive social barriers embodied in Shylock's retentive household. These underlying attitudes are later affirmed by the actions of the major characters who, like Launcelot himself, are not punished but rewarded for their cupidity and deceit.

Thus, although the commercial wizards of both Shakespeare's *Merchant of Venice* and Jonson's *Alchemist* practice coining, casting, projecting or prospecting gold solely to the detriment of the social unit, and although these wizards *seem* to be punished as scapegoats for the sins of the self-made man, the ethical basis of their scapegoating is actually no more unambiguously traditional than are the real arts of Jonson's fake alchemist. As Knights himself has suggested, frauds like Subtle represented the common public quest for a "more accessible El Dorado," an activity as plainly contemporary as Shylock's money lending (124). Equally contemporary, however, is the commercial speculation of other characters from whom the frauds are only faintly distinguished in terms of practice, but strongly distinguished in terms of remuneration. In fact, the audience views a steady stream of venal characters whose rewards are bewilderingly dissimilar. What, then, actually preserves the successful charlatans from the fate dealt to a Subtle, a Shylock or a Morocco, who fatuously believes he has a natural right to win at Portia's "marriage lottery" because he knows a *"golden mind stoops not to shows of dross"* (2.7.20; italics supplied)? Are not the latter's methods and desires as base as those used by Bassanio in his quest for the same "golden fleece?" Applying Greenblatt's influential "self-fashioning" formula, to which Cohen also seems to subscribe, Morocco would here function as the Oriental "Other" whose "golden desires" can be purged, neutralized and reappropriated as the "natural" aristocratic prerogative of the fair young Venetian.[9] Indeed, one must agree that only by a morally as well as theatrically dubious sleight-of-hand can the Christian virtues of the "angelic" Portia be divorced from the virtues of her inheritance as a lady "richly left" in the kind of angels both Morocco and Bassanio covet (2.7.55–59): the coin of the realm.

Of course, the superficial justification for this allotment is that Morocco gets "what many men desire," more "ore" but less bride, and his rival Arragon, that "silver'd o'er" and arrogant scion of France, his own silvered or mirror image, a blinking idiot. Yet Bassanio, the prodigal and "base" lover, who *also* chooses according to his own (if more modest) image, finds his scarcely "humble reward" in the leaden casket. His method thus seems essentially the same as theirs, although, ironically, it is actually more selfish; *his* hazard is undertaken at the expense of another's gold, happiness, and perhaps life itself. Hence if there is any traditional merit behind his claim to a "chance" as fair as his choice is "true," it rests in its rejection of gaudy upper-class "ornament" ("Hard food for Midas," 3.2.101–02), and pale middle-brow silver ("common drudge / 'Tween man and man," 3.2.103–04). The only consistent "virtue" of the openly entrepreneurial venture he contracts with Antonio (and probably with Portia herself) is thus also subtly *untraditional*: it rejects the trappings and the symbolic aura of wealth, not for ideal love, but for the abstract essence of a wealthy marriage, its exchange value.[10] Hence, when this "essence" is finally "translated" and "sublimed," its transformations will go beyond Greenblatt's formulation in ways illumined by an examination of Jonson's *Alchemist*.

In Jonson's comedy the Janus-like butler, Jeremy/Face— conman, captain and sorcerer's apprentice—engages in a joint enterprise similar to Bassanio's, but based on the self-interest of companions considerably more dubious than Antonio, Portia and Shylock combined. With the spurious alchemist, Subtle, and his whore, Doll Common, they form a "venture tripartite" (1.1.135) to increase their actual gold by marketing fictitious "interest" in the philosopher's stone and in other projects for instant accumulation. In this case the success of the venture is threatened by the competition between these suitors for the "golden bed" both of Doll and of the rich young widow, Dame Pliant, as well as by their excessive skill in "projecting" similar lusts into their victims. Yet once again the contest is won through a combination of the luck and skillful choice in the *basest* character, the temporarily humbled Face and his scarcely less altruistic if more canny double, Lovewit. In the process, Subtle is out-Faced by his own Morocco-like ego, while his chief rival, Surly, is undone by his arrogant underestimation of the powers of pretense, that is, by a pale and middle-brow faith in the power of truth to triumph over fiction. Additionally, while the phony wizard/conman is parted from his ill-gotten gains with as much despatch as Shylock is from his savings, his treacherous right-hand man and "Lungs," Face, is allowed to keep both his place as Jeremy the butler *and* the chest of their loot. In this case the winner even overgoes Launcelot and Bassanio in the moral flimsiness of his claim to triumph, both despite and due to his "baseness." While Jeremy, too, admits his participation in the generally "leaden" or "fallen" conditions of humankind, there is no Antonio-like Christian to shore up his claims, nor is there even a tenuous symmetry between his purported "sacrifice" and any traditional Christian notion. Not only is he forced into his newfound humility by the unexpected return of his employer, Lovewit, but the latter plainly rewards him for having an excess of the acquisitive spirit that damns his accomplices. Much like the minor embezzlers of *The Merchant of Venice*—Jessica, Lorenzo and Launcelot—the unscrupulous Face lives on to join the feast (5.5.159–65).

Again we must question why Face's enterprise is rewarded when Subtle's and the sour-but-honest Surly's are not. Surly, in fact, not only resists the lure of gold, but dislikes imposture to much the same extent as Shylock. Both these characters possess a certain crude wit and integrity that *should* in some sense be regarded as virtuous, but which is instead chastised. As René Girard remarks,

> Between Shylock's behavior and his words, the relationship is never ambiguous. His interpretation of the law may be narrow and negative but we can count on him for acting according to it and for speaking according to his actions. (106)

Girard explains these incongruities by regarding Shakespeare's play as essentially ambivalent and self-contradictory, a watershed of ethical evolution that at once celebrates and critiques the psychology of scapegoating. Yet while this explanation seems adequate to the first phase of the drama's dialectic, it is inconsistent with its synthetic conclusion, its transformation of both the "hazards" of Christian mercy and the false "certainties" of Jewish judgment. In this sense Shakespeare's Portia, much like Jonson's Face, is herself a Janus figure, a *reapportioner* rather than simply a metaphoric "princess" who "stand[s] for sacrifice" (3.2.57) in opposition to Shylock's "stand for judgment" (4.1.103). A theatrical as well as a figurative androgyne, in the end she not only stands for but enacts the exchange of dress, rings, wealth and beds, but not, significantly, of flesh and blood.[11]

Here a number of the inconsistencies underlying both dramas makes their audiences realize that the spurious freedom of the "merry bonds" and philosopher's stones that is being manipulated by the blocking characters actually blocks: this freedom halts rather than expands opportunity, and controls profits that will not "trickle down" but monopolize privilege and power. Opposing this are the exchange artists *par excellence*, who, if they swap daughters and sisters, angels and "pelf," deserve the victory in a game of wits that devalues ascribed meanings in order to reward free translation and improvisation in place of subtle lore and ancient enchantment. In league with their audiences, they put new spirit into the dead letter of the proverb that "all that glisters is not gold" (2.7.65), and in so doing they subvert the traditional aristocratic standard of naturalized or "use" value.[12] In the process, it becomes clear that it is not Bassanio so much as Shylock who equates human flesh with gold; Bassanio may be willing to wager his friend's capital, but only thoughtlessly risks his life, while Shylock can little distinguish between his ducats and his daughter (2.8.15-16), or between Antonio's flesh and any other forfeiture. Although Antonio's anti-Semitism provides one motive for his ruthlessness, Antonio himself glimpses another:

> He seeks my life. His reason well I know:
> I oft delivered from his forfeitures
> Many that have at times made moan to me.
> Therefore he hates me.
>
> (3.3.21–24)

Shylock thus prefers the one-sided profits of foreclosure to those derived from capital investment and shared returns, while Bassanio invests in a win-or-lose-all type of enterprise associated with venture rather than monopoly capitalism. Unlike Shylock, he seeks out merchant rather than princely allies, ones who have diversified and not landed interests. As Antonio assures him, "My ventures are not in one bottom trusted, / Nor to one place; nor is my whole estate / Upon the fortune of this present year" (1.1.42–44).

Hence, although as economic metaphors the forms of thrift practiced by Bassanio and Shylock are only marginally different, as economic plots they represent vastly different modes of activity. Shylock himself outlines his financial ideology, which is essentially a strategy of covertly cornering the market and eliminating the competition. Nor, as suggested above, is his procedure any different with his customers than with his daughter, whose will and interests he regards as completely bound up with his own. In contrast, the will drafted by Portia's father seems to have the opposite intent: to open a closed form of exchange by inserting a random and ambiguous element into the traditional authority of fathers over daughters and of gold over the lead, the common "mirror" in which Bassanio finds his own and Portia's reflection. This dual "insight," like the words hidden/ revealed by Portia's choice of "casket music," reflects more than a single surface and inner meaning.[13] While "base" metals like Bassanio's constitute the transmutable "soul" of free enterprise in this marriage lottery, the "refined" ones coveted by the Moroccos, Mammons, Subtles and Shylocks of these comedies represent the obstructing body of a unidimensional concept of property and tradition.

Similarly, although the deferred consummation of Portia's marriage and its elaborate re-legitimation with a new exchange of rings has generally seemed overly manipulative if not grossly patriarchal to many modern audiences, it also offers a less restrictive basis for distinguishing the tentative exchange of bodies from Shylock's exchange of flesh. Like Subtle's, Shylock's method of accumulation relies upon mysterious alignments of sexual and financial potency that only a secret "art can beget" (2.3.172). According to Subtle's hierarchy of analogies, gold is the "natural" offspring of mercury and sulfur, "the one / . . . supplying the place of male / The other of the female, in all metals" (2.3.161–63). Yet Shylock, too, subscribes to a superstitious method of propagating interest in kind—not based on metals, but on bonds that are as good, and in securing Antonio's pound of flesh, even better than gold. His precedent is Jacob's quasi-alchemical trick of producing an inordinate number of the "streaked and pied" animal assets in order to extract his proper "interest" from Laban's capital. These analogies between the organs and processes that generate precious metallic, human or animal species are based upon a medievalizing homeopathic magic. Hidden similarities in nature are manipulated to legitimate a form of social organization based upon stable universal homologies, and a form of "thrift" based upon hoarding. Yet according to Shylock's circular logic, "That was a way to thrive, and he was blest; / And thrift is blessing if man steal it not (1.3. 78–86). Antonio is outraged by this doubletalk as Subtle's less perceptive customers are not, yet in both cases the wizard/trickster retains the upper hand by blurring the distinction between different orders of nature, which in fact permits him to make his gold "breed as fast" as his customers.[14]

Thus while Knights's identification of these wizard/tricksters with the growing opportunism of the capitalist classes may be superficially convincing, a closer examination of their practices suggests otherwise. As he himself observes, by the early seventeenth century it was not private but government-sponsored enterprise that had become associated with the worst excesses of early industrial capitalism,[15] and the king himself was forced to promise "the removal of monopolies, of which there were at this time seven hundred in the kingdom, granted by letters patent under the broad seal, to the enriching of some few projectors, and the impoverishing of all the kingdom beside."[16] Not only were these projectors notoriously corrupt, but in the popular mind they were also associated with ruthless, quasi-cannibalistic brutality both in their own persons and in that of their agents, one of whom arrested a workman and "threatened 'to pull the flesh from his jaws and to starve his wife and children.'"[17] In this context, Shylock's insistence on extracting payment in kind—which Antonio and Bassanio only suspect but the audience soon knows means payment in flesh—takes on a subversively antiabsolutist significance. This is especially obvious in the example quoted above, where the precedent of Jacob's "wooly breeders" is used to reexamine the differences between "kind" and "kindness."[18] Shylock's assurance of his good faith in offering the loan, "This is kind I offer," ironically echoes Jacob's shifty stratagem for extracting payment from the hide of his shiftless kin, the same "kind" of trick that caused Laban to lose too much of *his* kind. Bassanio's eagerness to "convert" this into some form of kinship with Christian kindness (an attempt as misguided as his asking Shylock to share their dinner) causes him not only to miss Antonio's irony, but ultimately to distract both of them from the question of what "fair terms" may mean to someone who scarcely supports fair trade:

> *Antonio.* The Hebrew will turn Christian; he grows kind.
> *Bassanio.* I like not fair terms and a villain's mind.
> *Antonio.* Come on. In this there can be no dismay;
> My ships come home a month before the day.
>
> (1.3.174–77)

Yet if the two Christians remain oblivious to the implications of this deceptive rhetoric, the audience does not. By now they sense that not only Antonio's bond but his doom seems to have been sealed; that like Bassanio, he is too eager to gamble on a "merry venture" with one who is no merchant, after all, but a monopolist. Unlike Antonio, who trusts to the winds of chance (winds elaborately described in the first scene as possessing an unlimited potential for misfortune), Shylock's sport is to wager on one of two sure things, extracting payment in one kind or the other, in gold or in flesh. In this he allies himself not so much with honest speculation as with a *dictation* of exchange, an association that ties him to the feudal and neofeudal classes whose methods, if not whose land, he shares.[19] His implicit unwillingness to participate in any genuine mode of negotiation is made gradually more explicit throughout the play until in act 4 it amounts to a complete resistance. Here he reveals that his "humour" goes beyond the "due and forfeit" of his bond of flesh and even extends to a poisoning of rats and a detestation of pigs, cats, musical instruments—in fact, of *anything* capable of involuntarily loosing the rigid walls of his body physical or financial. Preferring to squeeze rather than be squeezed, to him there is no distinction between woolly breeders, woolly bagpipes, and the tissue around Antonio's heart (4.1.47–62).

Subtle is as skilled as Shylock in "engendering" life from metal and *vice versa*, and thus in producing an insidiously punning inversion of what his words appear to offer his victims. Both offer their "thrift" to the thriftless, which in effect means converting their assets and their wills (in both senses of the word) to gold. Like Shylock, Subtle is especially adept in propagating his own greed in all the customers who seek his skill for manipulating the "parents of all other metals" (2.3. 154). Even more outrageously, not only are both the parents and the children involved in this process illegitimate, but his whole line of descent produces an incestuous intermingling of customers and their cash, property and women. Yet since Subtle's alchemical, like Shylock's biblical, smokescreen is transparent to its secondary audience, for them his rhetorical hocus pocus becomes a theatrical shell game enacted for the straight man's loss and the public's gain. At the same time, for their stage victims and their actual worldly counterparts, the villains' ominous ability to supply the part of both male and female in "engendering" new gulls remains real enough, as is the cash value of these "offspring" in *both* audiences. Yet while Subtle can frame a living philosopher's stone from the children of all classes, these especially prove as good as gold when they spring from the wealthiest and greediest elements of society, such as those represented by Sir Epicure Mammon.

The unsubtle but also unsuspected duplicity of the referent *him* in Subtle's assurances to Mammon underscores the potency of his verbal "med'cine" among those whose rank only accelerates its operation, its speed surpassing even that with which Iago's verbal "poison" works upon Othello:

> Son, be not hasty. I exalt our med'cine
> By hanging him in *balneo vaporoso,*
> And giving him solution; then congel him;
> And then dissolve him; then again congel him:
> For look, how oft I iterate the work,
> So many times I add unto his virtue.
> As, if at first one ounce convert a hundred,
> After his second loose, he'll turn a thousand;
> His third solution, ten; his fourth, a hundred;
> After his fifth, a thousand thousand ounces
> Of any imperfect metal, into pure
> Silver or gold, in all examinations
> As good as any of the natural mine.

(3.2.103–14)

Because it is clearly *Mammon* who is the "stone" that will be dissolved to yield gold so many times as Subtle "iterates" the work—perhaps a hundred, perhaps a hundred thousand, all "as good as any of the natural mine"—the referent "he" is as shifty (and as thrifty) as Shylock's "kind." In this respect both Subtle and Shylock may be considered *neo*-usurers, which, according to Thomas Lodge, is chiefly any "subtill underminer" whose success depends not merely on the practice of lending and borrowing, but on his ability to make his wares (as Agnew points out) into "the image of its victims' deepest desires."[20]

As in *The Merchant of Venice*, these practices ultimately aim at "engendering" a rich woman, in this case a beautiful young widow in sad need of Portia's wit—Dame Pliant. In the "lottery" for her hand, Lovewit triumphs over the rest by an even more outrageous combination of chance, baseness, disguise and effrontery than Bassanio possesses, but the similar success of their strategies indicates an aptitude for interpretation and exchange is their common advantage. Thus, the superiority of the bonds both thereby "engender" lies chiefly in a negotiability detached from rhetorical enchantment *and* from the compulsive "iteration" of Subtle's formulas, if not from all disguise. The victor's form of disguise significantly differs from the methods of feudal or monopolistic accumulation by rejecting compulsive nonsense in favor of a "lottery" whose laws are subject to interpretation and change. Indeterminacy is thereby valorized over hoarding, reciprocity (even in lying) over one-sided mesmerism.[21] Here the traditional condemnation of the usurer on the basis that he does not, like "the merchant that crosse the seas, adventure,"[22] itself undergoes a quasi-alchemical transformation. Financial, theatrical, and even marital adventures are now conceived as legitimate transmutations if, and only if, they reject the strict accountability of the *lex talionis* in favor of a "liquidity" whose "hazards" may be thinly concealed, but not so thick as to "entrap the wisest" (*Merchant of Venice*, 3.2.101).[23] Although disguises are instrumental both to Face and Bassanio, then, their disguises are never meant to be permanent like Shylock's or Subtle's pretenses, but are continually stripped away and exchanged in the process of a progressive and imminent rather than a curtailed and immanent carnival.[24]

The fact that Bassanio, too, wears many "faces," only makes him more desirable than the stereotypical suitors Portia satirizes, suitors who, unlike either of the "true" lovers, claim to know their own worth (cf. 1.2.38–90 and 3.2). Bassanio, in contrast, reveals one disguise only to don another, which he will alter again. Thus as he advises Portia before their marriage is actually consummated,

> . . . Gentle lady,
> When I did first impart my love to you,
> I freely told you all the wealth I had
> Ran in my veins— I was a gentleman—
> And then I told you true; and yet, dear lady,
> Rating myself at nothing, you shall see
> How much I was a braggart. When I told you
> My state was nothing, I should then have told you
> That I was worse than nothing; for indeed
> I have engaged myself to a dear friend,
> Engaged my friend to his mere enemy
> To feed my means.

(3.2.252–63)

Yet this potentially damaging admission, like Bassanio's later self-incrimination, brings him not loss but gain. Particularly in view of the circumstances surrounding Lovewit's courtship, these results suggest that marriage itself is being reconceived as a form of exchange whose "profits" have been freed from their former compulsions; men and women give and receive as employers and employees, wage earners but not feudal slaves. If Dame Pliant, like Portia, is almost literally auctioned off to the cleverest bidder, she is not compelled by either a foolish brother or erring father to accept their choice of husbands. While Dame Pliant's choice is perhaps too whimsical to conform precisely to the "meeting of minds" that Agnew finds now replacing "earlier preoccupations with the physical delivery or transfer of goods or property" (82), nevertheless the independence of her action cannot be wholly divorced from what Cohen describes as Portia's primary concern in act 5: "a playful and graceful effort by the aristocratic heroine to carry out the serious business of reestablishing the bourgeois assumptions of her marriage" (778).

The general similarity of the two exchanges appears even more clearly when the characteristics of the less lucky aspirants to Dame Plaint's hand are compared to those of Portia's unsuitable suitors. Drawn from a variety of classes and religious persuasions, the admirers of either Doll, Dame Pliant or of Subtle himself are all comparably unpliant enthusiasts of antique forms of enchantment that promise to grant them economic rewards in spite of their pathetically underdeveloped capacity for verbal improvisation or mimetic art. Abel Drugger, Pliant's first admirer, is a plodding and superstitious merchant who hopes to "thrive" not by learning but by buying the necromancer's charms. Dapper, the weak-minded clerk who depends upon Subtle's magic charms as his only hope for winning at gentlemanly games of chance, or for gaining the still more illusive title of nephew to the "Queen of Fairy" (1.2.49–135), gambles away his rightful bequest for the prospect of a fictitious "aristocratic" inheritance. The lady's brother, Kastril, constitutes Dapper's wealthier double, in that his only hope of living up to the status of his recent inheritance depends upon buying a magic chart or instrument in order to gain the pseudo-ability (in more sense than one) of excelling in the fashionable art of "quarrelling" (3.4). These characters, like the materially and spiritually impoverished Puritans, Ananias and Wholesome, and like foolish Sir Epicure, fail not merely as incompetent hoarders of "gifts," which they lack the entrepreneurial talent to gain on their own, but like Surly, they fail as bad actors. While only Surly plunders the dated wardrobe of *The Spanish Tragedy* in his abortive courtship, all of Subtle's gulls in some sense resemble Hamlet's out-of-fashion acting trope. Their imaginative incapacity causes them to depend on antique rhetorical formulas that deflate rather than raise their real "stock," and position them as the consumers or consumed in a plot that they had hoped would gain them new customers.[25]

The scapegoating of this model of exchange and its replacement with a more adequate (or at least newer) one is most complexly developed in the final three acts of *The Merchant of Venice*. Portia's successive transformations from master/mistress (standing in for her father as well as herself) to suitor/lawyer (courting first Bassanio and then the court) are staged as freely encountered "hazards," the stakes waged in a game of multiple and potentially conflicting interests. In order for these simultaneously marital, legal and financial interests to be successfully balanced, a series of conversions has to take place whereby floating replace indenturing contracts. This exchange is clearly signalled in the opening scene of act 5, where Portia pointedly corrects Lorenzo, to whom music, like money, seems to have an *intrinsic* value. He expounds an essentially medieval scale of value in which

> The man that hath no music in himself,
> Nor is moved with concord of sweet sounds,
> Is fit for treasons, stratagems, and spoils;
> The motions of his spirit are dull as night,
> And his affections dark as Erebus.

> (5.1.83–87)

While this theory conveniently justifies the scapegoating of miscreants like Shylock, who hates music of all kinds, Portia asserts the intrinsic danger in assigning value to these traditional appearances. In fact, not only musical but *all* perceptions of magnitude, worth or power must henceforth be regarded as relative:

> A substitute shines brightly as a king
> Until a king be by, and then his state
> Empties itself, as doth an inland brook
> Into the main of waters...
> Nothing is good, I see, without respect...
>
> (5.1.93–97, 99)

Although Portia's correction recognizes some intrinsic superiority of king to substitute, or of master to man—as of Lovewit to Face—here the ultimate measure of all things is fast becoming its exchange value. Worth alters according to circumstance, supply and demand, so that although the music they now hear "sounds much sweeter than by day" (5.1.100), this impression is as flexible as the superiority of the songs of larks to those of crows (102). Context determines reception, whether musical or social, as Lorenzo's tardy reception of Portia due to his infatuation with Jessica reveals (113–14). Bonds of all kinds are thus established to be altered, just as stations are to be honored only to be exchanged.[26] Hence Portia's best "surety" in her marriage lies in reinforcing the mutuality of obligations so that Antonio now participates in her marriage contract with Bassanio as a kind of warrantor. Because she acknowledges that Bassanio should "be much bound to him, / For, as I hear, he was much bound for you" (5.1.134–37), Antonio feels compelled to "be bound again, / My soul upon the forfeit, that your lord / Will never more break faith advisedly" (5.1.251–53). And well might he feel free to "risk his soul," because the new terms of this "risk" are framed by a pun, a negotiable language game. Thus he can swear that Bassanio will never *intentionally* or "advisedly" break faith with Portia, that is, not on his *advice*.

These negotiations are already forecast in act 4, where the conditions of Portia's returning the ring with which

Bassanio had forsworn himself are established. Hence her final consent to move from orchestrator to orchestrated rests not only upon her correction of the essentialist fallacy of music, but upon the new exchange value of rings and bonds of all kinds. These conditions are emphasized both by the punning exchange discussed above, and by the event that immediately precedes it: Portia's *rejection* of Bassanio's traditional attempt to swear renewed fidelity by his lady's "fair eyes" (5.1.242). While Portia has nothing but ridicule for this plea—"Mark you but that! / In both my eyes he doubly sees himself, / In each eye one" (243–44)—she *is* willing to take him back if he swears by his "double self," which she deems a true "oath of credit" (245–46), insofar as this system now acknowledges credibility. Perhaps even more significantly, the same system is used to legitimize and spread the "interest" of Shylock's bonds, the "stock" that furnished the basis of Bassanio's Belmont expedition.[27] Shylock's renegotiated "thrift" thus becomes the humanly viable equivalent of Subtle's dehumanizing alchemy: here the economics of one form of exchange is appropriated *both* in order to displace the traditional taboo against usury *and* to renegotiate the proper use of interest. Thus if this process resembles Greenblatt's concept of "Othering," it also contrasts with its motivating force by mitigating or canceling rather than validating the traditional authority of the governing hierarchy, which turns out to be its *actual* Other.

In general, then, these plays testify to the tacit substitution of an essentialist, quasi-medieval ideology with an alternate ethos, the thinly disguised ideology of the rising as opposed to the entrenched entrepreneurial classes. Like their heroes, Bassanio and Face, both comedies exalt *and* expose their own sleight-of-hand, giving them a doubleness that provides their own figurative legitimacy, as well as their quite literal ability to transmute the "dross" of finance into the "golden fleece" of theatrical exchange. Although this self-justifying form of enterprise is certainly not disinterested—it can, after all, gain a coat-of-arms for a glover's son—and although this in turn justifies Girard's remark that in the process "Mankind has become a commodity, an exchange value like any other," it is just as certainly *not* lacking in egalitarian claims (101–02). The nonmagical conversions it pointedly displays benefit only those who negotiate, and exclude those who hoard, who are nearly always those who have inheritances or privileges to squander.

This formulation has the advantage both of explaining the apparently arbitrary separation of the two kinds of entrepreneurs featured in these comedies, and also of placing the theater of Shakespeare and Jonson in a broader historical context, one that recognizes the stakes that its playwrights and actors indeed had in valorizing the incipient ideology of the bourgeoisie.[28] That there is also considerable modern irony in Jonson's and Shakespeare's exchange of one form of bondage for a "freer" form should by now be equally obvious. Girard captures the cynicism but also the general dynamics of this ideology as follows:

> The generosity of the Venetians is not feigned. Real generosity makes the beneficiary more dependent on her generous friend than a regular loan. In Venice a new form of vassality prevails, grounded no longer in strict territorial borders but in vague financial terms. The lack of precise accounting makes personal indebtedness infinite. This is an art Shylock has not mastered. (103)

However, Girard forgets that Shylock *has* mastered the art of making people into property, of inscribing or attempting to inscribe them in "strict territorial borders," even if he remains outside the infinite circulation of money, vows and mutual obligation that demands of its subjects a quite different form of art, a form for which the theater at this time seems to supply the paradigm. The positive potential of this form of exchange is emphasized in the final acts of both comedies, where both Shylock's locked chest and that in which Subtle and Doll conceal their ill-gotten goods are unlocked and their contents distributed—either to the true merchants of Venice—Lorenzo, Jessica and Antonio—or to Jonson's even broader class of theatrical "merchants," Lovewit's true audience. Further, while the justification of Face's or Antonio's purported "sacrifice" remains metaphorically traditional, in practice it functions to exploit the form in order to change the content of what was contemporarily regarded as a repressive order of things. What the new order attempts to install in its place thus differs strikingly from Greenblatt's patriarchal self-fashioning, even while it shares some of its objectifications and displacements. In effect, it invokes an interpersonal project of *re*-fashioning favorable to economic individualism, a visionary form of enterprise adequate to the actorly roles of "new" men and women. While not casting hierarchy aside altogether, its successful entrepreneurs triumph by rejecting the simple recirculation of the old world's currency. They instead enter the brave new world of Belmont, a world that quite clearly stands for a remodeled island of exchange.

That the theatrical rapprochement between Venice and Belmont, Shylock and Portia, or between Face, Lovewit and their equally theatrical "customers," remains as ambiguously visionary as brutally realistic hardly needs commenting. Face concludes *The Alchemist* with as much cynically self-serving as communally beneficial generosity, and Gratiano concludes *The Merchant of Venice* with a similarly ironic gesture, a lewd pun on his future interest in "keeping safe Nerissa's ring" (5.1.307). Yet we must remind ourselves that cynicism and irony are, on the one hand, wholly in keeping with the double purposes of double selves, and on the other, with the double service that Jonson in particular wishes the theater to perform: that of applying "fair correctives" (prol. 18) to its audience in the process of pleasing them with a mixture of "gain and profit" (16), and of receiving in return a corresponding legitimacy and financial reward. Although the practices involved in gaining material rewards from the manipulation of fictions necessarily suggest that this theatrical exchange is often far more like theft than thrift, its ability to recirculate production and consumption equally insures that it is a theft not *unlike* thrift. Hence, as that paradigmatic double self, Jeremy/Face, concludes, "though I am clean / Got off from . . . all / With whom I traded,

> . . . yet I put myself
> On you, that are my country; and this self
> Which I have got, if you do quit me, rests
> To feast you often and invite new guests.
>
> (5.5.159–65)

Jonas Barish has commented upon some of the inevitable tensions and liabilities that result from the world vision of Jonson's Jeremy as follows:

> The positive standard, the ethical humanism and solid sense to which he is always appealing, remains for the most part in the background, and every effort to incarnate it dramatically (Bonario, Surly, Grace Wellborn) is a failure. (88)

Yet, ironically, in *The Alchemist* as in *The Merchant of Venice*, although these positive standards are nowhere "embodied," they permeate much of the background and at least some of the foreground of the dramas' comically mixed motives, a mixture that somehow conspires to redefine the meaning of "ethical humanism" itself. Even more jarringly, then, we find that the tensions within this remodeled commercial ideology are strangely consistent both with the classical Marxist claim that the bourgeoisie begins as a progressive class and ends as a reactionary one, *and* with Albert O. Hirschman's revision of this claim's teleology; the latter finds "that economic expansion is *simultaneously* ambivalent in its political effects, whereas Marxist thought imposes a temporal sequence with the positive effects necessarily antedating the negative ones" (124). Certainly, then, if any real precision in sorting out these claims is to be hoped for, we must reevaluate the subtle and heretofore invisible conflicts within what Weber called the "Protestant ethic," along with the often mixed-class affiliations (fictive as well as actual) of its agents. But we must also rethink the tendentious and tedious task of attempting to fit the complex comedies of Jonson and Shakespeare into clearly defined pro- or anticapitalist commercial ideologies—particularly as these are understood from an exclusively modern perspective—and finally abandon these attempts. What is needed is a whole new vocabulary of progress and regress, liberation and containment, a vocabulary at least tentatively freed from reductive, autotelic assumptions common both to Marxist histories and their supposed antitheses, the liberal critiques of capitalism whose conclusions have proved remarkably consistent from Knights and Greenblatt to those of their important, if often overlooked, ancestors—R. H. Tawney and Christopher Hill.

Thus, as David Little persuasively argues, although Tawney's name is often linked to the sociology of Weber, and Hill's to that of Marx, both tend more reductively than either Weber *or* Marx to insist that a self-conscious, dominant middle class had already emerged in England by the seventeenth century. Further, although Weber himself often writes as though he shares their assumptions about the point at which the middle class "takes over," he also argues explicitly against a simple identification of rational capitalism and the mere existence of a middle class (Little, 19–20, n. 47). More significantly still, Little finds Hill restating and extending two of Tawney's erroneous assumptions, that "individualism" and social order are necessarily antithetical, and that two distinct social classes (aristocratic and bourgeois) stand on either side of this great divide (110). Instead, as Little amply shows, it is far more accurate to regard the conflicts of this period as involving distinctly different views of society, Puritan inflected or "neotraditionalist," and Anglican inflected or "patrimonial traditionalist," that at this time are neither so clearly distinct nor so clearly class-based as in advanced capitalism (170–72). Thus, instead of a complete departure from the system of social authority that precedes but also coexists with it, Weber more correctly views Puritanism as providing for "the redirection and the reinterpretation of the place of moral authority in the social order[;] . . . not a one-sided emphasis on rights to the exclusion of obligations, but a redefinition of both rights and obligations in accord with a new system of meaning and values" (235).

What is particularly significant about Little's careful rereading of Weber is that his multivalent insights harmonize with those of Shakespeare and Jonson themselves. While both playwrights use the stage ruthlessly to debunk the hypocrisy and "secret" economic ambitions of Puritans (the characters of Angelo in *Measure for Measure*, Tribulation Wholesome in *The Alchemist*, and Zeal-of-the-Land-Busy in *Bartholomew Fair* come immediately to mind), Jonson for one seems rather blatantly to regard his interests less as antithetical to theirs than as their more pragmatic and viable counterpart. That he *should* do so is demonstrated by the language the Puritan Thomas Cartwright uses to advocate the preaching of the Word for the "common profit" of the congregation, language strikingly similar to that used in the prologue to *The Alchemist*. As Cartwright argues, preaching contributes to a beneficial spiritual economy insofar as "it pertaineth to the commodities off the whole body / that the part which he [the preacher] hath the nourishment off / be well preserved."[29] Jonson echoes these bodily metaphors for social "profit," but ironically underscores a more subterranean sense of profit by linking it to fiscal *gain*: although bad manners or "humours, [now] feed the stage," like a good or *successful* preacher he will improve his hearers with "wholesome remedies" in whose working "gain and profit meet" (9, 15–16). He thus calls attention to the fact that embedded in this discourse of "healthful" exchange is a form of social contract that promotes more than one kind of "commodity" transference between "the whole body."[30] In his view, the only real difference between theatrical and spiritual exchange can be found neither in their ideals of maximizing food and "profit," and still less in their common ideology of socioeconomic fluidity, but only in the purity of motive each assumes.

While Jonson's characters ultimately insist that thrift cannot consistently be separated from theft, and theft itself can be used for socially constructive purposes, no Puritan would admit so much. Most, like William Perkins, piously regarded business dealings as "a realm for special Christian responsibility over and above the prescriptions of the law" (Little, 123). Obviously, in spite of its royal patronage, the theater's very real marginality prevented its practitioners from holding equally lofty views of their own "callings."

On the contrary, this marginality drove one playwright to "redeem" his profession by restoring his family coat of arms, and the other to become the first to edit and publish his collected works. Yet as their plays themselves suggest, we should not overestimate the "aristocratic" overtones of their defensive measures; when most condemning they most compete with Puritans, and in so doing, they most contribute to the growing secularization of an evolving ideology of exchange.[31]

# 7 • Imagination and Ideology in *Macbeth*

*Arthur F. Kinney*

H istory functions for the people of Tudor England, according to one of their chief authorities, Cicero, as *"the light of trueth, the witnesse of tymes, the Mistresse of lyfe, the Messenger of antiquitie, and the lyfe of memorye, preservinge from oblivion deedes worthye of memorye, Atchieved thorough longe processes of tymes."*[1] The Latin translation is that of the French writer Matthieu Coignet, in his *Politique Discourses upon trueth and Lying*, which was in turn translated into English by Sir Edward Hoby in 1586. In the most recent paraphrase for our own time and culture by Phyllis Rackin in *Stages of History* published in 1990—"History, it seemed, could raise the dead, inspire the living, reveal the secrets of statecraft, teach the details of military tactics, expose the deceits of fortune, and illuminate the ways of providence" (3)—it could, that is, describe the chronicles of Hector Boece or Francis Thynne or the drama of Shakespeare in their construction, or reconstruction, of the events in the life of Macbeth. But, she continues, the progress of Renaissance historiography and theory of history was characterized by an increasing sense of alienation from the past, of its ineluctable otherness, even while the desire to know and recover that past remained intense, lending a deep poignancy to the entire historiographic enterprise. Historical fact was now open to question, and historical truth was now debatable. Records were subject to loss or distortion, witnesses could be biased, and all things were vulnerable to the ravages of time.... [Thus] Historiographic writing no longer had a direct, unequivocal relation with historical truth. Alternative accounts of historical events and opposed interpretations of their causes and significance now threatened each other's credibility, a process intensified by the development of the printing industry and the spread of literacy. (12–13)

For Rackin, history like theater, "where common players draped in the discarded clothes of aristocrats impersonated their betters" in playing out the past, "was deeply involved in the same destabilizing social transformations that produced the nostalgic desire for a stable, historical past" (22).

Yet "Art exists for a reason; it is not mere decoration, but a necessary worker in the necessary business of a human culture,"[2] and this is nowhere more urgently and persistently evident than in *Macbeth*. Here, Shakespeare is always conceiving and reconceiving the historical past, as his protagonist is, through the powerful and treacherous means of the imagination.

> Is this a dagger which I see before me,
> The handle toward my hand? Come, let me clutch thee.
> I have thee not, and yet I see thee still.
> Art thou not, fatal vision, sensible
> To feeling as to sight, or art thou but
> A dagger of the mind, a false creation,
> Proceeding from the heat-oppressed brain?
> I see thee yet, in form as palpable
> As this which now I draw.[3]
>
> (2.1.33.41)

*This* is *Shakespeare's* Macbeth, his "Secret'st man of blood" (3.4.127) who, he tells us of his own pitched life, alone had the ability to realize that "Stones have been known to move and trees to speak; / Augures and understood relations have / By maggot-pies and coughs and rooks brought forth" such secret knowledge (3.4.124–26). He towers, solitary in the play, a man, the poet Robert Bridges once remarked, "of magnificent qualities of mind." And his is a mind swirling in thoughts rendered forcefully as images of incandescent power.

> Thou canst not say I did it; never shake
> Thy gory locks at me. . . .
> Avaunt, and quit my sight! let the earth hide thee!
> Thy bones are marrowless, thy blood is cold;
> Thou hast no speculation in those eyes
> Which thou dost glare with! . . .
> What man dare, I dare.
> Approach thou like the rugged Russian bear,
> Th'armed Rhinoceros, or th'Hyrcan tiger,
> Take any shape but that, and my firm nerves
> Shall never tremble. Or be alive again,
> And dare me to the desert with thy sword;
> If trembling I inhabit them, protest me
> The baby of a girl. Hence, horrible shadow!
> Unreal Mock'ry hence!
>                              Why, so; being gone
> I am a man again.
>                              (3.4.49–50; 92–95; 99–106)

> . . . You make me strange
> Even to the disposition that I owe,
> When now I think you can behold such sights,
> And keep the natural ruby of your cheeks
> When mine is blanch'd with fear.
>                              (3.4.111–15)

In such irrevocable, such indelible lines as these, Shakespeare's royal historical tragedy moves beyond history, perhaps beyond tragedy, to concentrate on the issues of royalty, of regicide, usurpation, rule and tyranny, of "Vaulting ambition which o'erleaps itself" (1.7.27). And the means for all these is what Montaigne calls, in John Florio's translation published three years before Shakespeare's play, "the force of the Imagination." "*Fortis imaginatio generat casum,*" Montaigne tells us in one of the earliest essays of his first book, "*A strong imagination begetteth chance* . . . . I am one of those that feele a very great conflict and power of imagination. All men are shockt therewith, and some overthrowne by it. The impression of it pierceth me, and for want of strength to resist her, my endevour is to avoid it" (1.2., sig. E2v). Precisely what terrifies Montaigne, though, only attracts Macbeth: he takes chance, abstracts and personifies it, and then subjects it—or him, or her—to his own ends: "If Chance will have me King," he says, "why, Chance may crown me, / Without my stir" (1.3.144–45). Even Duncan, far from any battlefield, realizes, according to Rosse, that Macbeth is "Nothing afeard of . . . / Strange images of death" (1.3.96–97).

Michael Goldman makes a similar observation from both a critical and a theatrical perspective. "Macbeth is a brave soldier, an active physical man—but the most striking thing about him is his imagination," Goldman writes.

> Here the term applies in its most literal sense—Macbeth possesses an image-making faculty of nightmarish power. We get, in this play, as full a portrait of the workings of a human mind as we do in *Hamlet*, but Macbeth has none of Hamlet's interest in analysis. He doesn't tend to think abstractly, and he doesn't *like* to think about his situation in any form. But he cannot help thinking about it in images. When he is about to commit a murder, the image of a bloody dagger comes up before him unbidden; it is so vivid he thinks it is real. He wishes it would go away, but it will not. This is not a supernatural apparition, but, as he calls it, a dagger of the mind—the product of his imagination.[4]

But this is still only one in a chain of images projected by Macbeth's ardent imagination. "This supernatural soliciting / Cannot be ill; cannot be good," Macbeth remarks after *seeing* the unexpected three sisters (1.3.130–31), but the abstract titles they prophesy force him to question not them but an imagined regicide that will image, that will concretize what "strange intelligence" (1.3.76) they have given him: his mind elides from an initial "suggestion" to a fully imagined "murther." Almost at once, we hear Macbeth ask himself,

> ... why do I yield to that suggestion
> Whose horrid image doth unfix my hair,
> And make my seated heart knock at my ribs,
> Against the use of nature? Present fears
> Are less than horrible imaginings.
> My thought, whose murther yet is but fantastical,
> Shakes so my single state of man,
> That function is smother'd in surmise,
> And nothing is, but what is not—
>
> (1.3.134–42)

Nothing is but what is not, so that only the imagined truly is. To confirm the deed, he draws his own dagger from his side to realize the dagger of his mind ("I see thee yet, in form as palapable / As this which now I draw"). Led by his imagination, making what is not is, he transforms the abstraction—murder—into a personification, too, while he transforms his imagined look of horror into the image of the fierce Tarquin:

> ... Now o'er the one half-world
> Nature seems dead, and wicked dreams abuse
> The curtain'd sleep: Witchcraft celebrates
> Pale Hecate's off'rings; and wither'd Murther,
> Alarum'd by his sentinel, the wolf,
> Whose howl's his watch, thus with his stealthy pace,
> With Tarquin's ravishing strides, towards his design
> Moves like a ghost.
>
> (2.1.49–56)

Regicide and rape become inseparable, both politically imagined; and the "supernatural soliciting" is at one with his exterior and interior world, for when he hears a bell it is *his* bell, *his* signal—"the bell invites me. / Hear it not, Duncan" (2.1.62–63). The world conforms to and confirms the force of his imagination. Except, of course, the three weird sisters who did no *soliciting* at all—they merely prophesied the future. As James L. Calderwood has also observed, "Macbeth's imagination invents the murder of

Duncan,"[5] just as later, in 3.2, he will imagine and so invent the death of Banquo: "I will advise you where to plant yourselves, / Acquaint you with the perfect spy o'th'time, / The moment on't; for't must de done to-night / And something from the palace" (3.1.128–31).

The deathly trajectory of Macbeth's imagination reaches its highest pitch on stage with the appearance of the bloodied ghost of Banquo. Whether or not anyone other than Macbeth saw the ghost on stage in 1606 is a question beyond any extant documentation, regardless of how *our* imaginations might wish to amend the scene. The stage direction at 3.4.37 in folio 1 reads *"Enter the Ghost of Banquo, and sits in Macbeth's place,"* but the folio text, our first, is printed nearly two decades after the play was written and staged, perhaps rewritten and restaged. And in our one other bit of evidence, Simon Forman's account of a performance in 1611 in which he talks of the ghost, it is not clear whether it was corporeally on stage or in his remembered narrative of the event he describes. If the Ghost did appear, bloodied with clouts of blood and shaking his gory locks, he would have recalled to the early audiences the bloodied captain of 1.2: "I am faint, my gashes cry for help" (1.2.43), the deed of his maimed death recalling in turn the Captain's words of praise

> For brave Macbeth (well he deserves that name),
> [who] Disdaining Fortune, with his brandish'd steel,
> Which smok'd with bloody execution,
> Like Valour's minion, carv'd out his passage,
> Till he fac'd the slave."
>
> (1.2.16–20)

If, on the other hand, no one sees the Ghost—for he has no witnesses here, unlike the occasion of weird sisters on the heath—then we are left with Macbeth's now-diseased imagination. But this *is* a play about the force of the imagination—and we, witnessing a theatrical event, are hardly exempt. Indeed, even Macbeth's apparent admission to himself and his wife—"Strange things I have in head, that will to hand, / Which must be acted, ere they may be scann'd"

(3.4.138–39)—is really no admission at all: it not only invites, but it requires our imagination.

This is a crucial element of the play. The central event occurs out of the range of our imaging, if not of our imagining. Not witnesses to the regicide, "we are obliged," Robert Hapgood has recently written, "to join Lady Macbeth in imagining it, in straining to see what we are not allowed to see, as Macbeth is 'about it.'"[6] This forces us, while watching the play, to substitute for the event as well, as Calderwood has noted:

> It is one thing for us to know that Macbeth murders Duncan, but it is quite another for us to see him at it. Hence Macbeth's horrible but invisible imaginings must not be allowed to materialize on stage as a horrifying deed. But for Shakespeare to omit the deed entirely would be to break faith with his audience, who have been promised a regicide. The deed must be absent, but it must also be present. How is this managed? By substituting for the unstaged deed a speech by Lady Macbeth that mediates between us and it, obscuring and revealing it at once. For although Lady Macbeth is before us on stage, her own horrible imaginings are in the bedchamber with her husband. If Duncan had not resembled her father, she says, she would have done the deed herself. Now, in a sense, she does do it.
> And, alas, so do we. (52–53)

We must close the fissure, our imagination amending and healing the rift in the imaged presentation. But our imagination and reason in this are both confirmed by subsequent direction and events: the absent murder of the king is followed by the murder, in half-light, of Banquo; by the murder in full light of Macduff's son; and by the murder and mutilation of Macbeth himself. And just as we close these portions of the play, so we also supply two more related moments— related imaginatively and politically—the election of Macbeth and his coronation at Scone.

Such events are not guaranteed by the play's end, however; rather, they are catalysts for reopening our imagination. For when Malcolm returns to Scotland and invades Dunsinane, our own imaging and imagination both, now keenly aware of the crucial importance of absences, will note that someone is missing. It is Malcolm's younger brother Donalbaine, who, Holinshed tells us, will return at a later date to kill King Malcolm in turn to take the throne for himself. The final lines are equally unsettling. Malcolm is hailed three times by his troops just as Macbeth's troops, the three weird sisters, hailed him; and Malcolm closes the play by putting off proper rewards: "what needful else / That calls upon us, by the grace of Grace, / we will perform in measure, time, and place" (5.9.37–39). Rather, "thanks to all at once, and to each one, / Whom we invite to see us crown'd at Scone" (5.9.40–41). Once more we must imagine a coronation at Scone Abbey, just as we imagined Macbeth's.

*Macbeth* is thus a notoriously *incomplete* play—unless, of course, we find its ending not at its conclusion but near its middle, when the second prophecy of the sisters concludes with "*A show of eight Kings, the last with a glass in his hand; BANQUO following*" (4.1.111) that brings the play into the time of King James and of Shakespeare. And then oddly, if we locate the temporal conclusion in act 4, Banquo is part of the present time of Stuart England, too, for after following the ghostly presence of James, who disappears, he remains: "the blood-bolter'd Banquo smiles upon me / And points at them for his" (4.1.123–24). If this is the true ending of the play—as it might be argued chronologically—then the play lives on in the present, factual time for Shakespeare, but only with the eight kingly ghosts of the unliving, the "horrible imaginings" that Macbeth first had contemplating Duncan's death (1.3.138), now a "Horrible sight" (4.1.122) of the "two-fold balls and treble sceptres" (4.1.121) that clearly represent James VI and I and his Union of the Crowns. This is the "Horrible sight" that Macbeth imagines and then of which he says, "Now, I see, 'tis true."

II

The fact that Macbeth's imagination encompasses an

imaging of the anachronistic King James, and that our associated imagination must therefore do likewise, has not gone unnoticed nor unremarked. In what is the best study of the historiography of Shakespeare's *Macbeth* to date, David Norbrook notes that "The hallucinatory dagger that leads Macbeth toward the Murder" of Duncan, the imagining with which we began, had ideological significance in Shakespeare's time as "a stock republican emblem of tyrannicide"—clearly Shakespeare's chief concern in the play—and furthermore that "There is a heavy irony in Macbeth's comparison of himself to Tarquin, whose rape of Lucretia led to the fall of the Roman monarchy."[7] Neither pointed reference has any place at all in the actual life of MacBeth MacFindlaech, Mormaer of Moray, who in 1040 killed the High King of Scotland, Duncan MacCrinan, in a pitched battle at Burghead in Moray. According to *The Orygynale Cronykil of Scotland*, Andrew of Wyntoun tells us that "Duncan was a vicious, bloodthirsty, selfish tyrant,"[8] "an unpopular king" in the words of Macbeth's present-day biographer, Peter Berresford Ellis, "who was intent on pursuing an aggressive, expansionist war against England and, at the same time, against the Orkney jarldom" (43). The few meager records of Macbeth reported by Marianus Scottus, Tighernac, the *Ulster Annals* and the *Saxon Chronicle* all agree that the first ten years of the reign of Macbeth, a popular king, were peaceful, and that he visited Rome where he gave freely to the poor.

The fabled Macbeth—and quite possibly the only Macbeth Shakespeare knew—was filtered through a series of republican historians who, Norbrook shows, were at great pains to argue the case for popular resistance to tyranny. To this end, Wyntoun added to his "history" a dream in which Macbeth saw the weird sisters and received predictions of Birnam Wood and of his death from a man not born of woman; to this Fordun joined the name of Macduff, Thane of Fife, the sprawling land mass just north of Edinburgh; and Hector Boece added the wholly fictional genealogy of the Stuart line beginning with Banquo and Fleance (whom he also imagined). In writing the Scottish chronicles for

Holinshed, Francis Thynne largely followed Boece, turning Duncan into a "faint-hearted milksop" whose *"smal skil . . . in warklike affaires"* would justify removing him from rule.[9] But Macbeth himself turns tyrant in due course, planning ways *"to slea Banquho and his sonne . . .* as they returned from a supper at the palace, so that Macbeth might be held guiltless" (marginal note 33). Fearful of the increasing power of Macduff, who flees before he can be killed, Macbeth kills Macduff's family, setting in motion the rebellion led by Malcolm and Macduff with the support of English troops. "Siward the noble earle of Northumberland with a great power of horssemen went into Scotland, and, that doone, placed Malcolme surnamed Camoir, the sonne of Duncane, sometime king of Scotland, in the gouernement of that realme, who afterward slue the said Mackbeth, and then reigned in quiet" (44). In due course, according to Thynne, Malcolm

> was crowned at Scone, the 25 day of Aprill, in the yeere of our Lord 1057. Immediatlie after his coronation he called a parlement at Forfair, in the which he rewarded them with lands and liuings that had assisted him against Makbeth, aduancing them to fees and offices as he saw cause, & commanded that speciallie those, that bare the surname of anie offices or lands, should haue and inioy the same. He created manie earles, lards, barons, and knights. Manie of them, that before were thanes, were at this time made earles, as Fife, Menteth, . . . Leuenox, . . . Caithnes, Rosse, and Angus. These were the first earles that haue beene heard of amongst the Scotishmen (as their histories doo make mention.) (44–45).

Such rewards of English titles—with which Shakespeare also ends his play even before Malcolm is crowned at Scone—insure a succession that will eventually incorporate the descendants of Banquo and Fleance and the ancestors of James I. Thus the chronicle ends the story of Macbeth, and what follows is where the play extends or subverts it not to the moment of military victory at Dunsinane but at the more ideologically oriented site of *"A house in Forress"* (4.1.1), where Macbeth encounters the three sisters (now called witches) for the second time. And in this newly imagined space, Shakespeare puts within the long temporal spread of the *"show of eight Kings"* (4.1.111) ending with James—whose further line, Macbeth senses, "will . . . stretch out to th'crack of doom" (4.1.117)—a shorter chronology of three apparitions, *"an armed head," "a bloody child,"* and *"a child crowned, with a tree in his hand"* (4.1.68; 76; 86), clearly signifying Siward, Macduff and Malcolm.

Within the chronology up to Shakespeare's time and dependent on it, then, are clear republican images denoting tyranny and rebellion. But by combining these images and these concerns with the hallucinatory or willed visitation of the witches by Macbeth, Shakespeare extends his play of past regicide to present politics by asking fundamental questions about what we see and imagine because of what we believe, or wish to believe. At the site of the witches, and at the moment of prophecy, imagination and ideology are joined inextricably. And it is not just ideology as the examination of republicanism as opposed to monarchism, but, as Jonathan Dollimore puts it translating Louis Althusser, "the very terms in which we perceive the world, almost— and the Kantian emphasis is important here—the condition and grounds of consciousness itself."[10] The boundaries of imagination and ideology thus become blurred (and have been seen as reversible terms), since they both shape specific beliefs, ideas and values. But Shakespeare needed no Althusser to tell him that; Francis Bacon (among others) did. In Bacon's words, "methods of procedure are potentially things themselves,"[11] but he said so with a warning: the idols of the mind could distort thoughts by imagination. But they could not even conceive thoughts without the imagination.

Shakespeare's play about the imagination thus necessarily admits ideological concerns, what David Lee Miller calls "necessary fictions," "'double think' which we use to control the world."[12] In fact, the mirror carried by the eighth king in the witches' show, imaging James, might have recalled for some in Shakespeare's audience James's own book of advice to his son, Prince Henry, printed in England in several editions in 1603—the best seller of that year. In the book,

James tells the potential king, "as your company should bee a paterne to the rest of the people, so should your person bee a lampe and a mirrour to your companie"[13] while the whole of the *Basilikon Doron,* he writes, "must be taken of al men, for the true image of my very minde, and form of the rule which I have prescribed to my selfe and mine" (145). This image, moreover, should be public, should be presentational. "It is a trew old saying, That a king is as one set on a stage, whose smallest actions and gestures, all the people gazingly doe behold: and therefore although a King be neuer so praecise in the discharging of his Office, the people, who seeth but the outward part, will euer iudge of the substance, by the circumstances; and according to the outward appearance" (*Works* [1616], sig. P6v). While James goes on to urge collating the outward appearance with the inner disposition, it was just this outward appearance of his own behavior, like the outward appearance of Macbeth's in Shakespeare's play, that so upset Shakespeare's countrymen from the start of James's reign. "Having been schooled in Roman, not English constitutional law," Albert H. Tricomi writes, "James awakened suspicions early on that he had little regard, foreigner that he was, for English rights and liberties."[14] On his initial journey from Edinburgh to London, at Newark-upon-Trent, for instance, he summarily hanged a cutpurse without warning and without trial, much as any tyrant might. In less than his first six weeks in England—reminiscent of the titles Malcolm gives out in Shakespeare's play before he is actually crowned—the as-yet uncrowned James created 237 new knights, and another 432 a few days later; one morning at Belvoir, he created 46 new knights before breakfast. All told, he attempted (like Malcolm) to enlist support (as well as earn money for the depleted national treasury) by raising 1,161 men to knighthood by the end of his first full year. In addition, his refusal to keep court in London following the coronation—preferring instead to hunt in the country, leaving the government to Cecil—displayed the kind of aloofness that Macbeth displays. He was, it seems, immune to nobility, gentlemen and commoners alike, and the commoners at least began expressing their grievances openly by 1604.

> During one of James's hunting vacations at Royston, a now
> celebrated event occurred. The king had lost one of his prize
> hounds, Jowler, in the hunt. The next day the animal suddenly
> reappeared with a letter attached to its neck: "Good Mr.
> Jowler, we pray you speak to the King (for he hears you every
> day, and so doth he not us) that it will please his Majesty
> to go back to London, for else the country will be undone;
> all our provision is spent already and we are not able to
> entertain him longer."[15]

"What had begun as a prereogative of kingship," Tricomi
comments, "had become for the English a question of ethics,
of good government" (9).

But James's potential for distant and disdainful government, if not actual tyranny, was found not only in his actions
but in his published theory of government, *The trve Lawe
of free Monarchies: Or, The Reciprock and Mvtvall Dvtie
Betwixt a free King, and his naturall subiectes* (1598; 1603).
The pamphlet was unsettling, arguing as it did for an
absolutist government, never conceived by Elizabeth, on
scriptural, legal and natural grounds.[16] His own example
was, surprisingly, Samuel's prophecy of the tyrant Saul, whom
he defends before arguing more generally,

> Now then, since the erection of this kingdome and
> Monarchie among the Iewes, & the law thereof may, &
> ought to be a paterne to all Christian & well founded
> Monarchies, as being founded by God himselfe, who by his
> Oracle, and out of his owne mouth gaue the lawe therof:
> what libertie can broyling spirites, and rebellious mindes
> claime justly to against any Christian Monarchie: since they
> can claime to no greater liberty on their part, nor the people
> of God might haue done, and no greater tyrannie was euer
> executed by any Prince or tyrant [than Saul]? (67)

He was equally unforgiving when it came to the law of the
state.

> For as our Chronicles beare witnesse, this Ile, and espe-
> cially our parte of it, being skantly inhabited, but by very
> few, and they as barbarous and skant of ciuilitie, as number,

there comes our first King FERGVS, with a great number
with him, out of *Ireland*, which was long inhabited before
vs, and making himselfe maister of the countrie, by his owne
friendship, and force aswell of the *Ireland-men* that came
with him, as of the country-men that willingly fell to him,
he made him selfe King and Lorde as well of the whole
landes, as of the whole inhabitants within the same. Thereafter he had his successours, a long while after their being
Kinges, made & established their lawes from time to time,
and as the occasion required. So the trueth is directlie contrarie
in our state to the false affirmation of such seditious writers,
as would perswade vs, that the Lawes and state of our contrie
were established before the admitting of a King: where by
the contrarie ye see it plainely proued, that a wise King
comming in among barbares first established the estate and
forme of gouernement, and thereafter made lawes by himself, and his successours according thereto.

The Kings therefore in *Scotland* were before any estates,
or rankes of men within the same, before any Parliaments
were holden, or lawes made: and by them was the lande
distributed (which at the first was whole theirs) states erected
and decerned, & formes of gouernement deuised & established. And so it followes of necessitie, that the Kinges were
the authors & makers of the lawes, and not the lawes of
the Kings ... (70–71).

Thus "ye see it manifest, that [as] the king is ouer-Lord of
the whole land: so is he Maister ouer euery person that
inhabiteth the same, hauing power ouer the life, and death
of euery one of them" (72). He finds final support in natural
law.

And the proper office of a King towardes his subiectes agrees
very well with the office of the head towards the bodie, and
all members thereof. For from the head, being the seate of
judgement, proceedeth the care and foresight of guiding, and
preuenting all euill that may come to the bodie, or any parte
thereof. The head cares for the bodie: so doth the King for
his people. As the discourse and direction flowes from the
head, and the execution according therunto belongs to the
rest of the members, euerie one according to their office:
so is it betwixt a wise Prince, and his people ....

> And for the similitude of the head & the body, it may
> very wel fall out that the head will be forced to garre cut
> of some rotten member (as I haue already said) to keepe the
> rest of the body in integritie. But what state the body can
> be in, if the head, for any infirmity that can fall to it, be
> cut off, I leaue it to the readers judgement (74–75).

And if the argument is raised that a wicked man may become
king or tyrant, then that, James continues, is as it should be.

> Whereunto, for answere, I grant in deede that a wicked
> King is sent by GOD for a cursse to his people, and a plague
> for their sinnes. But that it is lawfull to them to shake off
> that cursse at their owne hande, which God hath layde on
> them, that I denie, and may so doe justly . . . . And as for
> vindicating to themselues their owne libertie, what lawfull
> power haue they to revoke to themselues againe those
> priuiledges, which by their owne consent before were so
> fully put out of their handes? for if a prince cannot justly
> bring back againe to himself the priviledges once bestowed
> by him, or his predecessours vpon any state, or ranck of his
> subjects: how much lesse may the subjects reaue out of the
> Princes hand that superiority, which he & his Predecessors
> haue so long brooked ouer them? (77).

Such absolutism, finally, is eternally binding on the people.
"And it is here likewise to be noted," James concludes, "that
the duty & allegeance, which the people sweareth to their
prince, is not only bound to themselues, but likewise to
their lawfull heires & posterity, the lineal succession of
crownes" (80). This succession of heirs and lineal succession
of crowns is the identical "line" that Macbeth proclaims
will "stretch out to th'crack of doom" (4.1.117).

Such a position led almost at once to the first constitutional document of the Jacobean period, *The Form of Apology
and Satisfaction* of 1604. It asserted, Tricomi says, that

> "The prerogatives of princes may easily, and do daily grow:
> the privileges of the subject are for the most part at an
> everlasting stand. They may be by good providence and care
> preserved, but being once lost are not recovered but with
> much disquiet." The signers even charged that James's

speeches were tending "to the utter overthrow" of "fundamental" House privileges and "of the rights and liberties of the whole Commons of your realm of England, which they and their ancestors from time immemorial have undoubtdly enjoyed" (287). The issue of absolutism they addressed directly to James, asserting that he had been "misinformed" if he had heard that the kings of England held absolute power in themselves (287).

It may indeed be true, as increasing numbers of historians have concluded, that this document deserves only a small place in parliamentary history—the document was later rejected as too extreme—but parliamentary history is one thing, political consciouness another. As a mark of the latter, *The Apology* reveals a zeal to safeguard the English political inheritance, a notable apprehension of despotism, and a disenchantment with James that is also evident in Jacobean satire and tragedy.[17]

James attempted, in argumentation and response, to build a seamless theory of absolutism allowing the divine right of kings by drawing on an unbroken history of Scripture, custom and law, the reversion of the prophecies at the heart of Shakespeare's play. But he meant then to function, nevertheless, as Keith Thomas has shown that prophecy then functioned, "to demonstrate that there was a link between contemporary aspirations and those of remote antiquity," to act as "a 'validating chapter' (to adopt the anthropologists' phrase) for new enterprises undertaken in the face of strong contemporary prohibitions."[18] "Ancient prophecies, like spurious history" such as Shakespeare's version of Macbeth, for instance, "also helped to mitigate the otherwise revolutionary doings of contemporaries," Thomas goes on. "By showing that current political activities were in accordance with the predictions of some long-dead figure, they took the sting out of them. Prophecies disguised the break with the past" (505). We may remember that James felt predictions in his dreams of the dead Buchanan—or his visions of being killed in *his* bed. Furthermore, Thomas adds, "Contempories also regarded ghosts," like the ghost of Banquo, presenting the show of eight kings with the witches, "as potential bearers of warning messages or prophetic utterances" (716).

This was surely the purpose of Dr. Matthew Gwinn, whose *Tres Sibyllae* was performed in Latin before King James during his visit to Oxford, on 27 August 1605, for here he fuses the story in Shakespeare's play with a prophecy that looks both backward and forward. The entertainment was offered by St. John's College; in it "Youths in habit and attire like nymphs or sibyls confronted the King, saluting him and putting him in mind of that ancient prophecy made unto Banquo, his majesty's ancestor, that though the sceptre should not come to him yet it should be for ever with his posterity."[19] The boys' staging thus reaches outward, breaking its own barriers of time and space: the present body of the king realizes and fulfills the future prophesied in the past. As in Shakespeare's play during the show of eight kings, "Genealogy and prophecy are made manifest in a visible display," as Steven Mullaney puts it succinctly in *The Place of the Stage*.[20] Hence Gwinn's *Tres Sibyllae* validates as well as honors King James, the work a celebratory act as well as, clearly, a deeply imaginative and ideological one. But in *Macbeth* "there is another genealogy in the air as well," Mullaney continues, "one heard rather than seen. Juxtaposed to the projection of James's line, the witches' riddles complicate its complimentary gesture with what amounts to a genealogy of treason and equivocation" (124). The vision of triumph is preceded by the three apparitions of rebellion and slaughter. For Shakespeare, prophecy—beginning with the witchcraft of Glendower in *I Henry IV*—links the supernatural with treason, even as Dr. Gwinn linked the supernatural to James.

To be fair, James developed his theory of divine right and his notion of absolutism while still in Scotland as a protection from and as a defense against attacks by Scottish Puritans and Catholics who threatened his rule from either side. His most formidable foe was the architect of the Scottish Reformed Church, the author of its *Confession of Faith*, *Book of Common Order* and *First Book of Discipline*, who had also been chaplain to the English King Edward VI and who had preached James's own coronation sermon when he was but a year old. This was John Knox, who in the popular English imagination of Shakespeare's time was the true founder of Scottish Puritanism but who was, to his own mind, a prophet sent from God. His thunderous voice deliberately imitated his predecessors in the Old Testament, and so did his writings: his *Letter to the Regent of Scotland* urging her to accept the Reformation; his *First Blast of the Trumpet Against the Monstrous Regiment of Women* warning against the ill fate of a woman's unnatural rule; and his *History of the Reformation in Scotland* recounting his confrontations with Mary Stuart, James's mother, all three constituting the largest important body of works of resistance theory in sixteenth century Scotland. Less well known but equally powerful is the fragmentary *Second Blast*, of which little remains but the outline:

1. It is not birth only nor propinquity of blood that maketh a king lawfully to reign above a people, professing Christ Jesus and his eternal verity, but in his election must the ordinance which God hath established in the election of inferior judges be observed.
2. No manifest idolater nor notorious transgressor of God's holy precepts ought to be promoted to any public regiment, honor, or dignity in any realm, province, or city that hath subjected the self to Christ Jesus and his blessed Evangel.
3. Neither can oath nor promise bind any such people to obey and maintain tyrants against God and against his truth known.
4. But, if either rashly they have promoted any manifest wicked person, or yet ignorantly have chosen such a one as after declareth himself unworthy of regiment above the people of God—and such be all idolaters and cruel persecutors, most justly may the same men depose and punish him that unadvisedly before they did nominate, appoint, and elect.[21]

On the Continent, and circulating widely in England by 1600, was the anonymous *Vindiciae contra Tyrannos*, the *Defence of Liberty against Tyrants*, now thought to be the work of Mornay. The *Vindiciae* argues from the authority of Scripture and the examples of martyrs that God's law must be obeyed above that of any earthly ruler and that any king who refuses to follow the laws of God ought to invite what would be true rebellion. As the people's duty is to choose a magistrate who represents and mirrors themselves and their will, any encroachment must be put down. "The King, therefore, is the delegate of the people for specific functions. The people is greater than the King"; "Popular sovereignty is therefore the basis of royal power."[22] In England, meantime, the early Reformer under Henry VIII, John Ponet, supplied the first work of resistance theory with his *Short Treatise of Politic Power* in 1556:

> I think it cannot be maintained by God's word that any private man may kill, except (where execution of just punishment upon tyrants, idolators and traitorous governors is either by the whole state utterly neglected, or the prince with the nobility and council conspire the subversion or alteration of their country and people) any private man have some special inward commandment or surely proved motion of God (as Moses had to kill the Egyptians) or be otherwise commanded or permitted by common authority upon just occasion and common necessity to kill (sig. G8v).

By 1594, with the publication of *A Conference About the Next Succession to the Crown of England*, the Jesuit Robert Parsons was urging the same thing: "Not only hath the commonwealth authority to put back the next inheritors upon lawful considerations, but also to dispossess them that been lawfully put in possession if they fulfil not the laws and conditions, by which and for which, their dignity was given them" (32).

In answer to such growing sentiment, James pulled back into a role of mystification. For him, "The holiness of power creates the power of holiness," as Debora Kuller Shuger has recently argued.[23] Both "the mysterie of the Kings power," as he put it, and his "absolute Prerogative" stemmed from the mystical knowledge that only divine rulers appointed by God came to have, the *arcana imperii,* or secrets of state, which surpassed discussion and dispute. "In James," Shuger adds, "this 'mystery' is equated with 'what a King may do in the height of his power,' that is with his *potentia absoluta*

and perhaps also with the Tacitean *arcana imperii,* where
it is implied that the prince's prerogative is not only sacred
... but involves a disparity between 'declared policy and
actual strategy'" (155–56). In time, James would declare before
the English Privy Council a "Mysticall reverence, that belongs
unto them that sit in the Throne of God" and in time,
Archbishop Whitgift would buckle. "The magistrate is holy
and not profane," James would add, "his authority holy, his
laws holy."[24]

## III

The tyranny central to *Macbeth,* then, which can prompt
acts of rebellion, spoke profoundly to Shakespeare's audiences when it was first performed in 1606. But this could,
in a general way, have come as no surprise: for a century
and more, tragedies had been associated with tyranny.
Dollimore notes that

> Thomas Elyot, in *The Governor,* asserted (in 1570) that, in
> reading tragedies, a man shall be led to "execrate and abhor
> the intollerable life of tyrants," and for Sidney tragedy made
> "Kings fear to be tyrants." Puttenham in *The Art of English
> Poesy* (1589) had said that tragedy revealed tyranny to "all
> the world," while the downfall of the tyrant disclosed (per-
> haps incongruously) both historical vicissitude ("the muta-
> bility of fortune") and God's providential order (his "just
> punishment").[25]

"The theater," Rebecca W. Bushnell sums, "locates the tyrant
at center stage, even though he was meant to be pushed
to the margins of political life and of humanity."[26]

In light of this, Shakespeare's *Macbeth* hardly seems
peculiar—but it is unusual in the specific resonances that
make the play especially chilling. There are, for instance,
uncanny echoes in Shakespeare's play of the Scottish historian George Buchanan's account of the death of Lord Henry
Darnley, James's father, at the hands of his mother, Queen
Mary Stuart, in league with the Earl of Bothwell.

In the middle of the evening's proceedings, the Frenchman Paris, one of [the Queen's] rascally servants, entered the King's chamber and placed himself, silently, so that he could be seen by the Queen. That was the signal agreed upon, that everything was ready.... On her return to the palace, she spoke for a considerable time with Bothwell. He was at length dismissed. He returned to his own chamber, changed his clothes, put on a military cloak, and passing through the guard, returned to the town with a few attendants. Two other groups of the conspirators came to the appointed place by different routes. A few of them went into the King's chambers, the keys of which, as I said before were in their possession. They fell upon him as he slumbered, and strangled him along with one of his servants, who slept on a little bed nearby. They carried the strangled bodies through a postern which they had made through the town wall for this purpose and into an adjacent garden. Then they set fire to gunpowder, and blew up the house from its foundations, with so great an explosion [the model, of course, for the 1605 Gunpowder Plot on Parliament House in Westminster]. ...

The Queen, who had been up waiting for the event of that night, called together the lords who were then in the palace, among them Bothwell.... Bothwell returned home, and with feigned amazement carried the news to the Queen, who went to her chamber, and for much of the next day she lay in deep and tranquil sleep.[27]

A number of details in Buchanan's account are also in *Macbeth*, but not in any of the chronicles thought to be Shakespeare's source for his play: the queen as hostess welcoming guests to a residence where she has already planned murder, her inability to accomplish the deed herself and her departure, the king killed along with a groom in their own beds, and the queen's subsequent feigned innocence even before her coconspirator, the Macbeth-like Bothwell.

This successful assassination also finds uncomfortable echoes in the Gowrie conspiracy. In 1604 Shakespeare's company, the King's Men, attempted to perform a play now lost and known only as the *Tragedy of Gowrie* about a similar event in James's own life, but they were required to remove it from the stage after only two performances. The official report of *The Earle of Gowries conspiracie against the Kings Maiestie of Scotland. At Saint Iohn-stoun vpon Tuesday the fift of August. 1600* was printed by Valentine Simmes, the printer of many of Shakespeare's plays, in London in 1600. It tells of the time early on the morning of Tuesday, 5 August when young Master Alexander Ruthven, "second brother to the late earle of Gowie," (sig. A2) who had been executed for his part in the Ruthven Raid against James years earlier, approached the king, who was preparing to go buck hunting at Falkland Palace. Ruthven told of meeting "a base like fellow, unknowne to him, with a cloke cast about his mouth" (sig. A2v) who, upon examination, was found to have "a great wide pot to be vnder his arme, all full of coyned gold in great peeces" (sig. A2v). The king began to think that it was Papist money intended for Jesuits, and agreed to come to Gowrie House, near Perth, to see it for himself. He was taken there, where he was apparently unexpected, given lunch and then led through a series of rooms, with each door locked behind him. Finally he arrived at "a little studie, where he saw standing with a very abased countenance, not a bond-man, but a free man, with a Dagger at his girdle" (sig B3). Master Ruthven then locked the study door, removed his hat and picked up the dagger, threatening to kill the king in revenge of his brother. When his appeal to Master Ruthven's conscience fell on deaf ears, the king managed to pull away, get open a turret window and shout for help below. Lennox, Mar and other members of the royal hunting party, who had been told by the porter that the king had departed, heard his shouts, forced open a stairway, and began pounding on the heavy study door—much as Shakespeare's Lennox and Macduff pound on the heavy door at Inverness to awaken a drunken porter. Another struggle ensued, and Ruthven fell. Inwardly, James knew the escape had been a very narrow one; but outwardly, he proclaimed it a miracle that confirmed the divinity of his rule. He wrote his own account of this miracle; he encouraged similar pamphlets; he ordered public holidays and public thanksgivings; and then, having learned his bloody instructions, he had Ruthven declared guilty of treason and his body hanged, drawn and quartered so that it could be exhibited, simultaneously, on poles fixed at Edinburgh, Perth, Dundee and Stirling.

Stanley J. Kozikowski has pointed out four features of Shakespeare's play of *Macbeth* that appear nowhere else except in this pamphlet: the dagger, the appeal to conscience, the banquet and the porter.[28] Shakespeare's play, set in 1040, seems deliberately tied to events in 1600 as well, and the king's miraculous escape here is, moreover, anticipatory— a prophetic event—of the Gunpowder Plot five years later in Westminster. But in the pamphlet on the Gowrie conspiracy, the salvation of the king is contrasted with the darker witchcraft of Gowrie:

> His maiestie hauing before his parting out of that towne, caused to search the said earle of Gowries pockets, in case any letters that might further the discouery of that conspiracy might bee found therein. But nothing was found in them, but a little close parchment bag, full of Magicall characters, and wordes of inchantment, wherein it seemed that hee had put his confidence, thinking himself neuer safe without them, and therefore euer caried them about with him: beeing also obserued, that while they were vpon him, his wound whereof he died, bled not, but incontinent after the taking of them away, the blood gushed out in great abundance, to the great admiration of all the beholders (sig. C2v).

This, then, is the *other* prophecy, one of demonic witchcraft, inside the larger prophetic warning of a conspiracy against the king like that we find in *Macbeth*. What the pamphlet leaves out, however, is the fact that the Gowries were the second-ranking family in Scotland whose own forces were rapidly growing. Once the Gowrie line is associated with treason and the earl himself killed, James's miracle will at least insure the security, if not the divinity, of his rule.

IV

The Gowrie conspiracy represented Scottish Puritan resistance at its most profound and most dangerous; much has been made elsewhere of the Catholic Gunpowder Plot as a similar influential reference and force behind Shakespeare's *Macbeth*. But there was another outspoken act of tyranny occurring between the two that had considerable impact on early Jacobean theater, but which until now has been overlooked in the chain of prophetic resonances that unite imagination and ideology near the time of Shakespeare's play. I refer to the Essex revolt of 1601. The best account I know is that by Mervyn James in *Society, Politics and Culture* (1986), a summary that is far more judicious than either Elizabeth I's detailed proclamation or Bacon's narrative in his *apologia pro sua vita*.[29] According to James, Essex was prompted to attempt his fatal march on the queen by the urgent pleas of his sister, Penelope Devereux Rich, acting on him as Queen Mary had on Bothwell. Her chief reason, much like that of the Gowries, was her sense of the Essex lineage, their bloodline now dominated and humiliated by an angry and spiteful Queen Elizabeth. There was a strong sense of religion, too, a Knoxlike sense of purpose and destiny alongside—as in the earlier case of Mary and the later Gunpowder Plot—a strong infusion of dissatisfied recusants. Moreover, like Macbeth, Essex was justifiably proud of his military prowess—and, in his case, his office as Earl Marshal of the realm. His attitude seems to us now straight out of the contemporary treatises on resistance: when urged to submit to the queen by Lord Keeper Egerton, he is said to have replied,

> that obedience could not be demanded beyond the bounds of honour, for "I owe Her majesty the duty of an earl and lord marshal . . . but I can never serve as a slave or villien." And in words which would reverberate into the seventeenth century, he repudiated a religious submission: "What, cannot princes err? Cannot subjects receive wrong? Is an earthly power infinite?"[30]

Ideology grants, then rescinds, identity. The march on the queen, as we know, was a dismal failure, for few would think of accompanying even Essex on such a mission of high treason against presumed tyranny. But once he was arrested, Essex had a remarkable conversion, and his solitary penance and his wish for a private death helped with unusual rapidity to return him to favor and to considerable popularity with the English people; by the time James arrived in London, the rebel Essex was already a folk hero. So forceful was his presence in death, in fact, that Samuel Daniel's play of *Philotas* (1605) follows, in its last two acts, an anatomy of heroic rebellion closely based on specific events in Essex's last days, as Laurence Michel has shown in considerable detail.[31] What Essex shares with Gowrie and Darnley, of course, as well as with Daniel's Philotas and Shakespeare's Macbeth, is his utter devotion and obedience to an ideological imagination and an imaginative ideology unrealized in the world in which he necessarily finds himself. Long before Althusser, they come to realize that ideology is an imagined, willed construct, while the imagination needs some sort of ideology, some culturally shaping beliefs, in order to exist.

In studying Shakespeare's *Macbeth*, we tend to forget that the play offers us two regicides, not one, and asks us whether the killing of King Macbeth is justified by the killing of King Duncan and sufficient to repair the state. In the *Basilikon Doron*, King James argues that such kings are placed on a stage where all the beholders' eyes are attentively bent to look and pry into the least circumstances of their secretest drifts.[32] It is just such an appeal to mystification as this that causes Annabel Patterson to remark in *Censorship and Interpretation* that "the institutionally unspeakable" nevertheless "makes itself heard inferentially, in the space between what is written or acted and what the audience, *knowing what they know*, might expect to read or see."[33] She goes on to note that "the text . . . becomes a matrix or holding pattern within which a series of widely differing events can and do occur"[34]—some legendary, some historic, some contemporary. It is the imagined text, to modify Michael D. Bristol slightly, that allows the ideological to "[make] possible the integration of functional and of dysfunctional elements within social [and political] reality."[35] With *Macbeth*, Shakespeare's large "wooden O" surrounds the somewhat smaller conjurer's circle where, magically, all time and no time meet as in prophecy, and this in turn surrounds the smallest circle of all in eternal tension—Macbeth's "fruitless crown" which, with "a barren sceptre" the three weird sisters put "in [the] gripe" (3.1.60–61) of his (and our) imagination.

# 8 • The Uses of Deception
## From Cromwell to Milton

*Sharon Achinstein*

B y 1647, Oliver Cromwell's revolutionary army had defeated King Charles's forces on the battlefied and had
forced the king to surrender at Oxford. Rather than celebrat-
ing their successes, however, Cromwell's army was dividing
into factions. The mutiny in the army began with the soldiers'
call for back pay, but soon, in their "Agreements of the
People," London radicals added their own demands for
"fundamental liberties of free-born Englishmen." Cromwell
believed that the Parliamentary cause could not survive such
divisions. By May, strong measures had to be taken to quell
the rebellion of the army, since any negotiations for peace
with the king could be put at risk by such disunity in the
Parliamentary cause. Responding to this new challenge,
Cromwell charged his Military Council not to use force
against the mutineers, but to wage a different kind of battle:
"keep a party of able pen-men at Oxford and the Army,"
he ordered, "where their presses be employed to satisfy and
undeceive the people." He further stipulated, "Do all things
upon public grounds for the good of the people, and with
expedition, to avoid divisions and for the prevention of
bloodshed."[1]

These injunctions amount to a propaganda campaign, authorized by a desperate Cromwell, who, like our own leaders, saw the necessity of good press coverage. As a supplement to the force of combat, he believed, war must also be won in the press. In requiring his supporters to pay attention to how their actions were represented, Cromwell tacitly acknowledged that rhetoric was a constitutive element of his own power, to be manipulated according to a desired political end.

Cromwell's public contradiction of his enemies belongs to a new era of political conduct, where allegiance was decided by airing issues, not by traditional patronage, and where leaders had to convince others of their legitimacy through public appeals.[2] For the first time in English history, readers were confronted with a variety of political positions in the press, not all of them state-sponsored; everything seemed "up for grabs," as J.H. Hexter puts it. The printing industry was crucial in this unprecedented political conflict.[3] During the English Revolution, over 22,000 pamphlets, sermons, newsbooks, speeches, broadside ballads and other ephemera were published in numbers surpassing the outpouring of books in the French Revolution.[4] The explosion of printed material after censorship lapsed in 1640 brought such subjects as religion, culture, law, finance, domestic relations and, inevitably, politics, to the attention of the public—an increasingly literate public, it appears. Historians believe 30 percent of adult males England in 1642 could read; in London, the figure was closer to 60 percent. These were extremely high figures compared to those of the rest of Europe.[5] The writers of the English Revolution were transforming their arguments about the people's rights and duties into actual practice by reaching out to an audience of the people, and by discussing political matters that had previously been censored.[6]

In Cromwell's emphases on action and mobilization, English Revolutionary propaganda may be traced back to the English Reformation, where propaganda was used by the state for the direction of the people.[7] The Protestant Reformation had first put the public into focus as an object of zeal, and Elizabeth's schemes for educational progress had made religion the impetus for widespread literacy. Reading pamphlets then was tied to action, all in the name of reform.[8] There are important differences between Reformation propaganda and that of Cromwell's "pen-men" that unsettle the comparison between Reformation propaganda and that of the Civil War period, however. Cromwell was ordering the dissemination of secular, political writing; many other pamphlet writers during the English Revolution were busy creating such literature. Yet the most significant difference between the propaganda of the English Reformation and that of the Revolution was the wider scope of opinion permitted in the press. Writers of the English Revolution wrote under conditions very like those of a free press, and the writing was engaged on many sides of an issue.

In of this torrent of opinions, readers had to grapple with conflicting perspectives. How were these readers going to avoid being taken in by propaganda, "deceived," as Cromwell put it? Many of the pamphlets of the English Revolution show that writers were deeply concerned that their readers be taught to resist enemy opinions or "deceptions." They felt a special pressure to teach this, since the audience for political choice was expanding to include new groups.[9]

In this essay, I demonstrate that politicians often used visual metaphors—figures of blindness and sight, as well as figures of telescopes, spectacles and other visual equipment— to register this concern that an audience make sense of the battle of opinions. This language of "seeing properly" reflects the authors' intense desire to control the interpretations of readers. I also argue that by their use of optical metaphors, the authors of the controversial literature of the English Revolution attempted to instruct readers how to read, encouraging their audiences to view any political text with critical eyes. In this way, *Paradise Lost* may be seen as a reflection of certain rhetorical practices of the English Revolution. As many critics have shown, Milton's *Paradise Lost* pursues a task of educating its readers. Milton, completing the epic poem after the failure of the Commonwealth and Protectorate, pursued a like task of responding to the practices of propaganda that had misled so many during the English Revolution. Like the other writers who engaged in the propaganda wars of the English Revolution, Milton wished to constitute subjects who were equipped with the reading skills to meet the challenge posed by propaganda. These writers conceived of political subjects as those who could root out truth among conflicting interpretations, who could make political choices based on a critical practice of reading.

Cromwell's program to "undeceive," part of his plan to defeat the mutiny among his soldiers, involved a battle over a public thought to be held captive by an enemy. In "undeceiving" the people, Cromwell used a word derived from the Latin root *capere*—"capture," taking prisoners— a military metaphor, befitting a war of words. As the volume of writings published during the Revolutionary period suggests, books were prime ammunition in that battle. Propaganda has had a long history, entering the mental lexicon with the Roman Catholic Church's response to the Reformation, its *Congregatio de propaganda fide* (Congregation for the Propagation of the Faith) in 1622.[10] For the most part, modern theorists of propaganda, both in the fields of communications studies and rhetoric, have slighted the early modern period, deriving their models from examples of twentieth century fascism. This has tended to essentialize and dehistoricize the study of propaganda. Today's theorists often invoke modern technologies (the communications systems of radio and television), forms of political organization and administration, and cultural norms (urbanism, secularity and "mass psychology")—all of which do not match the seventeenth century English experience of propaganda.[11] These conditions are so different from the conditions that Cromwell and Milton struggled with that it seems an anachronism to compare the two.[12]

What I have attempted to do in this essay is to suggest another method by which to understand propaganda. I have looked at propaganda from the perspective of those writing it, and have sought an understanding of propaganda in the language of those writers who recognized its power. Jürgen

Habermas has suggested that "the elimination of the institution of censorship marked a new stage in the development
of the public sphere" in Europe;[13] but it is clear that the
weakening of censorship in the 1640s in England did not
lead at once to the creation of a public sphere for free political
exchange. Rather, politicians struggled with the distortions
of propaganda, and this struggle infuses the early English
public sphere with its peculiar rhetorical character. The
construction of the political subject as a capable reader of
propaganda is one significant response to this torrent of
opinions, and it was one contribution of the English
Revolution to the history of political culture.

# I

English politicians during the Civil War period offered
many versions of the truth, and these versions were often
mutually contradictory, each clamoring for public acceptance. The press, whose freedom allowed the expression of
a much wider spectrum of political thought than had been
published before, was the vehicle of propaganda battles. We
do not know precisely how readers were affected by this
barrage of opinions—whether they changed opinions each
time they lay hands on a new pamphlet; whether "the whiff
of every new pamphlet should stagger them out of their
catechism," as Milton joked in his *Areopagitica;* or whether
readers were "fast reading, trying all things, assenting to the
force of reason and convincement," as Milton had hoped.[14]
But we do know that many writers were troubled by the
existence of contradictory opinions. While they sought to
attract readers to their own cause and to discredit all the
others along the way, they were also concerned about the
plight of their readers in the hands of their rivals' pamphlets.
Gaining a monopoly on truth was no easy task. The writers
of the English Revolution were aware that they were living
in a world glutted with deceptive stories. The author of the
weekly *Mercurius Civicus* (1643) warned readers against
enemies' distortion of truth. The newsbook's function was

made clear in the title: "Truth Impartially related . . . To prevent misinformation."[15] With "misinformation" circulating, this writer hoped to save readers from its effects. The author of a Royalist newsbook, *Mercurius Elencticus* announced, "I know 'tis the constant desire of the common-people to hear of News! Strange tidings! Be they never so untrue, ever relish with the multitude, provided they suit with their affections . . . to tickle the Ears of the giddy multitude; which are all of them false, and very unbecoming the Pen of any man that pretends the service of the King; because that by this means Truth itself is often blemished and obscured among such Lies and Forgeries; and things Real looked upon as futilous [sic] and absurd." The author added, "so good a Cause as we have shall (I hope) never stand in need of Lies to support it."[16]

The conflict in the press was especially worrisome to partisans because so many pamphlets were aimed at the populace. Henry Parker's anti-Royalist pamphlet called *The Contra-Replicant* (1643) feared that readers were being duped by the superior rhetoric of the king's writer: "None but the duller sort of people are to be catcht by pure Oratory," Parker writes, "the wiser sort are well enough instructed . . . [the King] aims not at the satisfying of wise men, but the dazzling of simple men."[17] Royalists and anti-Royalists alike expressed a particular nervousness about the force of pamphlets over the populace. As Milton scoffed, the king's portrait in *Eikon Basilike* was "set there to catch fools and silly gazers." Milton, again alarmed about the power of deceptions over a rude audience, feared that the king's supporters "intend [*Eikon Basilike*] not so much the defence of his former actions, as the promoting of their own future designes . . . to corrupt and disorder the mindes of weaker men, by new suggestions and narrations" (*CPW* 3:338). Royalists, too, worried about the susceptibility of the common folk to dangerous opinions culled from pamphlets, as the author of the *England's Remembrancer of Londons Integrity* noted:

> a generation of men are sprung up . . . whose employment is to write Pamphlets filled with false relations, to deceive

> the people, and to lay on fair beautiful colors upon the horrid and deformed faces of sedition, and faction, and to put the Ensign of Innocency and Peace into their hands, whose actions are guileful . . . O how are simple-hearted Readers abused with feigned stories, and shadows without substances, and all to hold them in suspense.[18]

Writers on all sides of the political spectrum represented their task as education of an audience of "simple men." They were concerned about a specific audience of the political illiterate: those unaccustomed to being the targets of political appeal.

The pamphlet battles during the English Revolution offered such uninitiated readers nothing less than competing images of the truth through various genres and tropes. Astrology books, long a medium associated with a popular audience, for example, could offer directly contradictory predictions to readers, predictions that would, of course, depend upon the political allegiance of the author.[19] The author of *Mercurius Vapulans* accused his enemy of "making cheating and lying pamphlets, and by the calculating of news for the meridian of Oxford," that is, of falsifying the truth according to the perspective of the Royalist stronghold.[20] George Wharton's Royalist almanac for 1645 read victory for the king's forces in the stars. Wharton summarized his sidereal deductions with this prediction:

> It is most apparant to every impartial and ingenuous Judgment; that (although His Majesty cannot expect to be secured from every trivial disaster . . .) yet several Positions of the Heavens duly considered and compared amongst themselves, as well as in the prefixed *Schemes* and *Quarterly Ingresses*, do generally render His Majesty and his whole Army unexpectedly victorious and successful in all his Designs.[21]

Parliament's astrologer, William Lilly, swiftly countered this, promising that if the king should take the march Wharton recommended, he would suffer "infinite loss on his party." Lilly vouched that "the Parliament's cause shall not want a Champion in Astrology to confute any thing in point of

Art that can be alleged from the greatest Clerks in Oxford."[22] John Booker's *Mercurius Coelicus* was another anti-Royalist response to Wharton's almanac, and Booker also interpreted the heavens according to his pro-Parliamentary stance, with results precisely opposite to Wharton's. The Royalist defeat in its first battle with the New Model Army at Naseby in June 1645 was to prove Wharton's prediction utterly wrong. What the readers of this popular genre thought at this point nobody knows.

Language itself was a political battleground, as authors accused their enemies of distorting words to suit their ends.[23] "Hard words, jealousies and fears,/ Set folks together by the ears": so runs the prologue to Bulter's *Hudibras*, an epic that reduces the very matter of the Civil Wars to insults. Booker, for example, represented the clash of opinions as a clash of terminologies, and urged that a correct dictionary was needed. "Victory" for Wharton's Royalist almanac was interpreted as "treachery" in Booker's *Mercurius Coelicus*. Booker explained, "I have gotten these base words by reading."[24] An ally of Wharton's was quick to respond to this pamphlet, avowing that Booker himself had stuffed his "perfidious pamphlets with Ambiguous phrases, thereby to beget new Feares and Jealousies amongst the people." This Royalist was troubled that Booker's language might mislead the people.[25] The anti-Royalist author of *Mercurius Vapulans* (1664) also focused on the question of interpretation of language, charging Royalist authors with "translating" the truth: "Your party are very sufficient *Railers*, even *Naturalized* into detraction and lying" (3). There were contradictory uses of language, as the author of *Mercurius Vapulans* asserted: "our grave and religious assembly of Divines, thou callest, *A schismatical Assembly of Taylors, Millers, Cobblers and Weavers, etc.* (so they sew up the rent which you Prelates and their adherents have made in the Church).[26] This author would have his audience "undeceived" by decoding the enemies' language.

Writers sought to steer their readers to the right interpretation—theirs—and they illustrated the possibilities for mistaken interpretation by different metaphors. One common figure denoting the resolution of a clash in perspectives is found in the cliché, "Religion is a Cloak for knavery," repeated so often during this period by Royalists. This figure of clothing and nakedness expresses a firm belief that truth, "knavery," lies hidden under layers, "a Cloak" that must be flung off. The anti-Royalist author of *Mercurius Vapulans* also used this metaphor: "For the truth of affairs must not walk abroad there, either naked, or in their own clothing, but must be translated into such a habit, as will be most pleasing and acceptable to the hearers." Special ways of interpretation were needed to expose the Royalist falsehoods, and the author of *Vapulans* wrote in order to "unbutton [Wharton] . . . to his Principles, and strip his libellous soul stark Naked, and lash him through the streets of London back again to Oxford" (2). By his use of this metaphor, the writer pointed to a situation rife with competing interpretations, but suggested that finally, there was only one true one, his own.

In a similar vein the metaphor of seeing was used by the English Revolutionary pamphleteers to represent the process of political interpretation. Sight is the chief metaphor on which I will now concentrate in the rest of this essay, because it subsumes all the others in its explicit recognition of rival interpretations. Yet the use of it touches upon several important epistemological issues. First, opinion is made to seem like truth. "True sight" as equivalent to "true knowledge" becomes the goal of the reader, and of course, true knowledge is what the writer believes he has. And second, the "truth" of the matter is to be attained through a process. Through their visual metaphors, writers represented that process of acquiring the truth.

## II

Rather than accusing their enemies of falsehood, the pamphlet writers who used metaphors of true sight spurred their readers to correct "faulty vision." The modern relativistic idea that "every image embodies a way of seeing" that is equally valid would be unheard of for the engaged writers of the English Revolution, however.[27] Some ways of seeing, they would argue, were right, and others were wrong, and it was most important to see the right way. It is significant, however, that the presence of "deceptions" was taken as a given. The clearest instance was the king. Was King Charles a traitor? This question alone was the issue in countless pamphlets, and the polemicists working to persuade an audience to fight against their king held that, though there were many images to choose from, there must be a *right* way of seeing him.

The debate over the right image of the king was central to *The Converted Cavaliers Confession*, which referred to changes in opinion as a matter of seeing properly, "opening eyes," "discovering" and "seeing." This pamphlet, published in 1644, presented the secrets of a "Cavalier" who recanted. This is a familiar form of propaganda to us, the "confession" narrative. In the title, the author represented a process of political enlightenment that echoed Parliament's 1642 Declaration of war, but in personal terms: *"The Converted Cavaliers' Confession of Their Design When first we drew the King away from his Parliament. As also (now our eyes are in some measure opened) that we see there was a deeper Plot and Design in hand, at that time by the Papists; who made use of us, to accomplish their own Design, which then lay hid from us, but now discovereth it selfe: With our Resolution to forsake the Papists."*[28] The Cavalier explained that the source of this new discovery was a book: as "Mr. Prynne in his late book at large setteth forth" (4), highlighting the place of reading, a process, in acquiring knowledge. Now awakened from his dream, the converted Cavalier urges others to see as clearly as he does, "that others that still prosecute the design that we did, may now take notice of the Papists, how they make use of us to our own destruction; and then I hope, you likewise will forsake them" (5). This Cavalier was to be a pattern for others to follow—others who must read, understand and see differently. "And this is my persuasion, and my Resolution is to adhere to the King's forces no more" (5).

It is doubtful that this was a "real" confession. The author used the device of a fictional persona, a reformed Royalist who now tows the Presbyterian line, in hopes of reaching other Royalists who might do the same thing. By this literary impersonation, the author could evade possible charges of treason ("after all," one might say in his defense, "it's only a fiction"), but the use of a fictional persona was a signal, too, of the structures embedded in the practices of ideological conflict. The Cavalier's confession revealed that a special way of reading Civil War events was necessary, with Mr. Prynne's book offering the key. By the use of this metaphor, the author invites readers to understand that finding the truth is a process of penetrating through mediations, and truth is not an immediately apprehensible fact.

Pamphleteers who used the metaphors of sight and seeing represented truth as mediated by acts of reading. The Royalist newsbook *Mercurius Elenticus* performed such a "reading," also using the metaphor of true vision. The author of this pamphlet offered an interpretaton of Parliament's restrictions on the press in October 1649, presenting his own meaning within brackets beside Parliament's language in italics. By this presentation, the author was able to give a running commentary on the language of Parliament, to direct the reader to interpret Parliament's words properly: "*God is pleased to bless our endeavors abroad,* [that you shall know anon] *and by that means to put an awe upon a great number* [the more Cowards they] *that wish us no good. And is pleases also to open mens Eyes by degrees* [to see your Perfidiousness and Treason] *to a discovery of their true Interest* [swallowed up by your State-Cormorants] . . . *some that were taken in their honest and Candid simplicity, by the cunning insinuation of a* [pretended, but a really Bloody] *Parliament, who lay in wait to deceive, have seen through the imposture, and delivered themselves from the Enchantment* [very properly indeed, for there is not much difference betwixt Rebellion and Witchcraft].[29] This author turns the Parliamentary gesture of "opening mens Eyes by degrees" back against Parliament, explaining that what men will see when their eyes are opened is "your Perfidiousness and

Treason." This author suggests that reading the Civil War pronouncements requires especially keen eyesight, an ability to "read between the lines."[30] This pamphleteer showed the reader just how to do so.

Writers fought over the political allegiances of their readers by acknowledging the mediation of truth through distorting perspectives, and by providing ways for them to overcome such distortions. As in the *Converted Cavalier's Confession*, the new perspective would offer a pattern for opposing the king. The language of perception is used to arm readers against being taken in, against being deceived, by others. Renaissance ideas about visual perspective underlie the recurrent metaphors of sight and deception in these Civil War pamphlets. We recall the application of systematic linear perspective, which arrived in fifteenth century Italy with Alberti. The "science" of perspective was a mechanical one, with rules about ratios and vanishing points providing geometrical certainty in the pictorial representation of space. Renaissance men and women were fascinated with games of illusion, games about multiple perspectives, such as anamorphic puzzles, as in the elongated skull shot across the lower portion of Holbein's *Ambassadors* (1533). This visual wit always depends upon *fixed* perspectives between which to shift; that's how the anamorphic skull, for example, may be "read" at all.[31] Once the "key" to the visual puzzle is known, the strange shape "looks like" a skull, and with the right point of view, the picture snaps into place. Visual ambiguities rely, then, on the beholder's knowledge of the conventions of seeing; the anamorphic skull may be read as a strange, elongated mark in the foreground of a painting and may also be read as a skull depending upon which vantage point it is viewed. The games played with perspective serve only to show how much perspective itself began to be seen as a convention, subject to manipulation and distortion.[32]

The authors of the pamphlets written during the English Revolution did not surrender their claims to true perspective by analogy to these games of multiple perspective, however. On the contrary, they wished to highlight the mediated quality of Civil War writing only to assert that once the mediations were recognized, readers would accept their truth as the only one, and that their enemies' power over an audience would slip away. Milton's *Eikonoklastes* is illustrative here. In *Eikonoklastes*, a pamphlet about destroying images, Milton replaces the king's image as a martyr with one of the king as tyrant.[33] Once the king is pictured as a tyrant, it becomes legitimate to topple his regime. This is a shift in perception, one that also effects a political change. By engaging the doubling effects of ironic language, these writers did not want to threaten the stability of their position by admitting a plurality of readings. Theirs was not skepticism about the possibility of a true perspective. Interpreting political events became troped as problems of proper "sight" not in order to make room for more interpretations, but rather to show readers that distortion was taking place.

By using visual metaphors to represent this process of discovering flawed mediations, writers forced readers to think of political opinions as if they were physical, material truths, truths of nature. The Royalist author of *Cuckoo's Nest at Westminster* (1648) makes use of this trope: "Therefore the People may now see (without spectacles) how grossly they have been deceived, and juggled out of their Lives and Estates," clearing away the deceptive writing of the Parliamentary press. Likewise, *The Eve Cleared: or a Preservative for the Sight* (1644) pictures a beaker filled with a potion, a "vial of preservative water for clearing eyes" on its title page, a medication that works to undo the damage of other pamphlets. The author recants "in honest English" of past mistakes: "now our eyes are open we cannot but confess that we have abus'd the King, abus'd the State and abus'd our selves all this while" (3).[34] Armed with new sight, the author admits he has succumbed to misprisions in the past: "How we have been cozened, how blinded, how enchanted? When we consider how unreasonably our reasons have miscarried, we cannot but doubt that there's more Art than honesty at Oxford" (3). Here the king and the Malignants are exposed for what they are by the metaphor of cleared vision.

Further, the optical metaphors and the mechanical aids to sight in many pamphlets—spectacles, telescopes, magnifying glasses—give the necessary equipment to readers to be able to see the defective mediations of their enemies. The pamphleteers' interest in the problems of mediation was an obsession, as revealed in the quantity of pamphlet titles using this figure: *A Prospective Glass. Wherein the Child in understanding is enabled to see what the wicked Counsellors did* (1644, Wing 379); *A Paire of Crystal Spectacles. Counsels of the Army* (1648); *A New Pair of Spectacles of the Old Fashion* (1649, Wing 696); *A New Invention, or, A paire of Cristall Spectacles* (1644, Wing 650)—all these put the matter of proper interpretation and mediation squarely on the title page.[35] Several of these pamphlets fill their title pages with a woodcut illustration of a pair of spectacles.[36] The author of *A New Invention* explains the value of this visual aid for the reader: "they have such a special virtue in them, that he that makes right use of them though he hath been blind three or four years will recover his sight very perfectly" (t.p.). The spectacles in *A New Invention* signal that a clearer "point of view" will be expressed than before, 20 times clearer, if we take the title page promise seriously. The "three or four years" of blindness in *A New Invention* refers to the "blindness" since the outbreak of conflict up to the moment of the pamphlet's publication in spring 1644. The moment was a crucial one for Parliament's surviving its own factional disputes after the deaths of a group of moderates, including Pym, Hampden and Brooke.

Yet this pamphlet, like many others that use this trope, doesn't make its position clear right away. Rather, readers must pierce a false image of the king by detecting the author's use of irony, rather than by simple persuasion through explicit political argument. By involving the reader in a game of correcting a false impression, the author of the pamphlet encourages a process of reading by which a reader becomes capable of resisting propagandistic assault. As an example of this process, *A New Invention* opens with a flattering portrait of the king, a posture that is increasingly called into question over the course of its pages. The author suggests that the Papists and Irish, traditional enemies of Protestant England, have been tamed by Charles, asking readers: "Dost thou not see the very Papists themselves that were wont to make nothing of stabbing and poisoning Princes, now become so pious and zealous that none are forwarder to take their King's part?" (A2). Despite the strong anti-Irish sentiment found at he end of the pamphlet, at the beginning the Irish are shown to be politically servile to this king: "that we in our rage pleased to call Rebels lately because they killed a few Roundheads there, come over as fast as they can possibly to protect the King here against the fury of Traitorous Schismaticks: Shall these exceed us in loyalty?" (A2). But when this author recommends, "let us join with those honest Irish, faithful Papists, and other loyal followers of his Majesty, and so make an end of these unnatural wars an unnatural way" (2), a tinge of irony can be detected.

With increasing venom, the author implies that the King of England himself had succumbed to Irish influence. The author questions the motives for King Charles's armistice with the Irish following the Scottish rebellion in 1644; in his view, such an accord is a sellout to the Catholics. When the author offers a picture of an England reconciled to its Catholic inhabitants and neighbors, the pamphlet's true political position becomes clear:

> That the Pope may domineer, his Majesty rejoice, and all his cut-throat Counsellors be as free from fear as they are from honesty; then will there be a brave new world for them that shall live in it, then there will be no Sects nor Schisms but all of one Religion ... This will be a Reformation indeed worth talking of, a Peace to the purpose, no more fears, no more jealousies, no more plots, no more Petitions then (3).

This peaceable kingdom is any English Protestant's nightmare, and when the author echoes Shakespeare's "O brave new world" speech in *The Tempest*, he signals to readers that this is yet a fantasy. That such a union would bring about a pleasant peace is only a fiction, one that the king and his supporters would *like* the people of England to believe.

In this dark fantasy of a Papist utopia, the author outlines the benefits to Protestants of the political arrangement, where "The Protestant Religion is to be maintained, and that it is the care and endeavor of the King's party to do it must and (no doubt) will be made apparent" (3). The speaker then brings out examples dating from the late 1620s that could hardly convince readers of the king's supposed protection of Protestant interests. Consider, he asks, the bungled attempt by the Duke of Buckingham's Commission at La Rochelle to relieve the Huguenots, where supplies were short, officers absent, and even instructions delayed. Or Charles's attempt to relive Elizabeth's victory over Spain, the failed mission at Cadiz of 1625, "we lost a lot of men there, but the honour we got is not to be spoke of" (3). These examples are hardly comforting, and they are followed by a list of others, all of which call the earlier pro-Irish position into question: "To what end was that Army readied against the Scots, Soldiers billeted in most parts of this Kingdom, an Army of eight thousand in Ireland in readiness, and the Protestants there disarmed . . . but only to maintain the Protestant Religion?" (6). The pamphlet writer has the luxury of never condemning the king outright (in 1644, after all, direct accusation against the Crown was still dangerous).

On the face of it, this is a Royalist pamphlet, with the king represented as a true defender of the Protestant religion. But the careful reader, one practicing "right use" of the *Spectacles*, concludes that this story is completely false. The pamphlet is laced with irony, so that readers "see" a true image of the king and "recover . . . sight very perfectly," as the title page had promised. All the contradictions between statements and reality—"the Pope was turned Protestant," (3) for example—must now be interpreted as false. The "crystal spectacles" lead the reader of this pamphlet to dispose of uncertainty about the king's real motives. The mechanical device signals to readers that they must employ special reading skills in order to grasp a *true* political picture.

Irony was a key method for writers in opposing their enemy's propaganda during the English Revolution. Irony required that readers recognize the simultaneous presence of two alternative accounts, between which the reader had to discern the correct one. Wayne Booth has called "stable irony" that wherein "the central meaning of the words is fixed and univocal, regardless of how many peripheral and even contradictory significances different readers might add," and the English Revolutionary use of the trope of vision is such an instance.[37] This kind of irony allows readers to have something to do with the construction of meaning, but the authors of the Revolutionary pamphlets limited the possible "contradictory significances" that different readers might add. The Civil War writers expressed anxieties precisely because of the existence of various possibilities for mis-interpretation of their words, and those who made use of these tropes of vision sought to *control* their readers' re-sponses by providing other possible readings, of which only one could be seen as true.

Attic drama gives us a formula for irony, by which we can see irony as the master-trope for literature in a world rife with propagandistic writing, according to Sue Curry Jansen: "In the comedic form, a contest *(agon)* takes place between two types of characters, the *alazon* or Imposter and the *eiron*. The Imposter enters the scene full of pretension, but is finally routed by the Ironical Man, who proves not to be the fool he originally seemed to be."[38] This drama of "unmasking" is analogous to the "undeception" performed by Booker's pamphlet, where Booker "stripped" his royalist enemy naked. Through this kind of unmasking, authors aimed to control their readers' interpretation of other texts.

This drama of unmasking is also the story of *Eikonoklastes*, Milton's response to *Eikon Basilike*, the "King's Book." Milton was ordered by the Council of State to respond to *Eikon Basilike*, which, published on the day of King Charles's execution, was an immediate publicity success, appearing in 40 English editions in its first year alone. Milton's reply, published in October 1649, took the king's book on its own terms, examining it chapter by chapter. Milton did not just replace the king's image as a martyr in *Eikon Basilike* with one as a tyrant in *Eikonoklastes*, but he also offered readers a way to perform such readings in the future, that "they that will, may now see at length how much they were deceiv'd in him, and were ever like to be hereafter" (*CPW*, 3:364); that readers "may find the grace and good guidance to bethink themselves, and recover" (601). Milton aimed to teach his own readers how to "read aright" such a piece of propaganda. He sought to provide readers not only with images, but also with strategies for reading, and with ways of seeing. He relied upon readers who wielded reason "sufficient both to judge aright and to examine each matter," as he put it in *Areopagitica* (*CPW* 2:511), to make their way through the forest of signs. These properly reading subjects would be able to resist propaganda by relying upon inner judgment to evaluate the statements before them. Milton sought to instruct readers politically in his *Eikonoklastes* by offering a completely different interpretation of an earlier text, and by urging readers to follow his alternative in both its methods and in its conclusions.[39]

## III

Just as Milton did in response to *Eikon Basilike*, many authors of pamphlets sought to educate their readers in ways of reading. They thought about conflicting points of view in perceptual terms. By using the figures of mechanical optical devices, writers signalled that readers had to practice special reading skills. Their pamphlets made the truth about the king, for example, into an issue of the activity of *perceiving* the king. The pamphlets offered mechanical means of "undeception" of some of the political rhetoric that was flying about during the early years of the Civil War. They worked to make readers "see" that rhetoric does not always equal reality, that when the king says he is fighting for the improvement of the Protestant Reformation, he may not be entirely truthful. Responding to the danger that propaganda might ensnare unwitting readers, writers used the figures of optical instruments to encourage readers to understand that what they were seeing might be merely an illusion created by a false interpretation or mediation.

The technique of forcing reader to make political distinctions is found in *The Second Part of the Spectacles* (1644, Wing S2316), which appeared around nine days after the previous spectacles pamphlet. It offered an illustration on the title page: a monocle, with the image of a tear-filled eye in the center, offering "this Multiplying Glass" [a magnifying glass] "in pity to those poor-blind Brutes." The author revises the viewer's perspective of the prior *Spectacles* pamphlet, explaining a bit of the irony in the previous pamphlet. This time, the speaker ventriloquizes a Royalist, repeatedly boasting of his "true Protestantism"—a phrase used by King Charles and by his enemies as justification for their actions. To call oneself a "True Protestant" would be to make a very specific claim at this time, when the Reformation of the Protestant Church was the aim of the Presbyterians, who called themselves "true Protestants." It was the Presbyterian belief that the king and his cohorts were not acting as "true Protestants," and Presbyterians made it their mission to bring England back to the "true Protestant" faith.

But this fictional character also identifies himself as a "Malignant," using the term of abuse coined by the Parliamentarians for their Royalist enemies, and the speaker thus immediately identifies himself with the *opposite* political allegiance. For someone to be identified as a "true Protestant" and then to claim one is a "Malignant," as the speaker here does, presents a paradox that would immediately be recognized by readers of the day. The answer to this paradox is that this presentation is meant to be read in a special way. The "Malignant" but nonetheless "True Protestant" speaker in *The Second Part of the Spectacles* goes on to give "an account of my faith, "and here we begin to resolve the paradox. If the reader perceives the conscious manipulation of key words, this text may be read as utterly ironic. "To be a *true Protestant*," the author explains, "it is very necessary first, that a man should be so far a Papist, as to maintain an implicit faith, and blind obedience to the Church" (3), invoking the image of "blindness" to talk about allegiance to Rome. This "blind obedience" is understood to negate the rhetoric of freedom of the real "True Protestants," whose very identities are pinned on independence from Rome. The author continues, "Nor will I believe, notwithstanding all the evidences, that they or His Majesties or Her Majesty, or her Priests, Friars and Jesuits, ever intended anything but the maintaining of the *true Protestant Religion*" (3). The author is self-incriminating, and also incriminating to the king, since to admit that the king and queen have a coterie of Papist characters—priests, friars, Jesuits—hanging about, is to expose the royal household as Catholic. The next five pages discuss the Spanish match and the Scottish war, and conclude that these seem incongruous with a true upholder of the Protestant faith.

The *"true Protestant"*—and now the words ring hollow—provides evidence to prove that the king is in no way disloyal to the Protestant cause, yet this cannot but accuse him. Letters between King Charles and the pope are said to show the king's friendliness to Catholics, and the marriage match between the king's son and the infanta of Spain are mentioned to prove his unswerving loyalty to the Protestant religion. Yet the mere fact of such a correspondence would condemn the king as a Papist, as would negotiations with archenemy Spain, as an interpreting reader would recognize. The meaning of this pamphlet is triggered by the key words, "true Protestant Religion," and these words are shown to be open to two competing interpretations. The text is finally to be understood as a savage anti-Royalist polemic. The pamphlet shows a "way of seeing" through the language of enemy Royalists, exposing the "Malignants" as hypocrites. *The Spectacles* then, provides two perspectives—the one narrated in the pamphlet that is the phony Malignant's version of the story, where the king is defended as a "True Protestant;" the other, revealed through irony, is quite the opposite. The capable reader would see that the ironic perspective wins.

By using metaphors of sight and images associated with seeing, the authors of these pamphlets signalled that propaganda needed to be decoded. Once true perspective became easy to distort, by shifting the physical position of the beholder, by the optical lens, and by the free press, writers found an image for the problem of the multiplicity of opinions. The Renaissance discovery of visual perspective and the seventeenth century refinement of scientific instruments like the telescope and optical lens gave authors figures for representing manipulated views. The seventeenth century political writers who used these figures asserted that once the mediating perspective was removed—either by an optical lens, or through cleansing the eyes by a potion—a correct and true account would result. In their use of the mechanical devices, authors admitted that there were more ways than one to see the world. "True Protestant" was a term that might be employed for opposite purposes. However, one thorny issue remained: how could writers be sure that their perspective was any more secure than the one they had displaced?

In *Paradise Lost,* Milton finds a solution by having Adam's faulty vision relieved through divine means. In book 11, Michael applies a potion to correct Adam's sight:

> . . . to nobler sights
> Michael from Adam's eyes the Film remov'd
> Which that false Fruit that promis'd clearer sight
> Had bred; then purg'd with Euphrasy and Rue
> The visual Nerve, for he had much to see;
> And from the Well of Life three drops instill'd.
> So deep the power of these Ingredients pierc'd
> Ev'n to the inmost seat of mental sight . .[40]

Michael's "Preservative for Sight," as the Civil War pamphlets might call it, gives Adam the perspective needed to view human history with clarity of true vision. Michael undeceives Adam of the distorting perspective "promised" as "clearer" by the "false Fruit." The language of this passage cannot but recall the rhetoric of the Civil War pamphlets, which also offered restoration for faulty vision.[41] Michael's educative mission to Adam and Eve provides a way for them to see, and books 11 and 12 of *Paradise Lost* chronicle that education in perception, guided by divine impulse. At other moments in *Paradise Lost* readers hear echoes of that Civil War trope of correcting eyesight. Milton converts it, however, into a spiritual condition, as when Adam exclaims to Michael, "I was far deceived; for now I see" (11.783); "now

I see" is repeated in 12.286; and in a redemptive moment, Adam reports, "Now first I find/ Mine eyes true op'ning, and my heart much eas'd" (12.273–74). Of course, greater than the scope of the poet, yet straining to be contained within his language, is the ultimate panoptical perspective, that of God, "beholding from his prospect high,/ Wherein past, present, future he beholds" (3.76–77).[42] In Milton's lexicon, sight is often a metaphor for spiritual enlightenment; humans strive for such a total perspective.

Milton takes his own blindness to be a spiritual advantage in his *Second Defense of the English People*, answering his supposed enemy, Alexander More:

> As to my blindness, I would rather have mine, if it be necessary, than either theirs . . . or yours. Your blindness, deeply implanted in the inmost faculties, obscures the mind, so that you may see nothing whole or real. Mine, which you make a reproach, merely deprives things of color and superficial appearance . . . there is hope that in this way I may approach more closely the mercy and protection of the Father Almighty . . . So in this darkness, may I be clothed in light (*CPW* 4.589–90).

We might contrast More's blindness, "deeply implanted in the inmost faculties," to Adam's cleared "inmost seat of mental sight." In Milton's *Second Defense*, some kinds of blindness offer a sign of "divine favor," a benefit: "Nor do these shadows around us seem to have been created so much by the dullness of our eyes as by the shade of angels' wings. And divine favor not infrequently is wont to lighten these shadows again, once made, by an inner and far more enduring light" (*CPW* 4.589–90).

Is this blindness also a political advantage, as Milton suggests in these remarks in *Second Defense*? That is, would the stripping of all mediations (including sight) lead to political truths? One would guess in his other works Milton would express this belief, especially given the rhetorical context of Civil War pamphleteering, where writers often alluded to the dangers of optical distortion, offering all sorts of restorative optical equipment to readers. In *Eikonoklastes*,

Milton supports the political value of "blindness," as evidenced in his scorn for the visual tricks of the frontispiece of the king's book. But Milton's *Paradise Lost* doesn't argue this line. In the last books of *Paradise Lost*, Adam does see truly; the problem for Milton is that his readers may not, lacking a divine interpreter. Without direct divine intervention—and such interventions don't happen frequently—sight may be a dangerous sense in Milton's line of thinking. For Milton, few had the special qualifications to be blind.

There are many examples of the difficulty in seeing properly in *Paradise Lost*, and indeed Satan exemplifies the dangerous power of deception.[43] As my final example, I take the optical metaphors in *Paradise Lost* by which Milton himself plays visual tricks on his reader in presenting Satan early on as an epic hero. Here is Satan's shield:

> . . . his ponderous shield
> Etherial temper, massy, large and round,
> Behind him cast; the broad circumference
> Hung on his shoulders like the Moon, whose Orb
> Through Optic Glass the *Tuscan* Artist views
> At Ev'ning from the top of *Fesole*,
> Or in *Valdarno*, to descry new Lands,
> Rivers or Mountains in her spotty Globe.[44]
>
> (1.284.91)

This passage relies on the double outlook of mock epic, which both asserts and takes away comparison with the shields of Homer's Achilles and Spenser's Radigund. But there is another tool of perspective at work here, namely, the telescope, and by using this figure, Milton seems to respond to the Civil War trope. Satan's shield looks "massy, large and round" like the moon, yet only when seen through the magnifying lens of a telescope. The line break in the poetry leads readers to expect an epic comparison between the shield's brightness and the moon's, but readers' hopes are dashed by the next line, which explains the optical illusion: "Hung on his shoulders like the Moon, whose Orb/ Through Optic Glass the Tuscan Artist views." We know as well as Milton how small the moon looks in the sky without optical aid. Satan's shield may appear a huge, massy and intolerably bright thing—Galileo's telescope in 1610 showed objects 30 times nearer and 1,000 times larger—but only from a perverted perspective.

Satan's false heroism is revealed by an act of visual perception; the image is mediated by a telescope. Just as the Civil War pamphleteers had used the figure, Milton exposes illusion of a specifically political kind through the simile. Like those authors, Milton provides the reader with a view of behind-the-scenes epic machinery: since we see the telescope magnifying Satan's shield to its epic proportions, Satan's heroism is diminished.

In *Paradise Lost*, Galileo's telescope does not necessarily lead to truth. As we follow the figure throughout the poem, as Annabel Patterson shows in her essay in this volume, we find a metaphoric structure based on the use of the telescope references. Patterson argues that because the new optics revealed imperfections in heavenly bodies, the new science could be allied to the work of "skeptical political analysis." Indeed, it is not clear from Milton's other use of telescope references that the perspective derived from the optical instrument is any truer than other perspectives, despite Milton's positive image of Galileo. Milton may share some of the skepticism of Thomas Hobbes, who asserted that philosophy was the truest form of knowledge, by contrasting it to science: "by opticks I can multiply at will."[45] In optics, Hobbes suggests, distortion and multiple perspectives could actually prevent the acquisition of true knowledge. That the telescope would not necessarily lead to a truer perspective is an opinion of at least one other Civil War writer. In the Royalist pamphlet, *The Great Assizes Holden in Parnassus* (1645), the author accuses the Parliamentary newsbook:

> Old Galileo's glasses to have used,
> Which represented objects to his eye,
> Beyond their measure, and just symmetry,
> Whereby the faults of many did appear,
> More and far greater, than indeed they were.[46]

In this allusion to Galileo's telescope, the author criticizes the interpretations of Parliamentary propagandists, who saw more than was actually there. The mechanical visual aids did not lead to a truer picture, but rather to a tainted one.

If we follow the telescope image in *Paradise Regained*, moreover, Milton's position is closer to this Royalist writer than to those writers who sought truth by means of these optical aids. In *Paradise Regained*, Satan employs an optical lens in order to display the kingdoms of the world to tempt the Son in book 4: "By what strange Parallax or optic skill/ Of vision multiplied through air, or glass/ Of Telescope" (4.40–42). Further on, Satan uses the telescope to give an impossible perspective: "Many a fair Edifice besides, more like/Houses of Gods (so well I have dispos'd/My Airy Microscope) thou mayst behold/Outside and inside both . . ." (4.55–58). In both allusions, the telescope *does* reveal more to see than the naked eye can behold. But it is not a *truer* vision. Rather, the Son must reject these perspectives.

In Milton's view, then, the telescope can only be a figure that represents an act of manipulation of sight. In the case of Satan's shield, the true perspective is reached by the reader who is capable of recognizing irony, who is able to distinguish the right reading from a distorted perspective. Satan himself appears like an epic hero only through a mechanical act of distortion, for which the act of proper reading itself will be a cure. Common to Milton's representation of Satan's shield and to the pamphleteers who made use of the optical metaphors is an invitation to readers that they read differently—that they read with the knowledge that what they are seeing *is* a perspective, a mediated representation, and not necessarily the truth.

Though authors of the pamphlets used the optical metaphors in order to clear the field for their own truth, Milton takes a more skeptical route. In both cases, however, readers were required to read between the lines. As we have seen, polemicists of the Civil War period struggled to replace the "erroneous" perspectives of their enemies with their own "true" ones, like Cromwell's "undeceptions" that attempted to cancel further "undeceptions." Milton's *Eikonoklastes* and the "Spectacles" pamphlets are two examples of just the kind of works that attempted to recover a "true" image, despite their use of metaphors that perhaps undermined their very efforts. Milton uses the figure of the telescope to call for action on the part of the reader, perhaps pointing out that the danger for political rhetoric was that there would always be another "deception" to "undeceive." Perhaps the readers of *Paradise Lost* would not come to political truths as a result of their reading, but they would become warier of mediated language, perhaps better able to defend themselves from the imprisonment of a single view.

Stanley Fish has shown us the effect of *Paradise Lost* to trip up the reader; I am concerned with the author's concern that readers be instructed in how to read and deflect propaganda, specifically in a political context.[47] I see Milton's education of readers in *Padise Lost* as a response to the problem of propagandistic writing, and I suggest that the poem be read through the pattern offered in *Eikonoklastes*, where Milton chose to present his education in perception as a lesson in reading, specifically setting aside a divine solution to the problem of political truth. I do not suggest that Milton rejected divine guidance in *Paradise Lost*. Yet in this epic Milton follows the implicit logic of the "spectacles" pamphlets to its skeptical conclusions, offering only methods, and not results, for the achievement of true sight. Milton pursued an option other than placing God as the source of all true perspective—that is, placing readers at the center of a new practice of polemical discourse.

Jürgen Habermas's claim that, in England, "censorship came to an end with the Licensing Act of 1695" may be made more complex by looking at the result of the partial lifting of censorship during the early years of the English Revolution. For the result was the startling arrival and widespread deployment of propaganda. New forms of control appeared within the press itself: Cromwell's call for his "pen-men" to act, or the trope of spectacles as a figure of control over interpretation, for example. The very conditions of the free press, the expression of contradictory views in the press and the ambiguity resulting in interpretations of events, may have actually prompted the widespread use of propaganda. As I have shown in this essay, writers also contrived to control their readers' responses to propaganda.

My pursuit of the uses of rhetoric during the English Revolution and my analysis of texts that display self-consciousness about the possibilities of rhetoric for ideological combat should contribute to the current debate over the function of ideology in the mid-seventeenth century. Attention to such rhetorical components of the rise of a public sphere might contribute not only to the postmodern interest in rhetoric and in the history of reading, but also to our understanding of the ideological component of the English Revolution. There is presently little agreement among historians about the role of ideology in the English Revolution. Revisionist historians are pursuing the idea that there was no profound ideological divide in the mid-seventeenth century, denying that there were long-term preconditions of conflict. There is an attempt to topple the Whig interpretive orthodoxy, which had seen the Revolution in terms of political progress toward constitutionalism. According to revisionists, it was not a revolution in the sense that we commonly think about revolutions.[48]

Our own deconstructive moment in literary criticism might demand that we undermine, by a more-than-rhetorical irony, the genuineness of such a rhetorical fight. On the contrary: the rhetorical effects of the Civil War period had very real consequences for individuals, parties and institutions, consequences that may be read in the blood spilled on the battlefields and in the villages. The rhetoric meant enough to warrant control by a politician like Cromwell. Historians may never come to agree whether or not the revolution was at root an ideological conflict—though I believe it was—but these examples show that writers saw it as one. Writers sought to arm readers with equipment with which to fend off enemy opinions. They invited readers to enter political debate by learning how to read and to understand political rhetoric. I hope that my interest in the ways that writers sought to equip readers to meet the challenge of propaganda will encourage further analysis of the impact of this new practice of public political conduct.

# 9 • Lady Falkland's Reentry into Writing
## Anglo-Catholic Consensual Discourse and Her *Edward II* as Historical Fiction

*Louise Schleiner*

T he present essay is part of a set of studies pursuing the general question, how—through what processes—did Tudor and Stuart Englishwomen become motivated and able to write anything beyond the private sphere, when so much stood against their efforts? What writerly self-concepts did they manage to construct, and how did gender operate and accommodate itself within these? The questions need answering in a fairly broad range of sociopolitical, affective and textual terms, the emphasis depending on which women are studied. One pattern is that women could begin writing at an outer edge of the sphere taxonomized by Gerard Genette as the "paratextual": that is, they could begin with translations, which function (among other ways) as paratexts—often culturally extensional paratexts—to their source texts.[1] Then, through having done translations, women sometimes gained an opportunity to speak in paratextual genres closer to a centered or framed textual space, genres such as prefaces and dedicatory poems, where they might find more distinct voices of their own. Finally, of those reaching this inner-paratextual sphere, a few went on to some centered textual space of their own, in publication or in more limited modes of circulation. The entrance to this pathway through the paratextual was religious activism.

It has been frequently observed, notably in Margaret Hannay's collection of essays *Silent but for the Word*, that translation of polemical religious works brought a number of women into print for the first time.[2] But to understand why they did such writing (and then how some of them moved on to other kinds), we must do more than note that zealous male coreligionists were, given the urgency of their cause, newly willing to accept women's written contributions: for it can be assumed that polemic intensity does not necessarily result in marginalized people's gaining a new voice. We must consider how women's socializing, activism and writing made them a part of the religious and political processes of their times.

It was not that, as in some cultures or subcultures, religion was "women's business"—far from it. To note two obvious points first, women were motivated to write about religion because such debates offered deeply engaging talk and action in which they were allowed to participate with men, albeit only marginally.[3] And from the male side, women were allowed to do so partly because, since the Reformation had set before every person a fearsome choice of churches—a choice held to determine one's eternal fate—some men came to see that it was scarcely fair to forbid women to talk over and even to write about that choice. As did a male editor of Susanna Hopton (a later seventeenth century religious writer), some could maintain that women as well as men ought to consider "a matter of that vast consequence" most carefully, and should not "take up, nor change their religion upon trust."[4]

But beyond these points, we can see a further explanation of women's entry into writing through religion if we consider it in the light of Jürgen Habermas's concept of consensual discourse—that is, discourse on select topics that takes place among people talking to and writing for each other who share a group identity that is important to their personal identities.[5] In the late 1610s and early 1620s, certain Arminian Anglicans and English Roman Catholics were contesting something within such a "we / you-and-I" identity, just as in the 1560s and 1570s the same kind of group-internal contestation had occurred among English Protestants of varying reformist stripes, a scene in which the humanistically educated Cooke sisters had been active.[6] That is, the Anglican Durham House group, their Catholic associates and other like-minded people,[7] were at work on Hugo Grotius's and Isaac Casaubon's dream of an ecumenical council and a *rapprochement* between Canterbury and Rome, whereby they hoped that Rome could be brought to some measure of compromise, and the English church would establish a relationship with the Roman like that between Rome and the Eastern or Uniate churches. As it turned out, through this process they were contesting just how far toward Catholic polity and liturgy the English church would go.

The clergy and court gentry involved in the socializing and the theological discussions of Bishop Richard Neile's Durham House crossed paths for a while in the 1620s, from both the river and street sides, with English Catholics going to Mass at the French ambassador's chapel. This proximity would soon lose its temporarily harmonious character, and at one point constables were accused of violating diplomatic terrain to arrest English Catholics.[8] The Anglicans of this scene considered themselves to be the true, doctrinal "catholics" (the word meaning "universal"), faithful to the nature of the church as it had been in the time of St. Augustine but unable to submit to the present corrupt rule of the Bishop of Rome. Among these was Elizabeth Cary—after 1621, Lady Falkland—who had long been attracted to Roman Catholicism but had been persuaded by the Durham House circle that Arminian Anglicans were the truer catholics. From time to time, people would indeed go over to "Romanism," having already seen it as within the "we / you-and-I" identity in which they had emotionally invested

themselves. In 1621, King James's mighty favorite Buckingham thought about doing so (only an intense personal effort
by Archbishop William Laud and others "saved" him).

In the mid-1620s, that broadly catholic "we" identity had
collapsed (the state of affairs reflected in the constable
incident), with the entrenchment of the Arminians into a
structured and for many unpalatable court faction of Laud,
Cousen and Buckingham. Lady Falkland fell out on the side
of militant popery, and there found the written voice she
had conceived for herself through the Durham House conversations and activism. Her daughter's biography shows the
youthful Elizabeth Cary experimenting with translations and
many original poems (the latter not extant, though one of
the former is—her Ortelius geography at the Burford Parish
church), then trying a leap into book publication with the
release of her play *Mariam* in 1613, which she was obliged
to recall (Cary, *Life*, 117). Fifteen years later, after these
forays into paratext and text, and having converted to Roman
Catholicism, she could find a successful entry way into public
and semipublic spaces for writing. She began translating a
treatise by the former Huguenot Jacques Davy, Cardinal du
Perron, contesting the theology of King James. In Habermas's
terms, she shifted from consensual communicative action
within the Arminian group to strategic action (Habermas,
117, 209)[9] against her former fellow travelers, in what she
considered the correct continuation of their cause. In other
words, Habermas proposes that when consensual discourse
has continued for a time, enabling some conflicts to be
resolved, a point may come when the consensus starts to
break down. Then opposing subgroups move into what he
calls "discourse" (proper), i.e., argumentation attempting to
reach some new, mutually acceptable base definitions from
which to *rebuild* consensus (209, on "action" vs. "discourse").
A flurry of back-and-forth argumentative documents (pub-
licized or circulated) typically signals this stage of things
as with the debate between King James and Davy. If such
efforts fail to achieve consensus, the "we" identity eventually collapses; some of the people one formerly identified
with become a "they," the opponents, and the former group

members, if able to do so, turn to confrontational strategic action against each other.

Exactly in the argumentative stretch of that sequence, I suggest, a sense of urgency may open the way for previously silent people within the group to think of themselves differently, and thus to find marginal or paratextual spaces for writing. This idea naturally arises from Habermas's analysis because at the point where consensual speech action starts to break down and semiadversarial discourse (in the above sense) to begin, fissures can open that allow an element of the group's identity to become newly visible, namely the otherwise suppressed borders of the "system of domination" (Habermas, xv) operative within the "we/you-and-I" group.

Having in this way found a voice in religiopolitical polemic, some women became able to move on and say more. As Lady Falkland in the 1620s worked on her translation of the treatise by Davy, Cardinal du Perron, she found herself also able to write something more her own, a fictionalized prose *History of . . . Edward II*, interspersed at dramatic moments with ringing iambic speeches, and sunk to the hilt in her frustrations under Buckingham's regime.[10] We can examine it shortly, but first let us review her rendition of the Cardinal's treatise, to see what she so delighted to write as a Catholic, wishing to persuade her formerly like-minded associates to take the same step she had. The work exhibits the kind of proposal, answer, counteranswer and counter-counteranswer process that Habermas sees as indicative of a collapsing ideological identity. Its preface presents a letter that Davy wrote to King James, transmitted by the refugee Protestant scholar Casaubon, which the king answered in detail. Those answers are summarized at the beginning of each section, and then in turn rebuffed at great length by Davy.

Lady Falkland's sentence style is forceful, and one can sense her enjoyment of Davy's polemic strategies and skillful light irony. He is especially good at epitomizing major points with some entertaining mythological anecdote taken as a simile. In chapter 2, for example, having begun epigraphically by showing the king claiming that it is he who belongs to the true catholic church, Davy then gives his answer: "Now the king belieues simplie . . . that the Church of God is one only by name and effect Catholicke and vniuersall, Spread ouer all the world, out of which he affirmes himselfe, there can be noe hope of Saluation: he condemnes and detestes those which . . . haue departed from the faith of the Catholicke Church & are become heretickes, as the Manichees, etc." "The Replie" begins:

> Telesius a Stripling of Greece, hauing won the prize and victorie of the Combate in the Pythian games, when there was question of leadinge him in triumph, there arose such a dispute betweene the diuers nations there present, euery one being earnest to haue him for theire owne, as the one drawing him one waie, the other an other waie, instead of receiuing the honor which was prepared for him, he was torne and dismembred euen by those that stroue who should honor him most. Soe, happenes it to the Church: . . . [when Christians] come to debate of the true bodie of this societie, then euery sect desirous to draw her to themselues, they rent and teare her in peeces . . . (*Replie of . . . Perron*, 18)

Davy then argues that sects basing their identity on newly devised creeds and separate national institutions, yet claiming a hold on the "true spiritual, worldwide church" of all times and places, are like the destructive mob of the tale.

Or again, starting the chapter on predestination, Davy says that King James has brought it up as a digressive issue to get the debate off the nature of the true church:

> Heere the most excellent Kinge behaues himself like *Hippomanes*, who runninge with *Atalanta* for masterie, cast out golden apples in her way, to delaie her with takinge them vp: soe his Maiestie putts rubbes in this discourse, to staie the course of my pen, and to stoppe me to examine them. But I hope to remoue them so quickly, that I shall be time enough at the end of my carrere, (*Replie of . . . Perron*, 52).

He goes on to say that St. Paul, in speaking of Christians' assurance that they will not be separated from the love of Christ, is using a rhetorical figure that must be recognized as such for the passage to be rightly interpreted:

> ... he speakes there of all the predestinate in generall, into whose number he puts himselfe, and those to whom he writes, by a figure which the grammarians call *syllepsis*; and accordinge to the rule, not of Faith, but of Charitie, which wills, that in all thinges concealed from vs, we should iudge in the better parte ... For betweene the certaintie of saluation, and despaire, there is a middle way, which is *hope*, that while it lastes, (as it ought alwaies to laste in a Christian man) is incompatible with despaire, and suffizeth to comforte vs ... (54–55)

As one would suppose from these instances, the central issue of the treatise is whether the true church consists, as King James alleged, in an invisible spiritual unity of all the people predestined to salvation and holding the essential Christian doctrines (though with diverse institutions of governance), or rather in an institution with continuity of social existence reaching back to the time of the apostles. In arguing the latter view, Davy adopted in one chapter a strategy that Lady Falkland probably enjoyed as delicious irony. The king had proposed that his English church was closer to the nature of the church in St. Augustine's time than was the modern Roman Catholic church, with all its corruptions. Taking the Protestants' own doctrine of sacraments as "outward and visible signs" of "inward and invisible" grace, Davy says in effect well, let us consider the outward signs of Augustine's church, and see whose church now exhibits them. He then rolls down a catalogue that becomes more and more persuasive as it continues, from adoration of the Eucharist as the real body of Christ, to the use of altars dedicated in memory of martyrs, prayers for the dead, the keeping of Lent, clerical celibacy, etc., all in quite concrete detail of "outward signs."

> [it was] A Church which in the Ceremonies of baptisme vsed oyle, salte, waxe lights, exorcismes, the signe of the Crose, the word *Epheta* ... A Church that used *holy water*, consecrated by certaine wordes and ceremonies ... A Church that held free will, for a doctrine of faith, & reuealed in the

> holy scripture ... A Church wherein their seruice was said throughout the East in *Greeke,* and through the west ... in *Latine,* ... a church ... that accompanied the dead to their sepulcher with wax tapers in sign of ioy and future certainty of their resurrection. ... And finally a Church which held, that the Catholicke Church had the infallible promise, that she should be *perpetually visible and eminent in her communion* ... [Now] let his Maiestie see, whether by these features he can knowe the face of Caluines Church, or of ours. (72–73)

Such was the treatise of over 400 pages that Lady Falkland delightedly rushed through, translating from French, and claimed that the copyist had spent four times as long on it as she had.

She had converted in late 1626, and by early 1628 had begun to write again, namely the two works here noted. During the intervening 15 years since the publication and recall of *Mariam,* she may have written occasional poems, but most of what her daughter lists from before her conversion is attributed to her early married years. As for publication or any detectable coterie circulation, she had spent 15 years of silence since the publication of *Mariam.* That play had, while portraying Mariam's dilemma sympathetically, celebrated an ideal of extravagantly submissive wifeliness, whereby the queen, though innocent of the alleged adultery for which her husband killed her, was yet censured for not having cheerfully welcomed him home, even though he had murdered her father and brother![11] Later, as soon as Lady Falkland had made the break to Rome and thus permitted herself one little tiny exception to that astonishing ideal of wifely duty, namely that only "for the sake of conscience" would she ever at all cross her husband, she could find a written voice again. What she found was the voice she had conceived for herself as part of the Durham House process described above. And according to her daughter, none of the hardships she suffered while her husband and the court tried to reassert their authority—betrayal by close friends, house arrest, and loss of her children and all income—none of these could hold a candle to the pleasure she found, through a late winter in a tumbled-down house by the Thames with only fish and bread and one loyal serving woman, writing and writing as much as she pleased.

The daughter's biography says that after becoming a Catholic, Lady Falkland spoke those prayers that the church most valued (perhaps the *Gloria*, "Our Father," *Ave Maria* and Act of Contrition?) as if they were especially her own, for "she did more hope to be heard as a child of the church."[12] The gaining of a voice is here explicitly noted. To see what this means in the daughter's terms, we must look at a deliberately obscure and cautious passage early in the *Life* (16–17) concerning two episodes of severe depression, identified only as having occurred when Lady Falkland was pregnant with her second and fourth children. The passage focuses primarily on the latter of these two episodes, since it says that in the years afterward, always "but once" she was able to control depression by excess sleeping. The fourth pregnancy I calculate to have been in 1613 to early 1614.[13] At that time, says the biography, she ate or drank nothing for two weeks but a little beer until the child ceased to move. The added comment that afterwards she was always but once able to control depression is left mysterious, without explanation of the one exception. It had been in 1613 that *Mariam* was published, and as the daughter elsewhere mentions, Lady Falkland had officially recalled a work of hers surely the only work, besides the much later Perron treatise, that she ever published, her play *Mariam*[14]—she declared, so the biography reports, that this work had been stolen from a friend's rooms and published against her will. This stock claim goes so completely against the attitudes she everywhere else expressed toward her own wrting that she must have been pressured to the recall, though apparently she did for some reason get angry with her sister-in-law and dear friend Elizabeth Bland Cary at about this time (the dedicatee of *Mariam*, who named her first daughter Mirial; Dunstan, xvii–xix); the *Life* tells of a breach between them, afterwards healed. In short, Lady Falkland suffered a time of painful self-contradiction, severe depression, anger at her closest friend (apparently for carrying out her own

wish to publish), and probably a debilitating effort to inter-
nalize the rightness of her silencing.

Then, after 15 years, ironically, the saying of some ancient
ritual prayers restored a written individual voice to Lady
Falkland, not without one last time of severe depression—
that "but one more"—while she learned what her conversion was costing her. That the leap into the freedom to say
those prayers, which so many a Catholic schoolchild has
considered the ultimate bondage, should have restored a
voice of her own must show that, for her, they meant the
chance at long last to make an assertion—an assertion
addressing the intragroup conflicts of the Catholicizing
Anglicans who were or had been her friends, and one that
threw off the constraints of English male authority. Susan
Feilding, Countess of Denbigh, Buckingham's sister, had
promised to take the momentous step with her (and much
later would convert), but at this time instead, out of fear,
tried to have her restrained by force from going to Lord
Ormond's stable, where the "reconciliation" took place; once
it had, Lady Denbigh immediately ran and tattled the event
to her brother and King Charles.[15]

I believe it was her friends' betrayals, especially Lady
Denbigh's, along with her lack of money and loss of her
children, that sent her into a severe depression in late 1627.
She wrote her way out of it in the Lenten fast of 1628: "to
out-run those weary hours of a deep and sad Passion, my
melancholy Pen fell accidentally on this Historical Relation;
which speaks a King, our own, though one of the most
Unfortunate; and shews the Pride and Fall of his Inglorious
Minions. . . . E. F." (*Life . . . of Edward II*, Preface).[16]

Her *History of the Life, Reign, and Death of Edward II*
(pub. 1680), begun or written in February 1628, is, as her
preface terms it, a "historical relation," not a history *per
se*.[17] We may consider it fictionalized history or historical
fiction, prototypically akin to the modern historical novel:
it treats researched characters and events through invented
thoughts, motives and conversations, with a focus on a certain
character's perspective, in this case that of Edward's French
queen, Isabella. It incorporates,[18] among other techniques,

the mode of prose "charactery" that had recently been developed in court conversational games of James's reign where women were major players,[19] and popularized by Sir Thomas Overbury (poisoning victim of James's first favorite Somerset and his countess). Furthermore, in the manner of the ancient historians that Lady Falkland liked to read in translation, her history invents suitable speeches for moments of high emotion. As for theme, it tacitly treats the medieval King Edward II and his successive homosexual favorites Piers Gaveston and Hugh de Spencer as analogues of King James, Somerset and Buckingham; as might be expected, the tale gives vent to a pronounced disapproval of homoerotic royal favoritism. (We should remember that not only Buckingham's sister, Lady Denbigh, but also Somerset's sister-in-law, Elizabeth Howard Knollys, Lady Banbury, were close friends of Lady Falkland's; her perspective was an insider's.) Her general moral in *Edward II* is that homosexuality—like any other personal indulgence in royalty— if it is not to ruin the kingdom, must be kept private and inconsequential, and not cause the favorites to acquire powers far beyond their competence. The history's epigraph is a revision of King James's motto, "Qui nescit dissimulare nescit regnare" (He who does not know how to dissimulate does not know how to reign) to "Qui nescit Dissimulare, nequit vivere, perire melius" (He who does not know how to dissimulate cannot live, rather will perish).

Lady Falkland's "Epitaph upon the death of the Duke of Buckingham," of 1629 or later, expresses her attitude toward that favorite turned *de facto* king with an ingenious ambiguity, covering her tracks in case the verses should come to the eyes of his family, on whose good will she remained dependent in her desperate financial plight:

> Reader stand still and see, loe, here I am
> Who was of late the mighty Buckingham;
> God gave to me my being, and my breath;
> Two kings their favours, and a slave my death
> That for my Fame I challenge, and not crave
> That thou beleeve two kinges, before one slave.[20]

A reader expecting the epitaph to be flattering to Buckingham would take the last two lines to mean: "I wish my fame to be that two kings [James and his son Charles] favored me while only a low-ranking fellow killed me; I do not care whether you prefer the kings' opinion over that of the low fellow." But quite another reading readily suggests itself: "I wish my fame to be that two kings favored me while only a low-ranking fellow killed me, rather than asking you to believe that two kings were emotionally subjected before one low-ranking fellow" [in the second case Buckingham himself]. The intimation that both Kings James and Charles were erotically or emotionally subject to a man of relatively low birth here finds a barely safe expression, illustrating her wit and verbal ability.

In its latter half, her *Edward II* narrative focuses on the plight of Queen Isabella, caught between the duty to remain a faithful wife and the need to do something about a husband who is ruining his kingdom. Her wifely dilemma is similar to that explored in *Mariam*, where the queen likewise ought to try to tolerate and support her husband, even in his tyranny, but this time with the opposite outcome: the husband's rather than the wife's death. Queen Isabella's maneuverings and escape to France, her royal brother's betrayal of her, her bringing of an army from Flanders, her successful capture of England, her fall to the temptations of an affair with Mortimer and even her tearful consent to her husband's death, are all brought about by her husband's extreme failures. A painful saga of the destructive effects of Somerset and Buckingham has been constructed by fictional displacement: an assertive French queen of England, albeit a tainted one, of whom the current Queen Henrietta Maria is a potential superior analogue,[21] takes action. Isabella is tainted because she violates wifely duty, even conspiring in her husband's death; yet she is irresistible as a role model because she succeeds politically and militarily against the ruinous favorite. The keynote of Isabella's centrality to the whole narrative is caught in a terse early sentence, concluding the account of Edward's marriage in France: "The Solemnity ended, and a Farewel taken, he hastens homewards, returning seised of a Jewel, which not being rightly valued, wrought his ruine."[22] What he had thought an object, a royal possession, became a human agent and deposed him and his sycophantic favorites.

All this is not to say that the queen's faults fail to meet with due judgment at Lady Falkland's hands. Especially her actions in publicly parading, demeaning and torturing Spencer after her victory are roundly denounced. She had declined so far from her earlier virtue that her actions showed "a savage, tyrannical disposition"; she should have respected his station as a peer, though only "by creation" (one of many instances of marked aristocratic bias in the history). Just as it had been said of Mariam in the play that she should have forgiven her husband and not shown "sourness," the narrator declares that Queen Isabella should have shown "a kinde of Sweetness in the disposition" that would "pity his [Spencer's] Misfortune," if not the man himself. Her vindictiveness was "too great and deep a blemish to suit a Queen, a Woman, and a Victor" (129). Lady Falkland even gets so carried away with denouncing the queen's cruelty on this occasion as to have her narrator declare that "we may not properly expect Reason in Womens actions" (130). The queen also, of course, should not have consented to her husband's deposition and murder, but the treatment of that episode is oddly milder in its critique.

On the whole, the treatment of the queen is sympathetic, agreeing with the history's conclusion that even though it was Edward's own wife and son who brought him down, "had he not indeed been a Traytor to himself, they could not all have wronged him" (160). For "it is much in a king to be himself dissolute, licentious and ill-affected; but when he falls into a second errour, making more delinquents Kings, where one is too much, he brings all into disorder, and makes his Kingdome rather a Stage of Oppression, than the Theater of Justice" (158).

Sensing the disastrous direction Charles's reign was taking in 1628, Lady Falkland shows that she harbors a wish to see Queen Henrietta Maria and the French Crown follow in the steps of Queen Isabella, though doubtless only so far as to take some decisive action to rid England of its canker, the royal favorite, not to depose the king (which deed, as noted, she condemns in Isabella's party, even after having shown how hopelessly incompetent a ruler Edward was). At several points in this *Edward II*, and especially in the moralizing conclusion, the narrator recounts the medieval story in terms that refer just as well or better to the contemporary case.[23] For example, a mention of the king's first favorite as skilled at poisoning is more reminiscent of the Overbury murder than of anything in Gaveston's career. Similarly, the portrayal of a groom of the royal chamber flattering his way into power fits the Jacobean better than the medieval situation, for Edward and Gaveston were already lovers before Edward became king, and the latter had served as a master of revels. Or again, a secondary mention of another deposed king, Henry VI, notes that he "had a *Suffolk* and a *Somerset* that could teach the same way" to deposition (156). James's Somerset (Robert Carr) and Suffolk (Thomas Howard, scandalous and impeached Lord Treasurer) had cashiered his credibility as a ruler.

Lady Falkland does not hesitate to speak directly of "Gaveston his [the King's] Ganymede" (4) and to speculate on the origins and nature of a homosexual disposition, as well as its functioning in a powerful man: her narrator wonders whether it might be hereditary, but finds that improbable since neither Edward's parents nor son showed signs of it. She supposes, too, that once it becomes "confirmed by continuance of Practice, and made habituary by custom," even the will of the man himself cannot alter it (3 ff.). As to its impact on the ruler's ability to govern, it is seen as a special instance of "the general Disease of Greatness, and a kinde of Royal Fever, when they fall upon an indulgent Dotage, to patronize and advance the corrupt ends of their Minions, though the whole Society of State and Body of the Kingdom run in a direct opposition" (16), a particularly dangerous instance when the favorites are male, since they can acquire ruinous powers.[24]

As for Lady Falkland's personal situation under Buckingham's regime, just when Parliament was trying to impeach him and Yelverton was there branding him a latter-day Hugh de Spencer, Lady Falkland found herself in the enormously painful position of having to depend on Buckingham and his creatures. She was a Catholic convert and still, in some measure, a friend of Susan Denbigh's. No one else would help her. Her *Edward II* was an attempt to cope with that situation. To get a concluding, more concrete impression of it, let us consider two excerpts. In the first, Edward has just married the base-born Gaveston to a daughter of the Earl of Gloucester, who is greatly distressed:

> To take away that doubt, the new-married man is advanced to the Earldom of *Cornwal*; . . . so that now in Title he had no just exception; and for conditions, it must be thought enough his Master loved him. To shew himself thankful, and to seem worthy of such gracious favour, *Gaveston* applies himself wholly to the Kings humour, feeding it with the variety of his proper appetite, without so much as question or contradiction: Not a word fell from his Sovereign's tongue, but he applauds it as an Oracle, . . . . If the King maintain'd the party, the servant . . . sung the same Tune to a Crochet. The discourse being in the commendation of Arms, the eccho stiles it an Heroick Vertue; if Peace, it was an Heavenly Blessing; unlawful Pleasures, a noble Recreation; and Actions most unjust, a Royal Goodness. These parasitical Gloses so betray'd the itching ear that heard them, that no Honour or Preferment is conceited great and good enough for the Relator. A short time invests in his person or disposure all the principal offices and Dignities of the Kingdom . . . . In the view of these strange passages, the King appear'd so little himself, that the Subjects thought him a Royal Shadow without a Real Substance. This Pageant, too weak a Jade for so weighty a burden, had not a brain in it self able enough to manage such great Actions; neither would he entertain those of ability to guide him, whose honest freedom might have made him go through-stitch with more reputation. He esteems it a gross oversight, and too deep a disparagement, to have any creature of his own thought wiser than himself . . . . This made him chuse his Servants as his Master chose him, of a smooth fawning temper, such as might cry ayme, and approve his actions, but not dispute them. Hence flew a world of wilde disorder. (19–21)

Here we see, among other stylistic features, a profusion of metaphors, sometimes tumbling over each other: in one sentence Gaveston is a "pageant" (a mere Skinnerian repertoire of behaviors), a feeble horse, a fellow of little brain, and then a seamstress who might have gone "through-stitch" through his affairs if he had at least sought competent sewing advice. Notice the progressive diminution effected by this series, which makes him in the end a quasi-woman—and an incompetent one at that.

And as a sample of the dramatic, as it were arioso speeches, consider the queen's as she leaves France, having been cast off by a brother who fears to start a war over a mere "female passion":

> Farewel (quoth she) farewel, thou glorious Climate, where I first saw the World, and first did hate it; thou gavest me Birth, and yet denyest me Being; and Royal Kinred, but no Friends were real. Would I had never sought thy Help or Succour, I might have still believ'd thee kinde, not cruel: but thou to me art like a graceless mother, that suckles not, but basely sells her children. Alas! what have I done, or how offended, thou shouldst deny my life her native harbour? Was't not enough for thee in my Distresses to yeeld no Comfort, but thou must Expel me, and, which was worse, Betray me to my, Ruine? The poorest soul that claims in thee a dwelling, is far more happie than thy Royal Issue: but time will come thou wilt repent this Errour, if thou remember this my just Prediction; my Off-spring will revenge a Mothers Quarrel, a Mothers Quarrel just and fit for Vengeance. Then shalt thou seek and sue, yet finde more favour from him thy Foe, than I could win, a Sister. (*History*, 108)

These arioso speeches, set as italicized prose in the printed folio, could easily be printed as blank verse;[25] we recognize the dramatist of *Mariam* and its twin Sicilian play that has not survived (some 20 years old when she wrote those plays), now in her maturity with more potential as a writer, inventing a generic format for something that she can imagine existing only among the manuscripts of a few friends. Perhaps she understood that it would not survive even there unless she left it with her husband's papers, where it could be mistaken for a work of his. Thus it was published and preserved in 1680.

From the biography's account, we see that Elizabeth Cary had been a bookish only child, allowed by her indulgent father to read and to study languages. Her youthful dedication of her Ortelius translation to her Uncle Henry Lee, where she promises more and better efforts in writing, shows that out of this private childhood world she had taken a completely nonviable self-image, an ambition to be a thinker and writer; naively she tried to pursue it in the adolescent years before she began to live with her husband and have yearly babies. Going to the theater and watching plays, she thought she could be allowed to write plays and narrative poems. The attempt to publish *Mariam* must have sent her into emotional shock; after that she understood that a woman's aspiration to write could not be reconciled with wifely duty. Years later, her longstanding attraction to the countercultural identity of popery finally supplied a way in—or shall we say a way out—to the place for a written voice.

# 10 • "This Giant Has Wounded Me as Well as Thee"
## Reading Bunyan's Violence and/as Authority

*Sid Sondergard*

T he legal net thrown over England upon the Restoration of Charles II, aimed at immobilizing dissidents and sectarians, succeeded in capturing nonconformist preacher John Bunyan on 12 November 1660. Bunyan was a tinker whose only education consisted of modest training in reading and writing received under his father's roof. Sensitive to his precarious position as a spiritual leader under such circumstances, over the following 12 years Bunyan regularly introduced and manipulated images of violence in his writings for didactic ends, filling the void of his physical absence with a signifying system that would continue to assert his ministerial authority to the Bedford congregation. That this system was constructed without the benefit of formal rhetorical training may explain why it seems designed to address its audiences at the level of human empathy and experience;[1] Bunyan's encoding of violence as narrative signifier functions as an assertion of his authority, but it is also employed didactically, modeling unpleasant physical experience fictively to deter his audience from sinful activity. This essay will examine Bunyan's continuing reconfiguration of his prison experience through a semiotics—that is, through a systematic sign code—of violence in work published both during, and in some cases long after, his imprisonment.

Early Bunyan scholarship developed the convention of reading Bunyan's years of imprisonment as a relative inconvenience rather than as the protracted torment his works suggest it to have been.[2] Editor Edmund Venables may be this perspective's most succinct speaker. While conceding that the post-Restoration incarceration of nonconformists was predicated on expediency rather than concern for humane treatment of prisoners, Venables seems strangely resistant to the reality of Bunyan's personal suffering, writing that

> Prisons at the best were foul, dark, miserable places in those days, and one who visited Bunyan during his confinement speaks of Bedford gaol as "an uncomfortable and close prison": but his own narrative contains no complaint of it, and *we may reasonably believe that his condition was by no means so wretched as many of his biographers represent*, especially after he had gained the favour of his gaoler, who at a later time was ready to imperil himself to grant indulgence to his notable prisoner. (xx, my italics)

More recent critics have been inclined to authenticate the trauma of Bunyan's imprisonment, though with quite different conclusions about its ultimate effect on the writer. Henri A. Talon argues that if "the virility of a man" is a quality which serves to "give distinction to his writing, the most creative experience in Bunyan's life was his imprisonment, and total renunciation".[3] Richard L. Greaves has observed the "obvious personal bitterness" of Bunyan's prison writings, commenting that "Bunyan clearly had his tormentors in mind" when he wrote *One Thing is Needful: Or, Serious Meditations upon the Four Last Things, Death and Judgment, Heaven and Hell* (1665), an "exercise in apocalyptic vengeance"[4]; at the same time, Greaves emphasizes "the rich experience of the prison years," for the resultant growth in Bunyan's self-confidence became "the basis for the exuberance of his subsequent ministry and writing."[5] Christopher Hill believes Bunyan's exercise of rhetorical violence to have been essentially therapeutic: instead of "tearing himself to pieces, he attacked an external enemy in order to help others on the path to salvation."[6]

I wish to examine the sign structures that communicate Bunyan's rhetorical violence as virility to Talon, as confidence to Greaves and as self-preservation to Hill; not to mediate these variations in reader response, nor, in James Jakób Liszka's words, "to replace one dogma by another, but simply to disclose the rules of the symbolic processes by which symbols become such."[7] There is a systematic logic to Bunyan's rhetoric of violence, for it is, as Teresa de Lauretis explains in discussing representations of violence, "an order of language which speaks violence," which "constructs objects and subjects of violence."[8] The object of Bunyan's rhetorical violence is the authentication of his spiritual authority; its archetypal subject is his prison experience.

The enthusiastic Restoration persecution of nonconformists ensured that Bunyan's prison experience was not an isolated incident, yet few of his peers experienced sentences either as severe as Bunyan's or were as understated in their discussion of them. Nearly 20 percent of all beneficed ministers lost their livings, and lay dissenters like Bunyan "had to endure nearly thirty years of sporadic but often very damaging persecution."[9] Edward Burrough (1634–1663), already marked as an outspoken man and imprisoned for it prior to the Restoration, was arrested at a meeting in 1662 and

> violently dragged through the streets to Newgate, to which prison he was committed for the offense of holding an illegal meeting. . . . He was thrust into the felon's dungeon, which was so crowded that some of the prisoners died for suffocation, while the remainder became seriously ill. (*DNB* 3:444)

Burrough died in Newgate. Isaac Penington the Younger

(1616–1679) was confined in Aylesbury jail with other Quakers (late 1660, early 1661) "in a decayed building behind the gaol, once a malt-house, 'but not fit for a dog-house'" (*DNB* 15:743). Penington was incarcerated for 17 weeks in 1664, and over the years 1665–1667 served three stretches of a month, almost a year, and approximately 18 months. The *DNB* emphasizes that the "long imprisonments and exposure to prison damps and fare" contributed to undermine "Penington's already weak constitution" (15:743). Although there is evidence of local authorities and townspeople "protecting dissenters," such instances "were exceptions to the sufferings many dissenters—especially Quakers—had to endure during the great persecution" (Hill, *Experience*, 295). George Fox (1624–1691) records in his journal that his prison in Lancaster "was so bad they would put no creature they had in it . . . . [W]hen they came, they durst hardly go in, the floor was so bad and dangerous, and the place so open to wind and rain. Some that came up said, 'Sure it is a jakes-house.'"[10] Though Fox was unfortunate enough to face Sir Thomas Twisden (1602–1683) as judge— the same justice who would ultimately reject Elizabeth Bunyan's appeals on behalf of her husband—his journal proudly recounts his courtroom battles and rhetorical victories over his persecutors.

The Man in the Iron Cage of Despair, from *The Pilgrim's Progress from This World to That Which is to Come* (1678), replies, when asked to identify himself, "I am what I was not once. . . . I was once a fair and flourishing Professor, both in mine own eyes, and also in the eyes of others."[11] In his autobiography *Grace Abounding to the Chief of Sinners* (1666), Bunyan encodes his prison experience as a triumph of Christian fortitude over physical misfortune (supporting thereby the various readings by Talon, Greaves and Hill), associating his "Fears, and Doubts, and sad Months with Comfort; they are as the head of Goliath in my Hand" (Venables, 295). This comfort, however, is a rhetorical construct, produced as compensation for the author who initially shared the Man of Despair's terror of reading his incarceration as God's "threatnings, dreadful threatnings, fearful threatnings of certain Judgement and firy Indignation" (Keeble, 29). Greaves has observed a subsequent incorporation of "eschatological themes as a direct outgrowth of the fear of death which troubled Bunyan as he faced imprisonment" ("Conscience," 25). From his spiritual crises and fears for personal safety, Bunyan synthesizes a compelling persuasive structure that appropriates the emotional immediacy of such "fearful threatnings" to serve his doctrinal ends. In a passage from *The Resurrection of the Dead, and Eternall Judgement* (c. 1665), fear of death combines metaphorically with the experience of the prisoner to warn unrepentant sinners of the horrors awaiting them:

> a living death shall feed upon them, they shall never be spiritually alive, nor yet absolutely dead.... You know, though a Felon go forth of the Goal [*sic*], when he is going to the Bar for his Arraignment, yet he is not out of prison, or out of his Irons for that; his Fetters are still making a noise on his heels, and the thoughts of what he is to hear by and by from the Judge, is still frighting and afflicting his heart.... Thus I say, will the wicked come out of their Graves, having yet the Chains of eternal death hanging on them, and the talons of that dreadful Ghost fastned in their Souls.[12]

Shackling guilty others with the "Chains of eternal death," Bunyan the Innocent Prisoner recodes himself as Bunyan the Authoritative Judge, "*Thus I say.*" Knowing that this author has felt the grip of the fetter and the trepidation of approaching "the Bar for his Arraignment," is also to know that "the talons of that dreadful Ghost fastned in their Souls" is a metaphor of intimidation and Christian indoctrination for Bunyan the Judge—but also an expression of the personal terrors of Bunyan the Prisoner.

Prison metaphors occur systematically in Bunyan's works and fulfill didactic functions whenever they appear. A 1684 broadsheet including his *A Caution to Stir Up To watch against Sin* signifies sin as an agency of torture by depicting it as a personified incarceration, as both prison and person:

> SIN is a Prison, hath its bolts and chains,
> Brings into Bondage who it entertains; . . .
> Wherefore look to it, keep it out of Door,
> If once its slave, thou may'st be free no more.[13]

The suggestion here that the experience of imprisonment precludes the possibility of ever being truly free again is more specifically asserted in *The Life and Death of Mr. Badman* (1680): "The Prisoner that is to dye at the Gallows for his wickedness, must first have his Irons knock'd off his legs; so he seems to goe most at liberty, when indeed he is going to be executed for his transgressions."[14]

Perhaps the most explicit, and most telling, of these metaphors appears in *One Thing is Needful: Or, Serious Meditations Upon the Four Last Things, Death and Judgment, Heaven and Hell* (1665), signifying Hell as the archetypal prison:

> 25. Wherefore Hell in another place,
> Is call'd a Prison too,
> And all to shew the evil case,
> Of all sin doth undoe. (Midgley, 92)

It is no coincidence that the key that releases Christian and Hopeful from the dungeon of Despair is "Promise." Without the conviction that his imprisonment would ultimately serve to secure his position as one of the elect (Hill, *Tinker*, 103–10), or that it could become a vehicle for continuing his ministry while separated from his congregation, Bunyan might not have survived, or might have become as embittered by the experience as other long-term political prisoner/authors, another Sir Walter Ralegh.

As a strategy central to his rhetorical structure, Bunyan ostensibly encodes his spiritual tracts with his prison experiences not to establish authority, but rather to compensate for prior authority displaced by his imprisonment.[15] His principal rationale for nonconformity is "his insistence that the ultimate authority in matters religious [is] the working of the Holy Spirit through the Bible and in the believer" despite "the claims of the state to govern religious behavior"

(Greaves,"Conscience," 23–24). Denied the freedom to demonstrate his faith evangelically, Bunyan instead proposes his prison context as the greatest test of the believer's ability to commune with the Holy Spirit, as in his *Prison Meditations Directed to the Heart of Suffering Saints and Reigning Sinners* (1663):

> 14. This was the work I was about,
>       When Hands on me they laid,
>     'Twas *this* from which they pluck'd me out,
>       And vilely to me said,
> 15. You Heretick, Deceiver, come
>       To Prison you must go,
>     You preach abroad, and keep not home,
>       You are the Churches foe.
> 16. But having Peace within my Soul,
>       And Truth on every side,
>     I could with comfort them controul,
>       And at their charge deride.
> 17. Wherefore to Prison they me sent,
>       Where to this day I lie;
>     And can with very much content
>       For my profession die.
> 18. The Prison very sweet to me
>       Hath been, since I came here,
>     And so would also hanging be,
>       If God will there appear. (Midgley, 43–45)

The objectification of prison as physical but not intellectual reality, and his rationalization of it as relatively "very sweet," are revealed as defense mechanisms by Bunyan's caustic description of the officials responsible for his imprisonment. His martyr-like faith and conviction empower him to steal victory from undeniable defeat, such that "I could with comfort them controul." Perhaps most significant, in terms of recoding undesired experience as desired, is another stanza depicting an unambiguous semantic shift in the prisoner as signifier: "I am most free, that Men should see / A hole cut through mine Ear; / If others will ascertain me / They'll hang a *Jewel* there" (Midgley 48). Scarred in the ear as a felon, Bunyan is forced into a choice between rationalization and despair, and decides to read—and to encode for his readers—victory in his trials.

The physical experience of arrest, trial and incarceration, particularly as exacerbated by the emotional agonies of shame and separation, produces images in Bunyan's works of penal extremity rather than of justice served, as when Christian and Faithful are condemned at Vanity Fair: "So they beat them pitifully, and hanged Irons upon them, and led them in Chaines up and down the fair, for an example and a terror to others" (Keeble, 75). Even the author's attempt to scorn corporal suffering and imprisonment as merely relative serves to signify the opposite; in *The Resurrection of the Dead*, Bunyan argues that just as "those petty judgements among men, as putting in the stocks, whipping, or burning in the hand" are proportionately much lighter than "beheading, shooting to death, hanging, drawing, and quartering," so the punishments decreed by humanity are nothing in comparison to those assigned by God (McGee, 289). The quintessential example of injustice signified through the deprivations and torments of penal extremity appears in *The Pilgrim's Progress*. After Christian and Hopeful are captured by the giant Despair, they are thrown into his dungeon and so horribly beaten that "by reason of the Wounds they received when he beat them, they could do little but breath[e]." Hopeful responds to the weary Christian as the author himself may have responded upon looking at the others suffering with him:

> Thou seest I am in the Dungeon with thee, a far weaker man by nature than thou art: Also this Giant has wounded me as well as thee; and hath also cut off the Bread and Water from my mouth; and with thee I mourn without the light: but let's exercise a little more patience. (Keeble, 95)

To combat the torment of the prison experience and of his vulnerability to the wills and caprices of others, Bunyan presents imprisonment as a homiletic affirmation of courage in the face of persecution. Bread and water cut off, living in darkness, physically branded and beaten, faced with "the possibility of a death sentence" (Hill, *Tinker*, 109)—regardless of how much of the fictional account reflects the factual experience of its author, Bunyan is witnessing through suffering. He thereby controls the semiosis of experience, if not the experience proper, as he recodes punishment to be read as reward.

Acknowledging the relationship between wayfaring and warfaring in Bunyan's narratives, Nick Shrimpton writes that, despite their bloodshed being allegorical, "the violence will not entirely vanish into rhetorical smoke."[16] Anne Hunsaker Hawkins believes that the insistent presence of Bunyan's narrative violence—a presence evoking the visceral in its depiction of the horrors of physical experience— derives from the fact that the evangelist combatting Satan, with the soul as the spoils, "is a variant on the warrior archetype," a "religious ethos that emphasizes the battle of the soul with the principle of evil, and that casts the hero in the role of warrior."[17] To empower this allegory, Bunyan draws upon his own episodes of suffering, constructing from them an experiential discourse intelligible to every reader. Elaine Scarry writes that pain "is a pure physical experience of negation, an immediate sensory rendering of `against,' of something being against one, and of something one must be against."[18] To authorize his words, Bunyan rhetorically draws his reader into participating imaginatively with him in the most essential of human experiences, physical suffering. *The Resurrection of the Dead* comments that "it is the body that feels the stocks, the whip, hunger and cold, the fire and rack, and a thousand calamities: it is the body in which we have the dying marks of the Lord Jesus" (McGee, 210). To be human is to understand pain as read in the book of the body. *One Thing is Needful: Or, Serious Meditations upon the Four Last Things, Death and Judgment, Heaven and Hell* (1665) versifies this conception of the human condition:

> A block, a stock, a stone, or clot,
> Is happier than I:
> For they know neither cold or hot,
> To live, nor yet to die. (Midgley, 100)

The physical torments of the body, however, merely provide the morphemes of Bunyan's discourse of violence, structurally facilitating its assimilation; its semantics are constituted by his attempts to express spiritual anxiety through physical experience. A written account of the life of lapsed Protestant Frances Spira,[19] considered in *Grace Abounding*, was "to my troubled spirit as salt when rubbed into a fresh wound; every sentence in that Book, every groan of that Man . . . was as knives and daggers in my soul . . . . I felt also such a clogging and heat at my stomach, by reason of this my terror, that I was, especially at some times, as if my breast bone would have split asunder" (Venables, 343).

In Bunyan's early works, authorial experience (read as universal human experience) is explicitly recoded as pedagogy, as spiritual instruction empowered largely by personal suffering and error honestly expressed. Three examples from *The Life and Death of Mr. Badman* demonstrate that the rhetorical structure of his later work shifts to confident pronouncements empowered by a strong sense of personal authority. In the first example, the author's book becomes a metaphorical gun, firing a scatter-shot theology:

> The Butt therefore, that at this time I shoot at, is wide; and 'twill be as impossible for this Book to go into several Families, and not to arrest some, as for the Kings Messenger to rush into an house full of Traitors, and find none but honest men there.
>
> I cannot but think that this shot will light upon many, since our fields are so full of this Game; but how many it will kill to Mr. Badmans course, and make alive to the Pilgrims Progress, that is not in me to determine . . . . However, I have put fire to the pan, and doubt not but the report will quickly be heard. (Forrest & Sharrock, 2)

The author displays great confidence in the affective power of his text ("impossible . . . not to arrest some"; "doubt not but the report will quickly be heard")—built noticeably upon public approval of his previous allegory (and hence citing his own celebrity as authority when proposing "the Pilgrims Progress" as the paradigm of spiritual growth)—and makes it clear that *he* is aiming this doctrinal weapon.

This self-empowerment is curiously followed by self-jeopardy, as Bunyan metaphorically places himself in physical danger on the reader's behalf:

> I know 'tis ill pudling in the *Cockatrices* den, and that they
> run hazards that hunt the *Wild Boar*. The man also that
> writeth *Mr. Badmans* life, had need be fenced with a *Coat
> of Mail*, and with the Staffe of a Spear, for that his surviving
> friends will know what he doth: but I have adventured to
> do it, and to play, at this time, at the hole of these Asps;
> if they bite, they bite; if they sting, they sting. Christ sends
> his *Lambs* in the midst of *Wolves*, not to do like them, but
> to suffer by them for bearing plain testimony against their
> bad deeds.... (Forrest and Sharrock, 5)

A veteran of defiant activity in response to religious convictions (he reduces the risk of political retribution rhetorically here to games: hunting, playing), Bunyan derives
authentication from his previous suffering and is able to
project the authority necessary to make these claims read
like welcome opportunities for faith to triumph again.

The final and climactic example among the many first-
and second-hand anecdotes illustrating bad lives in *Mr.
Badman*, grotesque in its explicit violence, depicts the suicide
of John Cox, a sickly, despondent, impoverished man from
"Brafield by Northampton." Under the pretext of getting
some rest one morning, Cox asked his wife to leave the
room,

> so she went out: but he instead of sleeping, quickly took
> his Raisor, and therewith cut up a great hole in his side,
> out of which he pulled, and cut off some of his guts, and
> threw them, with the blood up and down the Chamber. But
> this not speeding of him so soon as he desired, he took the
> same Raisor and therewith cut his own throat .... [His wife
> and neighbors enter, begging him to pray for forgiveness.]
> At the hearing of which Exhortation, he seemed much
> offended, and in angry manner said, Pray! and with that
> flung himself away to the wall, and so after a few gasps died
> desperately. When he had turned him of his back, to the
> wall, the blood ran out of his belly as out of a boul ....
> (Forrest & Sharrock, 159)

Bunyan's is still the hand wielding the metaphorical weapon—

in this case Cox's story—and while he submerges his authority by advising "I cannot confirm all particulars," he retains the experiential impact of the example by authorizing it: "I had it from a sober and credible person, who himself was one that saw him in this bloody state, and that talked with him" (Forrest & Sharrock, 159).

The question of authenticity in action as well as in ideology is clearly important to Bunyan, who maintains his personal integrity and authority as writer through scrupulous documentation—even of the "facts" of his allegories. In *Mr. Badman*, the author bridges the gap between real-life experiences and the character "Mr. Badman" by explaining that

> Some notice therefore I have also here in this little discourse given the Reader, of them who were his Confederates in life, and Attendants at his Death . . . . All which are things either fully known by me, as being eye and ear-witness thereto, or that I have received from such hands, whose relation as to this, I am bound to believe. And that the Reader may know them from other things and passages herein contained, I have pointed at them in the Margent, as with a finger thus: (Forrest & Sharrock, 3–4; an illustrated hand with pointing index finger follows this passage.)

Similarly, *The Holy War made by Shaddai upon Diabolus for the Regaining of the Metropolis of the World. Or, The Losing and Taking Again of the Town of Mansoul* (1682) opens with Bunyan, soldier in the battles of the Church Militant, serving as witness to see and to hear the events of the battle for Mansoul:

> Let no man then count me a fable-maker,
> Nor make my name or credit a partaker
> Of their derision: what is here in view,
> Of mine own knowledge I dare say is true. . . .[20]

"The Author to the Reader" in *Mr. Badman* asserts Bunyan's authority while more explicitly communicating his expectations for the reader: "I do trace him in his Life, from his Childhood to his Death; that thou mayest, as in a Glass, behold with thine own eyes, the steps that take hold of Hell; and also discern, while thou art reading of Mr. Badmans

Death, whether thou thy self art treading in his path thereto"
(Forrest and Sharrock, 1).[21]

Authority appears to be an issue in Bunyan's works
primarily when it proves a practical necessity in support of
his program of textual violence as deterrent. Through the
disruptive agency of this violence, he attempts to intervene
in a degenerative process of spiritual corruption infecting the
reader, hoping thereby to preempt total loss by displacing
eternal pain with immediate, temporal pain. This pain,
Bunyan warns, is to be expected as intrinsically part of the
Christian experience: Evangelist warns Christian and Faithful as they approach Vanity Fair, "bonds and afflictions abide
in you; and therefore you cannot expect that you should
go long on your Pilgrimmage without them, in some sort
or other . . . . [B]e you sure that one or both of you must
seal the testimony which you hold, with blood" (Keeble,
72). Vincent Newey paraphrases this burden: "For the Puritan,
faith can be no less of a challenge and difficulty than sin."[22]

Bunyan's poem *Ebal and Gerizzim; Or, the Blessing and
the Curse: Being a short Exhortation to Sinners, by the
mercy and severity of God* (c. 1665) outlines the figurative
methodology for an experientially based expression of spiritual terrors:

> Indeed the holy Scriptures do make use
> Of many Metaphors, that do conduce
> Much to the symbolizing of the place, . . .
> Similitudes are but a shade and shew
> Of those, or that they signifie to you.
> The fire that doth within thine Oven burn,
> The prison where poor people sit and mourn,
> Chains, racks, and darkness, and such others, be
> As paintings on the wall, to let thee see
> By words and figures, the extremity
> Of such as shall within these burnings lye. (Midgley, 125)

It should come as little surprise now that at the signifying
heart of Bunyan's system of semiotic violence lies "The
prison where poor people sit and mourn."

*Christian Behaviour; Or the Fruits of True Christianity*
(1663) presents a model of chastisement for fathers that is

coopted and wielded by Bunyan even as he details it:

> If thou art driven to the Rod, then, 1. Strike advisedly in
> cool blood; and soberly shew them, 1. Their fault; 2. How
> much it is against thy heart thus to deal with them; 3. And
> that what thou dost, thou dost in conscience to God, and
> love to their Souls; 4. And tell them, that if fair means would
> have done, none of this severity should have been: This, I
> have proved it, will be a means to afflict their hearts as well
> as their bodies; and it being the way that God deals with
> his, it is the most likely to accomplish its end. (McGee, 30)

Bunyan commits himself to this program of violence-as-
deterrent because he genuinely feels, given his own experience, that this is precisely how "God deals with his." This
is outlined even more explicitly in *Mr. Badman:*

> Suppose that there was amongst us such a Law, (and such
> a Magistrate to inflict the penalty,) That for every open
> wickedness committed by thee, so much of thy flesh should
> with burning Pinchers be plucked away from thy Bones:
> Wouldest thou then go on in thy open way of Lying, Swearing,
> Drinking and Whoring, as thou with delight doest now?
> Surely, surely, No: The fear of the punishment would make
> thee forbear; yea, would make thee tremble, even then when
> thy lusts were powerfull, to think what a punishment thou
> wast sure to sustain, so soon as the pleasure was over. (Forrest
> & Sharrock, 6–7)

Fear based on God's inevitable punishment of unrepentant
sinners—*Seasonable Counsel*'s observation that "The consideration also that we have deserved these things, much
silences me as to what may yet happen unto me" (Watkins,
7)—plus hope of reward for individual sacrifice[23] motivates
Faithful, in the context of Vanity Fair, to profess his religion
in the face of his greatest enemies. His reward and/or
punishment is an archetypal death conflating the discrete
afflictions of Christ and the traditional treatment of heretics:
"They therefore brought him out, to do with him according
to their Law; and first they Scourged him, then they Buffetted
him, then they Lanced his flesh with Knives; after that they
Stoned him with Stones, then prickt him with their Swords,

and last of all they burned him to Ashes at the Stake"
(Keeble, 80). These icons of violence perpetrated by both the
enemies of the faith and by zealots are familiar to Bunyan's
every reader; the emphasis here, however, is again experiential rather than historical. Bunyan wishes to allow his
contemporaries no illusion of safety from this kind of cruel
persecution—for his own torments have proved the naiveté
of such complacency.

Violence of a culturally familiar nature also appears in
the two parts of *The Pilgrim's Progress* when Bunyan appropriates conflict patterns from epic and romance narratives to increase the accessibility and rhetorical impact of
his allegory for the reader.[24] Backscheider suggests that the
author animates his Christian didactics with images of martial
conflict because they are "mythic and charged with associations" that "give the narrative additional truth" (113).
Christian must learn the tactics of spiritual warfare before
he can defend the faith—and his own soul—against the
temptations of Satan. Interpreter provides him a practical
lesson with the vision of the man seeking entrance to a
palace inhabited by golden-clad figures: undaunted by armed
men opposing his entrance, he "fell to cutting and hacking
most fiercely; so after he had received and given many wounds
... he cut his way through them all" while a voice inside
encourages "'Come in, Come in; / Eternal Glory thou shalt
win'" (Keeble, 28). This model of the assertive individual
who dares to combat puissant opposition is echoed when
the Dreamer witnesses Christian's participation in a discussion "about the Lord of the Hill" that is reminiscent of the
Christ-as-Warrior motif so prominent in Old English poetry
(e.g., *The Dream of the Rood*) and its revisions by Christian
scops: "I perceived that he had been a great Warriour, and
had fought with and slain him that had the power of Death,
but not without great danger to himself, which made me
love him the more" (Keeble, 43). Bunyan's structural formula—self-sacrificing endangerment in spiritual battle earn-
ing love and respect—functions to inspire and empower
Christian in his pursuit of the Celestial City, implicitly
acknowledging and validating the author's own voluntary

exposure to "danger" in the church's factional wars waged over the previous two decades. That is, the allegory's genesis dates back to its author's imprisonment. Bunyan withheld *Pilgrim's Progress* from initial publication "for several years"[25]—hence the pronounced violence and portraits of incarceration in the allegory were likely framed by the immediacy of his own experience, 1660–1672 (and by a return to prison for the first six months of 1677).[26]

Despite the author's service in the Parliamentary Army from November 1644 to 21 July 1647, Hill has declared it "doubtful whether Bunyan saw much military action" (*Tinker*, 46). Indeed, the climactic battle between Christian and the monster Apollyon betrays more contact with martial literary narratives than with hand-to-hand combat. Sustaining wounds on all extremities, "Christian again took courage, and resisted as manfully as he could. . . . [Though] Christian, by reason of his wounds, must needs grow weaker and weaker" (Keeble, 49). Bunyan reminds his reader of the physical cost of Christian's "manful" resistance by creating a semantics of suffering, inviting participation by the reader in the fiction of Christian's flesh-and-blood experience. And recalling both the pain and the disenfranchisement resulting from his own "manful" sacrifices on behalf of the Church Militant, Bunyan encodes the indescribable horror of battle as further authentication for the "eyewitness" author: "In this Combat no man can imagine, unless he had seen and heard as I did, what yelling, and hideous roaring Apollyon made . . . . ['T]was the dreadfullest sight that ever I saw" (Keeble, 49–50). Note that while Bunyan's self-authorization here is marked by a rhetorical appropriation of power (generated through the reader's attempts to conceptualize the unspeakable terror of Apollyon), he also manipulates such rhetorical empowerment to secure self-destruction for agents of evil. The titular Vice of *The Life and Death of Mr. Badman,* for example, indulges in violent curses that doom his immortal soul: "He would wish that evil might befall others; he would wish their Necks broken, or that their Brains were out, or that the Pox, or Plague was upon them, and the like: All which is a devilish kind of cursing, and is become one of the common sins of our age." Indicting himself more specifically, Mr. Badman "would also as often wish a Curse to himself, saying, Would I might be hanged, or burned, or that the Devil might fetch me" (Forrest & Sharrock, 30).

This authorial imperative of connecting with the reader on the common level of human experience to disseminate spiritual lessons seems, in general, less emphatic as time passes and Bunyan's personal authority becomes firmly established. Hence *The Second Part of the Pilgrim's Progress* (1684) employs the battle imagery of epic and romance merely as convention, to exploit its cultural familiarity, rather than to negotiate a textual rapport between author and reader. Bunyan chooses not to convert Christiana into a spiritual warrior like her husband, instead providing for her the chivalric champion Mr. Great-heart, who successively conquers the giants Grim (also called Bloody-man [Keeble, 181]), Maull (the telling blow occurs when Mr. Great-heart, "in the full heat of his Spirit ... pierceth him under the fifth rib" [Keeble, 203], bringing him within decapitation range), Slay-good (another decapitation [Keeble, 222]) and Dispair, whose severed head is used to signify the conquest of evil by Christian fortitude to all passersby (Keeble, 237). There is little semiotic difference between this signifier and the enormous head of Grendel, a trophy dredged up from the bottom of the bloody mere by Beowulf.

Lest all of this seem like mountains of carnage extrapolated from a molehill of individual suffering, we should be reminded that Bunyan's prison term had a profound experiential impact on his family as well. When his experiences are allowed the simple voice of personal narrative (or at least are not so explicitly introduced in the service of Christian pedagogy), Bunyan's separation from his family is portrayed with wrenching pathos. "A Brief Account of the Author's Imprisonment," from *Grace Abounding*, reveals that

> The parting with my Wife and poor Children hath often been to me in this place as the pulling of Flesh from my Bones; ...
> I should have often brought to my mind the many hardships, miseries and wants that my poor Family was like to meet with, should I be taken from them, *especially my poor blind*

*Child*, who lay nearer my heart than all I had besides. (Venables, 393)

More poignant yet is the suffering of his wife. *A Relation of the Imprisonment* recounts Elizabeth Bunyan's attempts to secure her husband's release, and at one point she testifies, "I was with child when my husband was first apprehended; but being young, and unaccustomed to such things, said she, I being smayed at the news, fell into labour, and so continued for eight days, and then was delivered, but my child died." Exacerbating the tragedy, unsympathetic justice Sir Thomas Twisden "told her, that she made poverty her cloak" (Venables, 426). The frustrated anger that must have been generated by such a loss finds diffused outlets throughout Bunyan's discourse of violence, but nowhere so explicitly as in his final allegory, *The Holy War*.

Bunyan's most overtly violent allegory dialectically asserts that there are no permanent solutions in the battle of the Church Militant, that the efforts of the individual in this conflict, those both "historical and the transhistorical, are in a state of tension"[27] unlikely to find permanent resolution within, or without, the text. This, however, is not to say that Bunyan ceases to emphasize the violence of the wars of the Church Militant through explicitly experiential structures. By fictively creating contact with violent experience, Bunyan creates fear of that contact (and hence of the ideas facilitating the fictive experience), as in this description of the fighting in the town of Mansoul:

> She saw the swords of fighting men made red,
> And heard the cries of those with them wounded;
> Must not their frights then be much more by far
> Than theirs who to such doings strangers are? (Forrest, 4)

The author increases such intimidation by detailed iconographical descriptions of the horrifying Diabolonian troops, including individual commanders, their standard-bearers and their scutcheons (Forrest, 211–14, 260–61), and by providing frequent casualty lists from both sides of the conflict (Forrest, 17, 18, 30, 69, 70, 86, 93–95, 103, 121, 225–26). Bunyan's voice of textual authority interrupts the narrative at certain points to remind the reader of the threats facing the unwary: "I told you before, how that these Diabolonian Doubters turned the men of Mansoul out of their beds, and now I will add, they wounded them, they mauled them, yea, and almost brained many of them" (Forrest, 232). Archetypal cruelty reigns once Diabolus exhorts his legions to "distress this town of Mansoul, and vex it with your wiles, ravish their women, deflower their virgins, slay their children, brain their ancients, fire their town, and what other mischief you can" (Forrest, 238)—yet the consequent, and inevitably triumphant, opposition mounted by Prince Emmanuel, son of high king Shaddai, reminds the reader that the most physically painful trials of the faith are answered with spiritual comfort.

Humbly, implicitly, Bunyan recalls the stoic resolve of his political imprisonment as the fundamental sign and authority in *The Holy War* when he depicts a resistant prisoner, Incredulity, who lacks the courage of his convictions and manages, while awaiting execution, to break out of prison and flee Mansoul. The coward resorts to "lurking in such places and holes, as he might, until he should again have opportunity to do to the town of Mansoul a mischief for their thus handling of him as they did" (Forrest, 151). Bunyan the prisoner did not seek revenge as Incredulity does, but looked beyond his immediate, mortal oppressors to the Satanic evil animating them. Wielding the most powerful icon of the faith for which he has suffered—and without conceiving this action as even remotely paradoxical or impious—Bunyan the author executes the captured Diabolonian war criminals by crucifixion (Forrest, 153–54, 222–24). Then to complete his victory over the diabolical forces that have oppressed him, Bunyan first devalues the Diabolonians as signifiers of evil ("there was not left so much as one Doubter alive; they lay spread upon the ground dead men, as one would spead dung upon the land" [Forrest, 252]), and then erases them from history altogether:

> They that buried them, buried also with them their arms, which were cruel instruments of death (their weapons were

arrows, darts, mauls, fire-brands, and the like). They buried also their armour, their colours, banners, with the standard of Diabolus, and what else soever they could find that did smell of a Diabolonian Doubter. (Forrest, 257–58)

In a war that has witnessed reversal after reversal, repeated diabolical triumph after what has appeared to be its permanent defeat, Bunyan completes his victory by semiotic manipulation, making it possible for subsequent generations of citizens in Mansoul to live without ever experiencing the horrors of Diabolus. How curious that in erasing these signs, Bunyan has somehow obscured the evidence of much of his own suffering—or so it would seem in the experience of those readers who continue to read his words, but not his pain.

# 11 • Imagining New Worlds
## Milton, Galileo, and the "Good Old Cause"

### Annabel Patterson

I n 1618, in the course of a dispute with the Jesuit mathematician Orazio Grassi over the comets of that year, Galileo was provoked into defining the epistemological problem we now refer to as a paradigm shift—or, more precisely, the problems caused by the knowledge that knowledge might be alterable, problems that were themselves rendered visible by a development in optics. It is no accident that terms we take for granted in our attempts to understand mental phenomena are related to sight, and some specifically to optics: perception, vision, perspective, focus, lens, speculation. Grassi had taken issue with Galileo's (to us) reasonable statement that the discovery of the fixed stars resulted from the use of the telescope, and had suggested that it might have other causes. In response, Galileo sardonically described the various alternatives proposed by the Roman Catholic Church in its resistance to the new science. His point was that the denial of the cause-and-effect relation between telescopic vision and new information about the heavens had created an absurd series of hypotheses that the new astronomer was required to refute—and that, given their absurdity, he never could. He would have to prove that he had not achieved his revolutionary results by, for example, "bringing down of the stars to earth or a venturing forth on our part into the sky, by which the interval between would be diminished" or by making "the stars swell up so as to enlarge and become more easily visible." Most threatening, however, of the impossible proofs demanded was that his experiment was "not an opening of closed eyes," a claim that, if not disproved, would have opened Galileo to the charge of interfering with the divine prerogative of blinding the eyes of fallen humanity.[1]

I begin with this as a colorful instance of how a paradigm shift—which requires us to see differently—may encounter resistance, not because the eyes of the opponents are themselves closed, but because they can envisage all too clearly what effects such a reinterpretation of the data must have on their traditional mode of operations. In this essay, I call not so much for a new paradigm but for a shift *back* to a much older one that became, for interesting reasons, discredited. This paradigm concerns our understanding of England during the seventeenth century, a topic of perpetual debate in the British academy, and one that ought to be of more interest in the American academy than it is. It was, after all, opposition to Stuart constitutional theory and religious intolerance that provided the initial sanction for the New England settlements and ultimately the rationale for the Constitution and the Bill of Rights. For if the relationship is Oedipal, a regular analysis of how we are currently construing our political origins is at the very least intellectual good housekeeping.

The paradigm in need of recovery has the virtue of being represented by a memorable phrase, the early modern equivalent of a soundbite: the *Good Old Cause*. Taken at its word, this formula stood for a broad ranging political and religious program: the attempt of a large part of the English nation in the mid-century to recover from Charles I "their just natural rights in civil things, and true freedom in matters of conscience," phrases that sound like second nature in late twentieth century America. But when Sir Henry Vane named the Cause both Good and Old in 1656, in his famous pamphlet *A Healing Question propounded and resolved,* it was already inflected with a mixture of nostalgia and defeatism. By the mid-1650s, the difficulty in reaching agreement as to what these noble goals meant to the differently motivated groups who had defeated and deposed the king had already led to extreme sectarianism and the autocracy of Cromwell's Protectorate.

As the Restoration approached, and the twin ideals receded, the phrase became ubiquitous. A nostalgic version appeared in R. Fitz-Brian's tract *The Good Old Cause Dress'd in its Primitive Lustre* (1659), implicitly an argument for support of the Rump as the natural descendant of the Long Parliament: "There was in those virgin (i.e. pre-Cromwellian) daies such a mutuall, strict and lovely harmony and agreement . . . between the Parliament and the honest unbiass'd people of the Nation" (5). Conversely, the phrase was rendered stigmatic in William Prynne's *The Republicans and Others Spurious Good Old Cause . . . Anatomized* (May 1659), or the anonymous *A Coffin for the Good Old Cause* (1660), or the broadside, *An Exit to the Exit Tyrannus,* which claimed that "their Good old Cause / Was only made for a pretence, / To banish all our freedome hence, / And overthrow our Lawes."[2]

## Resistance Among Historians

But to traduce the Cause, as seventeenth century partisanship was more than willing to do, was at least to admit its earlier existence and its efficacy. In our own time, a more subtle form of depreciation has been at work. Since the late 1960s, influential historians have questioned whether in the welter of motives that could be posited for the events of 1640–1660, there was any ideological clustering, anything that could still be identified as a "Cause."

There is surely a connection between the way people

construe historical causation and their capacity to accept the existence of a supervening Cause, in the sense of a group commitment over time to a principled agenda, which in turn becomes the motive for political behavior. If one's primary theory of historical causation is that people are motivated by self-interest rather than principle, one will tend to disbelieve in a unifying Cause; if, on the other hand, one believes that people are capable of suppressing immediate self-interest for the sake of a larger benefit, then one will tend to credit Cause-formations.

These generalizations are provoked by reflection on the revisionist history of early modern England initiated by Sir Geoffrey Elton, who in 1965 disturbed one of the long-established paradigms of Whig historiography. Elton, whose article was entitled "A high road to civil war?" doubted generally whether there were any structural causes for the events of 1640–1660, and especially whether there were any signs of approaching conflict in the Jacobean parliaments; specifically, he wished to refute the oppositional significance that had been attributed to the House of Commons *Apology* of 1604.[3] This was the beginning of a series of studies that appeared to demonstrate that whatever happened between 1640 and 1660, it was *not* a Puritan revolution, *not* the consequence of deepening parliamentary opposition, *not* the effect of class struggles with an economic base, and scarcely attributable to anything larger than accident, a runaway trainload of strategic mistakes and good intentions gone awry.[4] Thus, for example, John Morrill's *The Revolt of the Provinces* replaced religious ideology, republican theory and large-scale economic factors as causes with the study of local interests among the country gentry. We are left with the choice between an uninformed gentry (the majority) who failed to understand the issues on which the war was being fought, and a minority of brash and dogmatic men like John Pym whose excesses (in defining the issues) eventually drove some of the passive majority toward defense of the king.[5] Conrad Russell's *Unrevolutionary England, 1603–1642*, a title that speaks for itself, was one of the latest in this series, published in 1990.[6]

Now, while it is as reductive to assume a political motive behind every historical thesis as it is to assume that historians can attain complete objectivity, there does seem to have been an unstated agenda in some of these revisionist histories: to discredit not only the Whig historians of the past (and even, in the figure of J. E. Neale, the very recent past) but also the assumptions and achievements of the Marxist historian Christopher Hill, whose dedication to the revolutionary period and to left-wing religious splinter groups had been, we might say, keeping the Good Old Cause alive. Indeed, one of Hill's volumes of documents was published under that very title.[7] But a quarter of a century sufficed to absorb the revisionist paradigm, assess its contributions, and to render its political implications visible.[8]

In resuscitating the Good Old Cause as at least as reasonable an explanation for the events of the mid-century as those proposed to replace it (a move whose political implications must also by now be evident), I would also want to extend its reach chronologically. For the Cause was very old indeed by the time it came to be so named by Vane; and the binary principles that he had defined as "just natural rights in civil things, and true freedom in matters of conscience" had been articulated, though not always twinned like this, not merely under the early Stuarts but also in Elizabeth's reign, and Mary's, and Edward's, and their father's. In fact, we should probably look for them at least as far back as the late fourteenth century, in the well-documented story of Richard II's parliaments, as well as in the Rising of 1381. I am also convinced that the Cause supposedly dead by 1660 was, on the contrary, *still* being fought for openly and surreptitiously throughout the Restoration. I would hope eventually to demonstrate that one of the reasons that the age and continuity of this cause has not been observed or credited by historians is that they seldom investigate "literary" evidence; the very sort of evidence, one might suppose, where the traces of ideology or Cause-formation might be found.

To give some indication of how this might work, we can now look through Galileo's telescope at John Milton, a writer on whom both historians and literary critics have made claims of different proportions. Milton himself made claims on Galileo. One might even say that he enlisted Galileo in the Good Old Cause as early as 1644 when, in arguing in *Areopagitica* that the Long Parliament should repeal its Licensing Act, he suggested a favorable comparison between England, as "a place of philosophic freedom," and the "servile condition" of Italy. "There it was that I found and visited the famous Galileo, grown old, a prisoner to the Inquisition, for thinking in Astronomy otherwise then the Franciscan and Dominican licencers thought." "And though," he added, "I knew that England then [i.e. in 1638–1639] was groaning loudest under the Prelaticall yoak, neverthelesse I took it as a pledge of future happines, that other Nations were so perswaded of her liberty."[9]

In early 1660, however, in desperation at the seeming inevitability of the Restoration, Milton concluded the pamphlet ironically entitled *The Readie and Easie Way to Establish a Free Commonwealth* as follows:

> What I have spoken is the language of that which is not called amiss "The Good Old Cause" ... nay, though what I have spoke should happen ... to be the last words of our expiring liberty. (7:387–88)

These two statements roughly span the entire period of the civil war and its republican and Cromwellian aftermath, especially since *Areopagatica* looks back in this allusion to Milton's travels just before the war broke out. They demonstrate that Milton, at least, believed in the existence of the Good Old Cause, most clearly when it was about to become defunct. And it is relatively easy to prove from elsewhere in his polemical tracts how old he thought the Cause was, and how instinctively he merged in its genealogy the religious and political history of the nation. Thus in *Of Reformation* (a Puritan title if there ever was one), he wrote:

> We know that Monarchy is made up of two parts, the Liberty of the subject, and the supremacie of the King ... Yet these devout Prelates, spight of our great Charter, and the soules

of our Progenitors that wrested their liberties out of the Normane gripe with their dearest blood and highest prowesse, for these many years have not ceas't in their Pulpits wrinching, and spraining the text, to set at nought and trample under foot all the most sacred, and life blood Lawes, Statutes, and Acts of Parliament that are the holy Cov'nant of Union, and Marriage betweene the King and his Realme, by proscribing, and confiscating from us all the right we have to our owne bodies, goods and liberties," (1:592–93)

And in 1642 he celebrated the expulsion of these same prelates (the bishops) from the House of Lords as a constitutional victory in the spirit of Magna Carta: "With one stroke winning againe our lost liberties and Charters, which our forefathers after so many battels could scarce maintaine" (1:924).

Historians who overlook such language in Milton's polemical prose miss an opening into a net of motivation no more coherent in the aggregate, perhaps, than that discovered by Morrill among his gentry, but in which ideology (a structure of conviction) is clearly evident. Yet Morrill would probably not place Milton, even the Milton of the 1640s and 1650s, among his radical minority, the group of "extremists" represented by Pym. It would seem that we need another category of persons—and perhaps quite a large one (this is not the place to start listing possible candidates for its membership)—in order to account for this way of thinking and for the fact that Milton could cite so many precedents for it, including several from the sixteenth century. George Buchanan, Christopher Goodman, Dudley Fenner, John Ponet, Thomas Cartwright and Raphael Holinshed's *Chronicles* are a few of his authorities.

## RESISTANCE AMONG LITERARY CRITICS

Among literary critics, the evidence for Milton's republicanism in the pamphlets written between 1640 and 1660 has not exactly been overlooked, but it has been subjected to a different sort of repression. Milton's own statement that during this period his real genius was on hold and that he was writing at a disadvantage, with his left hand, has been widely taken as authorization for the belief that literature and politics are incompatible imperatives. Even Joan Webber, who recognized the importance of Milton's prose, wondered how he "sustained his vision" of the poetic life during those years and concluded that that vision was sustained in the digressive spaces between the fighting words where he spoke of his poetic vocation, and thereby "evoked a timeless world where contemplation and harmony are possible."[10] The anxious statements quoted above from the *Readie and Easie Way* have often been taken as support for the notion that *Paradise Lost* was written in a mood of profound political disillusionment, and that it redirects its readers' aspirations to apolitical, interior and transcendent values. This theory goes back, as does so much else in literary tradition, to Coleridge. "Finding it impossible," wrote Coleridge, "to realize his own aspirations, either in religion, or in politics, or society, [Milton] gave up his heart to the living spirit and light within him, and avenged himself on the world by enriching it with this record of his own transcendent ideal."[11]

Coleridge was himself far from transcending politics, and in the aftermath of Waterloo had become embroiled in an antiradical, anti-Jacobin polemic, conducted in his *Lay Sermons* and through journal publication.[12] We can begin to see signs of this guilty knowledge long embedded in "criticism" at the moment when, a century later, T. S. Eliot attempted to remove Milton from the literary canon. Eliot was himself influenced by F. R. Leavis, and together they provoked a "Milton quarrel" among British intelligentsia that spanned two decades. Milton's demotion was initially expressed in exclusively aesthetic or rhetorical terms. In 1936 Eliot laid against him the "serious charge" of being a bad influence on poets; of indulging in "rhetoric," as opposed to the conversational style that was carried forward by Dryden, to the extent of creating a barrier of style between his meaning and his reader.[13] In 1947, however, Eliot delivered another statement on Milton, supposedly to correct the misjudgments of his previous one, but actually to restate his misgivings in terms that rendered his own motivation

almost visible. Milton was, after all, a great poet whose
influence might be less noxious than he had supposed.[14]
Understandably, modern poets like himself, who had been
carrying out "another revolution in idiom," had been biased.
Their bias depreciated Milton while contributing to the
"taste" for Donne; but a decade later, Eliot felt, "we cannot,
in literature, any more than in the rest of life, live in a
perpetual state of revolution" (148). This political language
was scarcely coincidental. Milton's language, now strangely
described as "a perpetual sequence of original acts of lawlessness" (141) (another not-so-dead political metaphor), is
seen as the source of his greatness.

But Eliot was still more revelatory now about why Milton
made him anxious. His candor appears to have been unin-
tentional, the product of an attempt to establish his own
scientific perspective (his telescope) in contrast to Dr.
Johnson's more primitive cognitive tools:

> There is one prejudice against Milton, apparent on almost
> every page of Johnson's *Life of Milton*, which I imagine is
> still general: we, however, with a longer historical perspec-
> tive, are in a better position than was Johnson to recognize
> it and to make allowance for it. This is a prejudice which
> I share myself: an antipathy towards Milton the man . . . .
> But this prejudice is often involved with another, more
> obscure: and I do not think that Johnson had disengaged the
> two in his own mind. The fact is simply that the Civil War
> of the seventeenth century, in which Milton is a symbolic
> figure, has never been concluded. The Civil War is not ended:
> I question whether any serious civil war ever does end . . . .
> Reading Johnson's essay one is always aware that Johnson
> was obstinately and passionately of another party. No other
> English poet, not Wordsworth, or Shelley, lived through or
> took sides in such momentous events as did Milton; of no
> other poet is it so difficult to consider the poetry as poetry,
> without our theological and political dispositions, conscious
> and unconscious, inherited or acquired, making an unlawful
> entry. (134)

Reading Eliot's essay with the unfair wisdom of hindsight,
it looks suspiciously as though he was more like than unlike

Dr. Johnson in his bias against Milton the republican polemicist. His insight that the civil war in England is not ended has been confirmed not only by the developments in British historiography described above, but by a standardized school curriculum proposed by the Conservative government in which (at least in 1993) Milton is conspicuous by his absence. In this recent skirmish, the party of Eliot appears to have won a strategic victory.

It is one of the stranger facets of this 400-year-old conflict, however, that the alternative critical tradition, the "Whig" tradition of Hazlitt as distinct from Coleridge, should not have been able to recuperate *Paradise Lost* as a canonical text of classical or biblical republicanism. It is especially disconcerting, though understandable, that Christopher Hill (whose role as one of the implied targets of revisionist history was mentioned earlier) produced an account of Milton's late poems that finally differs very little from the Coleridgean theory of frustrated political ideals leading to their transcendence. The example is even more telling in view of the fact that Hill was one of the first modern historians of the seventeenth century to venture into "literary" territory, an experiment in interdisciplinary thinking that often makes the experimenter less capable of seeing the ingrown habits of the newly adopted discipline than those who were raised on them. In addition, Hill's own historiographical interest in the Levellers, the Diggers and other radical groups led him to read the Restoration as—to cite the title of one of his later books—*The Experience of Defeat*. In his final chapter there, Hill did argue, too late, and primarily from *Samson Agonistes*, that "there is no evidence that Milton ever adopted the post-1661 Quaker position of pacifism and abstention from politics."[15]

But Hill's major statement about Milton was already inscribed in the great biography, *Milton and the English Revolution*. Significantly, this appeared in 1977, at approximately the same time that the revisionist paradigm had achieved dominance.[16] And although in his early chapters Hill fought manfully for the notion that Milton was already a defender of the Good Old Cause in his early poems—an attempt that probably really was a lost cause, given the scantiness of the evidence[17]—when he turned to *Paradise Lost* he saw it as a message about acceptance of a superior wisdom that frustrates human intervention. In order to accommodate some version of the romantic thesis that Satan, the leader of a rebellion against his monarch, is the true hero of the poem, Hill imagined a chronological or compositional split in the poem, so that the early books, in which Satan is "wrong but grandly wrong" (365), were written before 1660, before Milton's despair was confirmed; but in general Hill believed that "the character of Satan alludes to some of the ways in which the Good Old Cause had gone wrong" (366).

This interpretation is, however, rendered unstable by Hill's simultaneous belief that Milton was, even in *Paradise Lost*, inhibited by the Restoration censorship. He relates the incident of 1686–1687, when Milton's friend Theodore Haak, who had translated the first three books of *Paradise Lost* into German, read them aloud to the Hanoverian pastor, H. L. Benthem, who understood them as a commentary on Restoration politics in England. According to Benthem, when Milton's friends heard the poem's title before it appeared, they assumed it would be a lament for the Good Old Cause and feared for his safety. When they actually read it, they were reassured and withdrew their objections to the poem's publication. But, continued Benthem, when Haak read the early books to him, he realized that "in fact 'this very wily politician' ('dieser sehr schlau Politicus') had concealed under this disguise exactly the sort of lament his friends had originally suspected."[18] How, precisely, we are not told. But Hill invokes this anecdote in support of one way of reading the poem: a microcriticism that looks beyond the narrative message (that rebellion is both demonic and doomed to fail) to tiny textual details that can be construed as hints of defiance. So, tucked into the expansive account of Creation in book 7 of the poem is one "parsimonious emmet," the ant that the poem sees as a "Pattern of just equality perhaps" (7.484–86). This detail Hill sees as a gesture toward a future republic, Milton "covering himself by an ambiguous 'perhaps'"

(408). Hill apparently did not notice the contradiction between his own two theories—the argument for defeat, expressed as spiritual obedience, and the covert or encoded argument for defiance.

Now, it must be admitted that *Paradise Lost* provokes such contradiction. Having rewritten the Fall, broadly speaking, in the political language of monarchy and rebellion and so incited the search for contemporary analogies, Milton refused to permit their unproblematic discovery in its details, which constantly contradict one other. Indeed, Mary Ann Radzinowicz claims that, while the poem will support both the theory of "politics abandoned" and that of "politics encrypted," it does so in order to teach its readers to avoid simple solutions. The poem is, then, a textbook in political education. Like Hill, Radzinowicz cites the "parsimonious emmet" as an ideologeme of Milton's program. Unlike Hill, she continues Milton's statement about the ant, to note that what immediately follows the word "perhaps" (which Hill had read as self-protection) is the word "hereafter," which Radzinowicz reads as deferral. A failed revolution is to be replaced by a better educated future—men progressively (in the tradition of Christian rationalism) "gaining illumination." Fixed meanings and single interpretations are coercive.

Radzinowicz's argument might itself, however, be recognized not as a genuine compromise, but as a skillful rewriting of the traditional argument for transcendence. In her hermeneutics, the poem's resistance to clear political solution, its linguistic ambiguity, are strategic; but in the last analysis, Christian rationalism and literary theory merge to produce a new version of the disengagement theory. Milton, she concludes, "has successfully resisted the temptation himself to appropriate 'the language of that which is not called amiss the good old Cause' for a utopian program." Praxis is displaced not merely into a better educated future, but into the philosophical space that is ultimately only lexis.

And what neither Hill nor Radzinowicz note is what happens if you continue Milton's statement about the ant a little further still:

> Pattern of just equality perhaps
> Hereafter, *joined in her popular tribes*
> *Of commonaltie.*
>
> (7.484–89)

The "pattern of just equality" is glossed by two values, "popular" and "commonaltie," that were far more radical in their implications than the republican movement as a whole had been capable of encompassing; witness the suppression of the Levellers. Even as turned on the lever of "perhaps," this tiny emblem gathers truly revolutionary force. It is not what we expect from a defeated Milton, from a transcendent Milton, from a prescient rationalist pedagogue or even from a somewhat muddled leftist intellectual; for what it implies (and this is a vision that Milton was at times seduced and at times repelled by) is the transformation of the many-headed multitude into a large, literate, industrious, self-determining middle class.

## Unchang'd/ To Hoarse or Mute, Though Fall'n on Evil Days

In what sense could Milton claim to be "unchanged" in 1667 from the frantic republican who had written *The Readie and Easie Way*? Having struggled myself with the resistance of *Paradise Lost* to political solution, I have concluded that the poem allows us all, no matter which party we belong to, to match it with our own convictions. This does *not* mean that it has no convictions of its own. In fact, signs of intentionality usually overlooked appear in the preliminaries to the poem as published in 1674. Most important of these was Andrew Marvell's introductory poem, which suggested that Milton was a latter-day Samson braced to bring down the pillars of his society upon the heads of its leaders—an act, moreover, of revenge. This reverberates strangely with Coleridge's statement that "Milton avenged himself upon the world by enriching it with this record of his own transcendent ideal." In what sense could *Paradise*

*Lost* possibly be conceived as a revenge, Marvell's poem provokes us to ask, and what connects that metaphor of violence to Marvell's pioneering definition of Milton's style as "sublime," the cause simultaneously of "delight and horror?" Eliot's reference to this style as "a perpetual sequence of original acts of lawlessness" allows us to posit that style might, after all, *stand for* something other than itself.

After Marvell's poem, which concludes by relating the sublime to the choice of blank verse, there appeared a note on "The Verse," whose last lines (which would therefore have been the last words a reader encountered before embarking on the poem) were:

> This neglect then of Rime so little is to be taken for a defect, though it may seem so perhaps to vulgar Readers, that it rather is to be esteemed an example set, the first in English, of *ancient liberty* recover'd to Heroic Poem from the troublesome and modern bondage of Riming.

This not only set Milton apart from the Royalist poets of the Restoration, who had made rhyme their mark of modernity, with Dryden as the chief exemplar and polemicist. By way of the phrase "ancient liberty," it also placed *Paradise Lost* and its refusal to rhyme in a political vocabulary of opposition that had been available from at least the later sixteenth century, and that Holinshed's *Chronicles*, to cite a text that we know Milton read with care, wrote into his description of the British rebellion led by Boadicea against the Romans in A.D. 62! In his otherwise economical account of ancient Britain, Holinshed paused to permit Boadicea to deliver a long speech on the subject of "ancient liberty," a speech that he had troubled to unearth in Dion Cassius:

> We therefore that inhabit this Iland, . . . are now contemned and troden under foot, of them who studie nothinge else but how to become lords & have rule of other men. Wherefore my welbeloved citizens, friendes, and kinsfolkes (for I thinke we are all of kin, since we were borne and dwell in this Ile, and have one name common to us all) let us now, even now (I saie, because we have not doone it heretofore, and

> *whilest the remembrance or our ancient libertie remaineth)*
> sticke togither, and performe that thing which dooth perteine
> to valiant and hardie courages, to the end we maie injoie,
> not onelie the name of libertie, but also freedome it selfe,
> and thereby leave our force and valiant acts for an example
> to our posteritie.[19]

In Milton's preliminary statement on his medium, blank
verse, openended, is enlisted (like Galileo, to whom Milton
alludes three times in the poem) in the service of the Good
Old Cause.[20]

But if Milton's untameable periods were a form of resistance—the poet like Samson shaking his invincible locks—
so too, perhaps, was his ambiguity, the refusal of his poem
to issue in facile political allegorization. It is in his focus
on "perhaps" as the key to the code, then, that Christopher
Hill is most helpful, rather than in his own attempts to
decode the poem or even in his emphasis on the Restoration
censorship, necessary though that reminder must be. For in
offering his readers a *choice* of interpretations, arising out
of a welter of conflicting textual directions, Milton created
the literary equivalent of Arminianism, hermeneutical free
will. Given free will in interpretation, an educated
commonalty could theoretically find themselves increasingly
confident in self-determination; a training that should, in
the long run, predispose them to Whiggish principles.

But interpretive choice is not to be mistaken for complete
textual indeterminacy. And, in fact, just as Milton's
Arminianism assumes that the regenerate will take "within
them as a guide / My Umpire Conscience," so his poem
as a whole assumes that its republican readers "will . . . to
the end persisting, safe arrive," (3.194–96). After their initial
disillusionment at Satan's evident betrayal of the revolutionary ethos, it is the *second* half of the poem that carries the
political message. Clearly, Milton's early interest in the story
of the Fall was intensified by the role played by Adam in
the absolutist monarchy theories of Robert Filmer. Although
Filmer's *Patriarcha* was not published until 1680, his *Observations upon Aristotle's Politiques* had been in print since
1652, and was therefore available to Milton. The preface of

Filmer's *Observations* already contains the crucial statement that Milton, through *his* Adam, was to deny:

> The first government in the world was monarchical, in the father of all flesh. Adam . . . having dominion given him over all creatures, was thereby the monarch of the whole world; none of his posterity had any right to possess anything, but by his grant or permission . . . There was never any such thing as an independent multitude who at first had a natural right to a community."[21]

Without any indirection at all, Milton rejected this theory in his account of Nimrod, the first biblical monarch, in book 12 of *Paradise Lost*. He makes it clear that the metaphors of rule applied to Adam's relation to the animals and to Eve were not extensible to political theory. As Radzinowicz notes, Nimrod is presented as the first to claim sovereignty over other men, "not content with fair equality, fraternal state," but "from Heaven claiming second sovereignty." And Milton's Adam thereupon repeats the arguments of *The Readie and Easie Way* against the return of monarchy:

> O execrable son so to aspire
> Above his brethren, to himself assuming
> Authority usurped, from God not given:
> He gave us only over beast, fish, fowl,
> Dominion absolute; that right we hold
> By his donation; but man over men
> He made not Lord; such title to himself
> Reserving, human left from human free.
>
> (12.64–71)

There could hardly be a clearer dismissal of the doctrine of the divine right of kings, with Adam as its father figure.

## TO THE END PERSISTING

This brings me to the last phase of my argument: that the Good Old Cause continued to operate, throughout the later seventeenth century, as an ideologeme of sufficient power and capaciousness to unite those who, if they agreed on nothing else, agreed that the Restoration of the Stuarts was a disaster for one or both of Vane's two principles, civil liberties and religious toleration. The Cause united those, like the regicide Edmund Ludlow, who believed that Cromwell had betrayed the revolution, as well as those who, like Milton and Marvell, had committed themselves to the Protectorate. And, as is equally significant, the Good Old Cause continually surfaces, in its stigmatic or demonized form, in the writings of those who, conversely, committed themselves to Charles II and James II, of whom John Dryden is the most interesting example. Particularly between 1680 and 1684, there is constantly asserted in pro-Stuart propaganda the very case that I have been making, that there had been a continuous radical tradition whose continuity increased its danger.

In 1683, for example, Robert Ferguson's *Lamentation for the Destruction of the Association and the Good Old Cause* is actually a crudely ironized attack on Shaftesbury and his supporters, who are made to define their cause as follows: "Interest is our Aim, Rebellion is our Doctrine, Hipocracy is our Cloak, Murder our Intention, Religion we have none, and the Devil is our Master" (3). "For our further proceedings we have the Presidents of the Late uncivil Civil strife from Forty One to Forty Eight, and the same Path was, and is our present Rode" (9). And it is interesting to hear Ferguson suggest that the only way to put an end to the Good Old Cause as he has redefined it would be a massive, apocalyptic enforced emigration to America:

> Were New England Wall'd round with brass, after our Banishment thither, that no Gate, Part, or any Place of Retreat could be made from it, and the whole Land become like (Mount Aetna) a Consuming Flame, that we might pass at one Sacrifice. Then, Quiet, Peace, Union, and Continual Concord might Inhabit the Earth. But till that happens, it is no more in our Power, to Alter our Natures (though the Mercy of the King should forgive us) then to Create our selves Angels of Light (9–10).

It may be only by coincidence that New England is here

envisaged in the imaginative terms of Milton's Hell. But is it also a coincidence when Dryden begins in the 1680s to equate the Fall of Lucifer with the Exclusion Crisis? Dryden, we know, wanted to rewrite the poem in that "modern bondage" of rhyme, and indeed reproduced it as *The State of Innocence*, an opera (planned in 1667, written in 1674, published in 1677) with a significantly different title and different effect, one that, unsurprisingly, makes no mention of Nimrod.

When Dryden's All *for Love: Or, the World Well Lost* was published in 1681, it appeared with a dedication to the Earl of Danby, Charles II's chief minister, and thereby became an occasion to inveigh against republicanism, past and present. "Both my Nature, as I am an Englishman," wrote Dryden, "And my Reason, as I am a Man, have bred in me a loathing to that specious Name of a Republick: that mock-appearance of a Liberty, where all who have not part in the Government, are Slaves." Citing Satan as the source of all rebellion, and clearly thereby alluding to Shaftesbury, Dryden also looked back to those "who began the late Rebellion," and who, when Cromwell emerged as the mastermind, "enjoy'd not the fruit of their undertaking, but were crush'd themselves by the Usurpation of their own Instrument."[22] This allusion to Satan as the first rebel, though in one way entirely conventional (it was an opening premise of the Elizabethan *Homily on Disobedience* first published in 1571) was repeated in Dryden's dedication of *Plutarch's Lives* (1683) to the duke of Ormonde. There Dryden wrote of the ingratitude of Shaftesbury and such of his followers who were former Royalists, and who had been lavishly rewarded since the Restoration:

> The greater and the stronger ties which some of them have had, are the deeper brands of their Apostacy: For Arch-Angels were the first and most glorious of the whole Creation: They were the morning work of God; and had the first impressions of his Image, what Creatures cou'd be made: ... Their fall was therefore more opprobrious than that of Man, because they had no clay for their excuse; Though I hope and wish

the latter part of the Allegory may not hold, and that repentance may yet be allow'd them.[23]

My point is that Dryden was here engaged in a reading of *Paradise Lost* that not only endorsed the first and most obvious level of political allegory—the Fall of the Angels as the Puritan Revolution—but imposed a second level of allegory from subsequent political history—the Fall of the Angels as the Exclusion Crisis, with Shaftesbury in the place of Cromwell. The effect of this move was to enroll Milton posthumously in a cause that was the very opposite of that which, I believe, he would at that time have espoused.

In the preface to *Religio Laici* (1682), Dryden had extended the retroactive history of party back to the 1580s, referring to "Martin Mar-Prelate (the Marvel of those times)" as "the first Presbyterian Scribler, who sanctify'd Libels and Scurrility to the use of the Good Old Cause" (b1). He thereby created a conceptual loop from the Admonition Controversy of 1572 and its immediate consequence in the Marprelate pamphlets to the Andrew Marvell whom he knew (and despised) as the author of the *Rehearsal Transpros'd* of 1672.[24]

In 1672, when Marvell took up the cause of religious toleration against Samuel Parker[25] (for which Dryden equated him with the Marprelate writers), he made it clear that he was engaging in but another phase of an ongoing struggle. On the one hand, the Anglican clergy who were now arguing for strict state-enforced conformity were illegitimately invoking the specter of the 1640s to demonize the nonconformists:

> "You represent them, to a man, to be all of them of Republican Principles, most pestilent, and, *eo nomine*, enemies to Monarchy . . . onely the memory of the late War serves for demonstration, and the detestable sentence & execution, of his late Majesty is represented again upon the Scaffold . . . to prove that the late War was wholly upon a Fanatical Cause, and the dissenting party do still goe big with the same Monster." (125)

On the other hand, much of Marvell's case against Parker

consists in aligning him with the Anglican clergy of the 1620s and 1630s, Robert Sibthorpe and Roger Manwaring, whose published sermons asserted the doctrine of monarchical absolutism and the irrelevance of Parliament (127–33) and whose destructive advice, culminating in the policies of Laud, Marvell holds responsible for the civil war.

This strategy permitted him to speak tactfully about Charles II, whose Declaration of Indulgence could certainly have been interpreted as an improper use of the prerogative. But one does not have to work very hard to detect, between the lines of the *Rehearsal Transpros'd*, a clear message to the king: if he continues to repeat the mistakes his father made, history may repeat itself. Looking back to the 1640s, Marvell wrote:

> Whether it were a War of Religion, or of Liberty, is not worth the labour to enquire . . . . but upon considering all, I think the Cause was too good to have been fought for. Men ought to have trusted God; they and ought and might have trusted the King with the whole matter. The Arms of the Church are Prayers and Tears, the Arms of the Subject are Patience and Petitions . . . . For men may spare their pains where Nature is at work, and the world will not go the faster for our driving. Even as his present Majesties happy Restauration did it self, so all things else happen in their best and proper time, without any need of our officiousness.[26]

At the very least, this statement retains the integrity of the Cause while denying the militancy that supported it. But the suspicious reader is certainly permitted to imagine another phase of historical development to follow in its "best and proper time," a suspicion not diminished by finding in the next sentence a distinct warning: that "the fatal Consequences of that Rebellion . . . can only serve as Sea-marks unto wise Princes to avoid the Causes."[27] Two kinds of Cause are thereby united in Marvell's argument. The first is the Good Old Cause that he still undeniably supports, and to which he would dedicate his *Account of the Growth of Popery and Arbitrary Government*; the second, the arbitrary behavior of monarchs that caused the first revolution of the seventeenth century and that could, in "proper time," also result in the second.

In the second part of the *Rehearsal Transpros'd*, there appears an account of Milton during the Restoration, which we should treat with the same suspicion as Marvell's disingenuous manifesto on the Good Old Cause itself. His motive was to protect his friend Milton from the charge of collaborating on the first part of the *Rehearsal*. His strategy is to imply that Milton, in the experience of defeat, had given up writing: having by "misfortune" been "toss'd on the wrong side" in the civil war, and having written "*Flagrante bello* certain dangerous Treatises . . . At his Majesties happy Return, J.M. did partake . . . of his Regal Clemency and has ever since expiated himself in a retired silence";[28] this was a rather misleading description, we must surely feel, of the man who, five years before, had published *Paradise Lost*. For certain readers, it could only have been a reminder of the invocation to book 7 of that poem, where Milton himself declared that his voice was "unchang'd / To hoarse or mute." I believe that Marvell and Dryden were each, from opposite points of view, aware of what Milton was up to in *Paradise Lost*, and that while Marvell assumed a role of protective disingenuity, Dryden tried to appropriate and tame the poem whose subversive force was impossible to define and, therefore, impossible to combat or suppress.

## THE BOLD TUBE

What does it mean that Galileo, with whom we began, is still a presence in Milton's poem in 1667 and 1674, present in no less than three references, in the last of which Galileo is named. The first of these allusions is the best known: In book 1 (287 ff.) Milton compares Satan's shield to the

> Moon, whose Orb
> Through Optic Glass the Tuscan Artist views
> At Ev'ning . . . to descry new Lands,
> Rivers or Mountains in her spotty Globe.

In book 3 (588 ff.) Milton imagines Satan landing on the sun as

> a spot like which perhaps
> Astronomer in the Sun's lucent Orb
> Through his glaz'd Optic Tube yet never saw.

In book 5 (261 ff.) Milton compares Raphael's vision of Earth to the moment

> when by night the Glass
> Of Galileo, less assur'd, observes
> Imagin'd Lands and Regions in the Moon:
> Or Pilot from amidst the Cyclades,
> Delos or Samos first appearing kens
> A cloudy spot.

Evidently these allusions are meant to form a sequence, establishing the astronomer's paradigm as one inseparable from the poem's own development. They are linked by the idea of spots, which the new optics reveals in heavenly bodies formerly thought perfect. In Marvell's *Last Instructions to a Painter*, written in the same year as *Paradise Lost*, the metaphor is specifically applied to the work of skeptical political analysis, though within a conventional reformist or petitioning model.

> So his bold Tube, Man, to the Sun apply'd,
> And Spots unknown to the bright Star descry'd;
> .....................................
> Through Optick Trunk the Planet seem'd to hear,
> And hurls them off, e're since, in his Career.
> And you, Great Sir, that with him Empire share,
> Sun of our world, as he the Charles is there.
> Blame not the Muse that brought those spots to sight.[29]

In *Paradise Lost* itself, the role of Galileo is more profound, and more revolutionary. His association is not with the demonic, but with fallen vision, which, though "less assur'd" than angelic sight, is nevertheless capable of "admitting" (Raphael's word) motion and change into the system.

This brings me back to the here-and-now perspective with

which this essay began, a perspective from which we can survey the vast changes that have occurred in at least western political thought since Milton and Marvell tried to come to terms with the Restoration. Richard L. Greaves, in the first of a three-stage counterrevisionary study of that period, concludes his study of the radical underground with the following commonsense conclusions:

> Although the radicals failed to attain their aims, their legacy was nevertheless significant . . . At root, the radical cause did not die, although some of its more parochial or unenlightened goals . . . mercifully did. But in its broadest principles—government under law, freedom, and toleration— it ultimately triumphed. Viewed in this light, their experience of defeat was only temporary.[30]

The Good Old Cause, in other words, gave us the principles of modern democracy. What for Milton was "perhaps" and "hereafter" we now take for granted. Let us not take them so much for granted that we fail to observe what it means when—according to either literary historians or historians proper—those who fought for our Cause are said to have abandoned it, or not to have believed in it at all.

# Notes

## Notes to Introduction / Keller

1. See Arthur F. Kinney, "Imagination and Ideology in *Macbeth*" (in this volume, 148–73) for the remainder of the quotation.

2. See Walter Benjamin, *Theses on the Philosophy of History*, reprinted in Hazard Adams and Leroy Searle, eds. *Critical Theory Since 1965*, (Tallahassee: University Presses of Florida, 1986).

3. Victor Turner, *From Ritual to Theatre: The Human Seriousness of Play* (New York: Performing Arts Journal Publications, 1982), 10.

4. Fredric Jameson, "Religion and Ideology: a political reading of *Paradise Lost*," in *Literature, Politics and Theory*, ed. Francis Barker, Peter Hulme, Margaret Iversen, Diana Loxley (London & New York: Methuen, 1986), 46.

5. For a clear statement of this distinction in historicist criticism, see Jonathan Goldberg, "The Politics of Renaissance Literature" ELH 49 (1982), 514–42.

## Notes to Chapter 1 / Bristol

1. Christopher Marlowe, *The Jew of Malta*, ed. N. W. Bawcutt (Baltimore: Johns Hopkins U P, 1978), I. 2. 161–62.

2. I am indebted to my colleague, Dean Frye, for pointing this out to me.

3. I have discussed ideology at greater length in my article "Where Does Ideology Hang Out?" in Ivo Kamps, ed. *Shakespeare*

*Left and Right* (New York: Routledge, 1991), 31–45.

4. Hans Barth, *Truth and Ideology*, trans. Frederic Lilge (Berkeley: U of California P, 1976).

5. See, for example, David Norbrook, *Poetry and Politics in the English Renaissance* (London: Routledge, 1984); *Shakespeare Reproduced: The Text in History and Ideology*, ed. Jean E. Howard and Marion F. O'Connor (London: Methuen, 1987); *Shakespeare Left and Right*, ed. Ivo Kamps (New York: Routledge, 1991), Heather Dubrow and Richard Strier, eds. *The Historical Renaissance: New Essays on Tudor and Stuart Literature and Culture.* (Chicago: U of Chicago P, 1988).

6. Jonathan Goldberg, *James I and the Politics of Literature* (Baltimore: Johns Hopkins U P, 1983); Leonard Tennenhouse, *Power on Display: The Politics of Shakespeare's Genres* (London: Methuen, 1986); Leah Marcus, *Puzzling Shakespeare: Local Reading and its Discontents* (Berkeley: U of California P, 1988).

7. See, for example, Annabel Patterson, *Censorship and Interpretation: The Conditions of Writing and Reading in Early Modern England* (Madison: U of Wisconsin P, 1984); Steven Mullaney, *The Place of the Stage: License, Play, and Power in Renaissance England* (Chicago:U of Chicago P, 1987); Arthur Marotti, *John Donne: Coterie Poet* (Madison: U of Wisconsin P, 1986).

8. See, for example, Alan Sinfield, *Literature in Protestant England: 1560–1660.* (Beckenham: Croom Helm, 1983); Jonathan Dollimore, *Radical Tragedy: Religion, Ideology, and Power in the Drama of Shakespeare and His Contemporaries* (Chicago: U of Chicago P, 1984); Debora Kuller Shuger, *Habits of Thought in the English Renaissance,* (Berkeley: U of California P, 1990).

9. Pierre Bourdieu, *Reproduction: In Education, Society, and Culture*, tr. Richard Nice. (London: Sage, 1977); Raymond Geuss, *The Idea of A Critical Theory: Habermas and the Frankfurt School* (Cambridge: Cambridge U P, 1981); John B. Thomson, *Studies in the Theory of Ideology,* (Berkeley: U of California P, 1984).

10. One of the more helpful recent discussions of modernity for the purposes of this essay is Robert Pippin, *Modernism_as a Philosophical Problem: On the Dissatisfactions of European High Culture,* (Oxford: Basil Blackwell, 1991).

11. A basic source for Herbert's life is *The Autobiography of Edward, Lord Herbert of Cherbury*. ed. Sidney Lee (London: George Routledge, 1906). The autobiography ends with the events of 1624, but Lee provides a detailed account of the remainder of Herbert's life. See also Eugene D. Hill, *Edward, Lord Herbert of Cherbury* (Boston: Twayne, 1987); John Butler, *Lord Herbert of Cherbury: An Intellectual Biography* (Queenston, Ontario: Edwin Mellen, 1990).

12. Eugene D. Hill, *Edward, Lord Herbert of Cherbury*, 78.

13. Robert Ashton, *The English Civil War: Conservatism and Revolution 1603–1649* (New York: Norton, 1971); J. P. Kenyon, *The Stuart Constitution: Documents and Commentary* (Cambridge: Cambridge U P, 1986).

14. Bruce Galloway, *The Union of England and Scotland: 1603–1608.* (Edinburgh: John Donald, 1986).

15. Christopher Hill, *The Century of Revolution: 1603–1714* (New York: Norton, 1966); B. A. Holderness, *Pre-Industrial England: Economy and Society from 1500 to 1750* (London: J. M. Dent, 1976).

16. Michael Walzer, *The Revolution of the Saints: A study in the Origins of Radical Politics* (New York: Atheneum 1976); Lawrence Stone, *The Causes of the English Revolution* (New York: Harper Torchbooks, 1972).

17. Louis Althusser, "Ideology and Ideological State Apparatuses (Notes Towards an Investigation)" in *Lenin and Philosophy and Other Essays*, trans. Ben Brewster (New York: Monthly Review Press, 1972) 121–73. See also Diane MacDonnell, *Theories of Discourse: An Introduction* (Oxford: Basil Blackwell, 1986).

18. See, for example, the discussion of the "post nati" as this is reflected in Shakespeare's *Cymbeline*, in Marcus, *Puzzling Shakespeare* 110–60. See also Galloway, *The Union of England and Scotland* and Brian Levack, *The Formation of the British State: England, Scotland, and the Union, 1603–1707* (Oxford: Oxford U P, 1987).

19. Frank Whigham, *Ambition and Privilege* (Berkeley: Univ. of California Press, 1984).

20. Linda Levy Peck, *Court Patronage and Corruption in Early Stuart England* (Boston: Unwin Hyman, 1990), 163–84.

21. Malcolm Smuts, *Court Culture and the Origins of a Royalist Tradition in Early Stuart England* (Philadelphia: U of Pennsylvania P, 1987).

22. Butler, *Edward Lord Herbert of Cherbury*, 1–6.

23. *The Autobiography of Edward, Lord Herbert of Cherbury.* ed. Sidney Lee, 22. Further citations to this work will be given in the text.

24. Peck, 241, n. 121.

25. Christopher Hill, *Intellectual Origins of the English Revolution* (Oxford: Clarendon Press, 1965); Barbara Shapiro, *Probability and Certainty in Seventeenth Century England* 1983); R. D. Bedford, *The Defence of Truth: Herbert of Cherbury and the Seventeenth Century* (Manchester: Manchester U P, 1979).

26. Edward, Lord Herbert of Cherbury, *De Veritate.* Trans. Meyrick H. Carré (Bristol: U of Bristol P, 1937), 76.

27. *The Poems English and Latin of Edward,Lord Herbert of Cherbury*, ed. G. C. Moore Smith (Oxford: Clarendon, 1923).

28. Edward, Lord Herbert of Cherbury, *De Religione Laici.* ed. and translated with *A Critical Discussion of His Life and Philosophy* by Haold R. Hutcheson (New Haven: Yale U P, 1944).

29. Edward, Lord Herbert of Cherbury, *A Dialogue Between a Tutor and His Pupil*, ed. Günter Gawlick (Stuttgart: Friedrich Frommann, 1971); *Autobiography*, 23–43.

## Notes to Chapter 2 / Nowak

1. William Barlow, *The Sermon Preached at Paules Crosse, the Tenth Day of November, Being the Next Sunday After the Discouerie of this Late Horrible Treason* [STC 1455] (London, 1606). See Joel Hurstfield, "Gunpowder Plot and the Politics of Dissent," *Early Stuart Studies*, ed. Howard S. Reinmuth, Jr. (Minneapolis: U of Minnesota P, 1970) and Paul Durst, *Intended Treason* (London: W.H. Allen, 1970).   Hugh Ross Williamson, *The Gunpowder Plot* (New York: Macmillan, 1952).

2. Millar Maclure. *The Paul's Cross Sermons, 1534–1642.* (Toronto: U of Toronto P, 1958), 5.

3. Robert Lacy, *Robert, Earl of Essex* (New York: Atheneum, 1971), 168.

4. Quoted from "The true copy, in substance, of the late earle of Essex, his behauior, speach, and prayer, at the time of his execution" by Barlow and Thomas Montford (another devine who attended upon Essex in his final days), "annexed" to Mathew Law's 1601 edition of Barlow's sermon. (William Barlow, *A Sermon Preached at Paules Crosse, on the First Sunday in Lent: Martij.1. 1600. With a Short Discourse of the Late Earle* . . . [London, 1601]. STC 1454). This brief appendix is primarily concerned with the details of the earl's execution, especially his confession and prayers upon the scaffold.

5. Cecil's actual role in Essex's execution is unclear. There is evidence that he may have helped Essex's wife seek a pardon for the earl. What his motive for such an action might have been, true compassion or a fear of creating a martyr, is unclear. What is clear is that through the persuasion of Sir Walter Raleigh, Cecil began to push for the execution once again. Stories about Cecil intercepting the ring that would have saved Essex would seem to be apocryphal, stemming from a historical romance first published a half century after the earl's death (DNB  6:887).

6. Alan Feger Herr, *The Elizabethan Sermon: A Survey and a Bibliography* (Philadelphia: U of Pennsylvania P, 1940), 53.

7. The preacher at Paul's Cross on 15 February 1601 was John Hayward, Rector of St. Mary Woolchurch, who worked directly from instructions from Richard Bancroft, Bishop of London, and

Cecil. In a letter to Cecil, Bancroft wrote, "The auditory was great . . . and the applause for her Majesty's deliverance from the mischiefs intended exceedingly great, loud and joyous. The traitor is now laid out well in colours to every man's satisfaction that heard the sermon" (qtd. in Maclure, 82). The sermon at the Cross on the following Sunday was also on the character of Essex, and was again prepared with the help of instructions from Bancroft (having first been approved by Cecil). The identity of the preacher is not known, but the content of his sermon must have been more moderate than that of Hayward's, especially with the earl's execution only three days away (221).

8. While Barlow is obviously making this connection between Jesus and Elizabeth, he would appear to be stating it implicitly because of the sticky matter of the queen's gender. The Gunpowder sermons, on the other hand, explicitly treat the link between God and James. Some of these sermons, most notably John Donne's (1622), even use this as their primary conceit.

9. In his *Like Angels from a Cloud,* Horton Davies (San Marino: Huntington Library, 1986) reads this conceit as referring to the short amount of time Barlow had to prepare this sermon (155); taken in context, however, this mushroom is clearly meant to signify the public's "false" perception of the rebellion.

10. Though the possibility of taking the Tower was raised by Essex's supporters a week before the actual uprising, Essex himself was not present at this meeting, and the rest of the rebels decided against it because they simply lacked sufficient strength to take both the court and the Tower (Lacey 280).

11. As Maclure puts it, "One wonders if Shakespeare was there, and noticed that" (85). Interestingly enough, if one accepts the chronology of Shakespeare's plays offered by G. Blakemore Evans in *The Riverside Shakespeare* (Boston: Houghton, 1974) (47–56), *Macbeth, Antony and Cleopatra* and *Coriolanus*—three plays that have to deal with the relationship of the individual to the state— were written soon after 5 November 1605. This suggests the possibilities for a new historical study tracing the effects of the Gunpowder Plot on the works of Shakespeare, or perhaps even the influence of these plays on the Gunpowder sermons.

12. Such a comparison becomes even more relevant when we consider that several of Essex's friends commissioned the Lord Chamberlain's company to stage a special performance of Shakespeare's *Richard II* for 40s the night before the actual uprising (Lacey, 282).

13. John Chandos, ed., *In God's Name: Examples of Preaching in England. 1534–1662.* (London: Hutchinson, 1971), 123.

14. William Barlow, *The Summe and Substance of the*

*Conference . . . at Hampton Court.* Introduction by William T. Costello and Charles Keenan. (Gainesville: Scholar's Facsmilies and Reprints, 1965), vi–viii.

15. Hugh Trevor-Roper, "King James and His Bishops," *History Today* 5 (1955): 581.

16. John Gerard, *What was the Gunpowder Plot? The Traditional Story Tested by Original Evidence.* (London, 1896), 129.

17. "A Discourse of the Maner of the Discouery of this Late Intended Treason." *Annexed to His Maiesties Speech in this Last Session of Parliament . . .* by King James I. STC 14392 (London, 1605), G4–G4v.

18. Hugh Ross Williamson, *The Gunpowder Plot* (New York: Macmillan, 1952) and Durst (see n. 1) have made the most detailed arguments for this conspiracy theory, but perhaps the most famous and influential one is that of the Jesuit John Gerard (n. 16).

19. Margaret Hotine, "Treason in The Winter's Tale," *Notes and Queries,* 30 (1983): 130.

20. Alan Haynes, *Robert Cecil, 1st Earl of Salisbury* (London: Peter Owen, 1989), 156. The connection between Catiline and the conspirators was actually first made by Henry Howard, Earl of Northampton and Lord Privy Seal, at the trial of Father Henry Garnet. See *A True and Perfect Relation of the Whole Proceedings against the Late Most Barbarous Traitors, Garnet a Iesuite, and His Confederates* [STC 11619] (London: 1606).

21. In "The English Catholic Community 1603–1625," *The Reign of James VI and I,* ed. Alan G.R. Smith (New York: St. Martin's P, 1973), John Bossy states, "I do not think that it was all got up by the Government, or that the conspirators were *agents provacateurs,* let loose by Robert Cecil on the Catholic community and the Jesuits to provide an excuse for delivering them a knock-out blow; no such blow followed" (95).

22. Of course, this Anglocentrism was not the only factor that brought about this renewal of anti-Catholic rhetoric in the Gunpowder sermons. A second factor puts more weight on just one man. In his excellent biography *King James VI and I* (London: Jonathan Cape, 1956), David Harris Wilson notes that James's first reaction to the thwarting of the Gunpowder Plot was one of pride and arrogance, for it gave proof to the world that he was divinely appointed by God to rule over Britain. This vanity quickly gave way to fear, however, once James came to realize that the entire scheme was primarily an attempt to kill him. According to Wilson, James's fear of assassination became so deep and profound that it altered his personality, causing him to become subdued and withdrawn. No longer did he eat in public; instead, he ate alone, confining himself to his innermost chambers, and accompanied only by his most loyal Scotsmen (227). The direct result of all

of this was his issuance of the Oath of Allegiance, which was designed to separate the loyal English Catholics from the disloyal ones. This oath, in turn, gave birth to the great paper war between England and the papacy, which was fought by such noteworthy generals as Lancelot Andrewes and Cardinal Bellarmine. The anti-Catholic rhetoric of this war filtered its way down through every level of society via the sermon, the most influential form of literature in the seventeenth century. As a result of this, Bellarmine quickly came to replace Guy Fawkes as the true enemy of God's chosen church.

## Notes to Chapter 3 / Tumbleson

1. William Wordsworth, *The Prelude,* 1805 version, 8:746–49, in *The Prelude 1799, 1805, 1850,* eds. Jonathan Wordworth, M. H. Abrams, and Stephen Gill (New York: Norton, 1979), 306.

2. Sheila Williams, "The Lord Mayor's Show in Tudor and Stuart Times," in *The Guildhall* Miscellany, 1 (1959), 4.

3. Margot Heinemann, *Puritanism and Theatre: Thomas Middleton and Opposition Drama under the Early Stuarts* (Cambridge: Cambridge UP, 1980), 4.

4. Theodore B. Leinwood's "London Triumphing: The Jacobean Lord Mayor's Show," in *Clio* 11 (1982): 137–53 supplies a useful historical bibliography and summary of the early history of the Lord Mayor's Day fetes.

5. Thomas Middleton, *The Trimphs of Truth,* in *The Works of Thomas Middleton,* ed. A. H. Bullen (Boston: Houghton, 1886), 7:233. All further references to Middleton's Lord Mayor's Day pageants are made in the text.

6. David Bergeron, "Middleton's *No Wit, No Help* and Civic Pageantry," in *Pageantry in the Shakespearean Theater,* ed. David Bergeron (Athens: U Georgia P, 1985), 165–80. For the symbolic function of masques, see Stephen Orgel's *The Illusion of Power* (Berkeley: U of California P, 1975).

7. Stephen Greenblatt, *Shakespearian Negotiations* (Berkeley: U of California P, 1988), 22, 136. See particularly the second and fifth chapters, "Invisible Bullets" and "Martial Law in the Land of Cockayne."

8. Franco Moretti, *Signs Taken for Wonders* (London: Verso, 1988), 42; and Jonathan Dollimore, *Radical Tragedy* (Chicago: U of Chicago P, 1984), 27. The issue of whether or not Middleton wrote *The Revenger's Tragedy* is a question of textual speculation that this paper will not and need not address.

9. Albert H. Tricomi, *Anticourt Drama in England 1603–1642* (Charlottesville: UP of Virginia, 1989), 152.

10. P. W. Thomas, "Two Cultures? Court and Country under Charles 1," in *The Origins of the English Civil War*, ed. C. Russell (New York Barnes and Noble, 1973), 184, qtd. in Christopher Hill, *Milton and the English Revolution* (London: Faber, 1977), 21.

11. Margot Heinemann, in *Puritanism and Theatre: Thomas Middleton and Opposition Drama under the Early Stuarts* (Cambridge: Cambridge UP, 1980), remarks, "There was an exceptional degree of social mobility, and contemporaries were very conscious of this shifting and changing—above all in London, the melting-pot for the whole kingdom" (3). In the *Huntington Library Quarterly* 47 (1984): 273–88, Thomas Cogswell attacks Heinemann's use of the idea of a unitary "Parliamentary Puritan opposition." Such revisionist historical analyses as Conrad Russell's *Parliaments and English Politics 1621–1629* (Oxford: Clarendon, 1979) have questioned the idea of an easy dichotomy between court and country, government and opposition, as at once "institutionally impossible" and "ideologically impossible" (9), because a member of Parliament needed both court and country support to get elected (6), and because a heterogeneous court was able to supply a patron for virtually any MP (10). As to the strength of the city, Macaulay records that when Elizabeth I and her council heard of the coming of the Spanish armada in 1588, the first person they sent for to request help was the Lord Mayor of London. The mayor and Common Council asked for 15 ships and 5,000 men, promised 30 ships and 10,000 men; Macaulay comments that those capable of giving such proofs of loyalty were not to be oppressed with impunity (Thomas Babington Macaulay, "Burleigh and his *Times*," *Critical and Historical Essays* [Boston: Houghton, 1900] 3:77–78). London possessed a pool of concentrated wealth, skills and labor found nowhere else in the three kingdoms.

12. Susan Wells, "Jacobean City Comedy and the Ideology of the City," in *ELH* 48 (1981): 37.

13. Cited in Heinemann, 171.

14. Frank C. Brown, *Elkanah Settle: His Lives and Works* (Chicago: U of Chicago P, 1910), the only book written about Settle, notes that Settle's *The Character of a Popish Successour* provoked more replies than any other work of the Exclusion Crisis except Titus Oates's *Narrative* and was regarded by Whigs as "unanswerable" (73), and that *The Female Prelate* "was perhaps referred to more often in dedication, prologue, and epilogue, than any other dramatic work produced between 1680 and 1700" (21).

15. See Annabel Patterson, *Censorship and Interpretation: The Conditions of Writing and Reading in Early Modern England* (Madison: U of Wisconsin P, 1984).

16. A footnote in the Bullen edition says "Old eds. 'must,'"

and the emendation to "most" obscures the obligation "must" reveals. The poor and dependent may not love the wealthy and powerful "most," but they "must" at least make a show of doing so. To make such an observation is not to claim that the modern sense of "must" need be the primary meaning here, although such could be argued, but that the original spelling allows a doubleness of denotation common in the variable orthography of the period that modernization of the text can erase.

17. Michael D. Bristol, in *Carnival and Theater: Plebeian Culture and the Structure of Authority in Renaissance England* (New York: Methuen, 1985), argues that "Plebeian culture . . . takes particular note of the arbitrary, ramshackle nature of authority and political power . . . . The grotesque physically oriented laughter of common people objectifies a preideological, implicit political doctrine. As Bakhtin describes it, that doctrine is 'the defeat of power, of earthly kings, of the earthly upper classes, of all that oppresses and restricts'" (138–39).

18. Oliver Goldsmith, "The Traveller," lines 387–88, in *Collected Works of Oliver Goldsmith*, ed. Arthur Friedman (Oxford: Clarendon P, 1966), 4:266.

19. Greenblatt, 29–30.

20. Hakluyt, 10:56, cited in Greenblatt, 29.

21. See Bristol, 21–22, for a discussion of univocal, multivocal and hybrid literary forms. Middleton's pageants are in form multivocal but in effect univocal: all roads lead to the Lord Mayor of London.

22. See Edward Said, *The World, the Text, and the Critic* (Cambridge, MA: Harvard UP, 1983), 53, for an examination of the textuality of the text as an instrument of domination.

23. A footnote in the *Diary* of Samuel Pepys, when soon after the Restoration he complains of "earthen pitchers and wooden dishes" at a Lord Mayor's Day feast, observes that "A great deal of city plate had been melted down during the Civil War" (Robert Latham and Mattle, eds., *The Diary of Samuel Pepys*, [Berkeley: U of California P, 1970–76], vol. 1 4:355. Some of the show of power had been expended in securing more of its substance.

24. It was of these works that Alexander Pope wrote (in *The Dunciad*, in *Pope: Poetical Works*, ed. Herbert Davis [London: Oxford, 1966], 477–78) that:

"Twas on the day, when **rich and grave,
Like Cimon, triumph'd both on land and wave:
(Pomps without guilt, of bloodless swords and maces,
Glad chains, warm furs, broad banners, and broad faces)
Now Night descending, the proud scene was o'er,
But liv'd, in Settle's numbers, one day more.

Settle appears in both *The Dunciad* and Dryden's *Absalom and Achitophel* as a result of his political and cultural identification with London.

25. Elkanah Settle, *Glory's Resurrection: Being the Triumphs of London Revived* (London, 1698), n.p. Further references to this work are made in the text.

26. See Nicholas Jose's *Ideas of the Restoration in English Literature* (Cambridge: Harvard UP, 1984) for a detailed discussion of such panegyrics.

27. Elkanah Settle, *The Triumphs of London* (London, 1701), 6.

## Notes to Chapter 4 / Campbell

1. See Jonathan Goldberg, *James I and the Politics of Literature* (Baltimore: Johns Hopkins U P, 1983); Jonathan Dollimore, *Radical Tragedy: Religion, Ideology, and Power in the Drama of Shakespeare and his Contemporaries* (Chicago: U of Chicago P, 1984). On the triumphal entry as an expression of monarchical power, see also Sidney Anglo, *Spectacle, Pageantry and Early Tudor Policy* (Oxford: Clarendon P, 1969); David M. Bergeron, *English Civic Pageantry, 1558–1642,* (London: Edward Arnold, 1971), and Roy Strong, *Art and Power: Renaissance Festivals 1450–1650* (Los Angeles: U of California P, 1984), 44 ff. On the masque as it reflects and authorizes the Jacobean power structure, see D. J. Gordon, "*Hymenae*: Jonson's Masque of Union," *Journal of the Warburg and Courtauld Institute* 8 (1945): 107–45; Stephen Orgel, *The Illusion of Power: Political Theater in the English Renaissance* (Berkeley: U of California P, 1975) and Joanne Altieri, *The Theater of Praise: The Panegyric Tradition in Seventeenth-Century English Drama* (Newark: U of Delaware P, 1986).

2. See Katherine Usher Henderson and Barbara F. McManus, *Half Humankind: Contexts and Texts of the Controversy about Women in England, 1540–1640* (Urbana: U of Illinois P, 1985). The proliferation of Protestant treatises on marriage during the late sixteenth and early seventeenth centuries attests to the enhanced status of wedlock as a divinely ordained condition, superseding the Catholic ideal of celibacy. Most of these were religious and philosophical texts written for men, but several contained a section addressed to the woman, enjoining her to humility and obedience. Also, in the controversy about women in the late sixteenth and early seventeenth centuries, women were widely characterized as having rapacious sexual appetites. See Suzanne W. Hull, *Chaste, Silent & Obedient: English Books for Women 1475–1640* (San Marino: Huntington, 1982), 47–56 and

110–22; Henderson and McManus, 47–97 and 133 ff.; R. Valerie Lucas, "Puritan Preaching and the Politics of the Family" in *The Renaissance Englishwoman in Print: Counterbalancing the Canon*, ed. Anne M. Haselkorn and Betty S. Travitsky (Amherst: U of Massachusetts P, 1990), 224–40; Margaret L. King, *Women of the Renaissance* (Chicago: U of Chicago P, 1991), chapters 1 and 3. For useful discussions of the representation of women in the drama, see Lisa Jardine, *Still Harping on Daughters: Women and Drama in the Age of Shakespeare* (New York: Columbia UP, 1989) and Karen Newman, *Fashioning Femininity and English Renaissance Drama* (Chicago: U of Chicago P, 1991).

3. References are to the New Arden edition of *The Tempest*, ed. Frank Kermode (London: Methuen, 1964).

4. Detailed descriptions of the characteristics of witches can be found in Heinrich Kramer and Jacob Sprenger, *Malleus Maleficarum*, trans. Montague Summers (1928; New York: Dover, 1971), 1–81. For an excellent discussion of witchcraft in the sixteenth and seventeenth century political context, see Stuart Clark, "Inversion, Misrule and the Meaning of Witchcraft," *Past and Present* 87 (1980): 98–127.

5. This point has been noted in a different context by Stephen Orgel, ed. *The Oxford Shakespeare: The Tempest* (Oxford: Oxford UP, 1987), 55–56.

## Notes to Chapter 5 / Rutledge

1. John Nichols, *The Progresses of James I* (London: The Society of Antiquaries, 1823), 1:370–72.

2. See Douglas F. Rutledge, "The Structural Parallel Between Rituals of Reversal, Jacobean Political Theory and *Measure for Measure*," *Iowa State Journal of Research* 62 (1988), 421–22.

3. Charles Howard McIlwain, ed. *The Political Works of James I*. Cambridge: Harvard U P, 1918.

4. Current anthropologists, such as Boon and Clifford, present more useful methodologies: James A. Boon, *Affinities and Extremes* (Chicago: U of Chicago P, 1990) and James Clifford and George E. Marcus, eds., *Writing Culture* (Berkeley: U of California P, 1986). However, Turner and Van Gennep offer a model for examining one of the signs Renaissance England consistently uses in the ceremonial language of change, that of inversion, chaos and misrule: Victor Turner, *The Ritual Process* (Ithaca: Cornell U P, 1977) and (author: supply info. on Van Gennep here)

5. Victor Turner, *The Ritual Process: Structure and Anti-Structure* (Ithaca: Cornell U P, 1977), 168.

6. Mircea Eliade, *Myths, Dreams and Mysteries*, trans. Philip Mariet (New York: Harper and Row, 1975), 80–81 and *Patterns in Comparative Religion*, trans. Rosemary Sheed (New York: New American Library, 1974), 404–06.

7. Mikhail Bakhtin, *Rabelais and His World*, trans. Helene Iswolsky (Bloomington: Indiana U P, 1984), 92.

8. Natalie Zemon Davis, "The Reasons of Misrule: Youth Groups and Chivaris in Sixteenth Century France," *Past and Present* 50 (1971), 50–55.

9. Victor Turner, *From Ritual to Theater* (New York: Performing Arts Journal Publications, 1982), 177–78.

10. The difference between ritual, festival and theater is early modern England is a difficult one to establish clearly, perhaps because the distinction is more modern than Renaissance. See Boon and Turner; Louis Montrose, "The Purpose of Playing: Reflections on a Shakespearean Anthropology," *Helios*, n.s. 8 (1980): 51–94; and especially Michael D. Bristol, *Carnival and Theatre* (New York: Methuen, 1985), 111–12. I emphasize the similarity of certain plays to rituals of transition, as opposed to Carnival, because those plays all appeared around the time James took the throne. I think it very likely that within the historical context these plays would have been taken as referring to rituals of transition into high office. In that case, the exchange between high and low and the release from social structure would have seemed more like the liminal aspects of rituals of transition into high office than the larger holiday, marketplace tension between Carnival and Lent that Bristol masterfully articulates.

11. Leonard Tennenhouse, *Power on Display* (New York: Methuen, 1986), 156.

12. For a related argument against Tennenhouse's claim that these plays can only reinforce the *status quo*, see Anthony B. Dawson, "*Measure fore Measure*, New Historicism and Theatrical Power," *Shakespeare Quarterly* 39 (1988), 328–41.

13. Rutledge, "*Respublica*: Rituals of Status Elevation and the Political Mythology of Mary Tudor," *Medieval and Renaissance Drama in England*, 5 (1990), 59.

14. Philip J. Finkelpearl, *John Marston and the Middle Temple* (Cambridge: Harvard U P, 1969), 3–70; 173–238.

15. For *The Phoenix* as royal entertainment, see Marilyn L. Williamson, "*The Phoenix*: Middleton's Comedy *de Regimine Principum*," *Renaissance News* 10 (1957), 182–87. See also N. W. Bawcutt, "Middleton's *The Phoenix* as a Royal Play, Notes and Queries, 201 (1956), 287–88.

16. Nichols I: Thomas Brodruie: "one Phoenix dead-another doth survive" (8); Thomas Cecil: "Or where as Phoenix dies; Phoenix is dead, /And so a Phoenix for Phoenix. . . " (16); Richard

Martin: Out of the ashes of the Phoenix wert thou, King James, borne for our good . . ." (129); Thomas Dekker: Thou being the sacred Phoenix that doest rise / From the sacred ashes of the first" (357); Ben Jonson (434). Also see Bawcutt, 287.

17. Thomas Middleton, *The Phoenix*, ed. John Bradbury Brooks (New York: Garland, 1980), 1.1.38–50.

18. Note the similarity between Falso's relationship to his niece and the notorious Court of Wards. According to feudal law, if the parent of a child died before the child became of age, he or she became a ward of the king, and as Stone explains, this became almost tantamount to slavery, as various peers could purchase and resell the wardship, while maintaining complete control of the ward's conjugal future. Moreover, Lawrence Stone points out that "the notorious abuses of the system were coming under increasing criticism at the end of the sixteenth and the beginning of the seventeenth centuries" (*The Crisis of the Aristocracy*, 1558–1641 (Oxford: Oxford U P, 1979), 603.

19. On the inflation of knighthoods and loss of honor by the Jacobean Court, see Stone, 77.

20. Peter Burke, *Popular Culture in Early Modern Europe* (New York: Harper and Row, 1978), 203.

21. Margot Heinemann, *Puritanism and the Theatre* (Cambridge: Cambridge U P, 1980), 86–87.

22. John Neville Figgis, *The Divine Right of Kings* (Cambridge: Cambridge U P, 1922), 86–87.

23. In the *Trew Law* James calls on "the old definition of a King, and of a law; which makes the king to bee a speaking law, and the lawe to be a dumbe king" (McIlwain, 63).

24. Alan C. Dessen, "Middleton's *The Phoenix* and the Allegorical Tradition," *SEL* 6 (1966), 303–05; here Dessen suggests that the success of the Phoenix as doctor and ideal ruler who cures the moral disease of society offers "an extended dramatic compliment to the new King . . . ." Dessen's examination of the disease imagery is excellent, but I want to see the possible compliment to James I as more problematic.

25. E. K. Chambers, *The Elizabethan Stage* (Oxford: Oxford U P, 1923), 1:302; 349–50.

26. John Marston, *The Malcontent*, ed. M. L. Wine (Lincoln: U of Nebraska P, 1964), 5.4.53–65.

27. See David Harris Willson, *King James VI and I* (New York: Oxford U P, 1967), 168–71 and Stone, 478.

28. Robert Eccleshall, *Order and Reason in Politics* (Oxford: Oxford U P, 1978), explains that late sixteenth and early seventeenth century theories of limited monarchy did not advocate representative democracy, but they did demystify political activity and suggested that "safegaurds to the common good were to

be discovered in cooperate wisdom, the mobilization of the members of the community by means of political institutions" (32–33). Also see Allen, 147–48.

29. Also see McIlwain, "Introduction to *The Political Works of James I*," xviii: "Calvin had declared that earthly princes who fought against God abdicated their power. . . and the extreme English Calvinists were inclined to look upon the retention of Romish forms and the assumption of the king's headship of the Church, alike, as little short of fighting against God."

30. Bishop John Overall, *The Convocation Book of 1606* (Oxford: John Henry Parker, 1844), 8.

31. Here Finkelpearl associates Marston's *The Fawn* with the seasonal rituals of inversion that took place every Christmas at the Inns of Court. See Joel Kaplan, "John Marston's *Fawn*: A Saturnalian Satire, *SEL* 9 (1969), 335–50.

32. Marston, *The Fawn*, ed. Gerald Smith (Lincoln: U of Nebraska P, 1965), Prologus, 9.

33. Steven Mullaney suggests that in the language of the city, the place of the stage itself argued for the fool's kind of ritual license: *The Place of the Stage* ( Chicago: U of Chicago P, 1988), 1–60.

34. See Richard Marienstras, *New Perspectives on the Shakespearean World*, trans. Janet Loyd (Cambridge: Cambridge U P, 1985), especially chapter 1, where he compares the king's absolute prerogative to wildness.

35. Finkelpearl, 222–27; see also Andrew W. Upton, "Allusions to James I and His Court in Marston's *Fawn* and Beaumont's *Woman Hater*, *PMLA* 44 (1929), 1048–065.

36. Lord Chancellor Ellesmere, "Tract on the Royal Prerogative," *Law and Politics in Jacobean England, the Tracts of Lord Chancellor Ellesmere*, ed. Louis A Knalfa. Cambridge: Cambridge U P, 1977), 200.

37. Mullaney explains that ambiguity itself can be treasonous (120).

38. Burke speaks of Renaissance carnival and rituals of inversion as both reinforcing or undermining the *status quo*: "There might be a 'switching' of codes, from the language of ritual to the language of rebellion. To move from the point of view of the authorities to that, more elusive, of ordinary people, it may well have been that some of those excluded from power saw Carnival as an opportunity to make their views known and so to bring about change" (204). Could structured inversion within the theater work the same way?

39. See Sir Philip Sidney, "An Apology for Poetry," *Elizabethan Critical Essays*, ed. Gregory Smith (London: Oxford U P, 1964), 1: 176–77 and Leah Marcus, *The Politics of Mirth* (Chicago: U of Chicago P, 1986), 26–27.

*Notes to Chapter 6 / Martin*

1. Robert Harcourt, *A Relation of a Voyage to Guiana* (London, 1613); see L.C. Knights' treatment of this and related episodes in *Drama and Society in the Age of Jonson* (London: Chatto, 1937), 54–55 ff.

2. The most notable exception to this tendency is Don Wayne's important critique of Knights, "Drama and Society in the Age of Jonson," *Renaissance Drama* 13 (1982): 103–29. Unfortunately, Wayne does not extend his revisionary remarks into the domain of historicist criticism as a whole, nor does he analyze either of the plays discussed here.

3. In describing the "incipient ideology" of this class, I follow the distinctions set forth by C. B. Macpherson, *The Political Theory of Possessive Individualism: Hobbes to Locke* (Oxford: Oxford UP, 1962). A useful summary of the evidence for the socioeconomic transition occurring in this period can be found in David Little's notes on "The Question of Economic Regulation in Pre-Revolutionary England," *Religion, Order, and Law: A Study in Pre-Revolutionary England* (New York: Harper & Row, 1969), 238–46.

4. Walter Cohen, "*The Merchant of Venice* and the Possibilities of Historical Criticism," *ELH* 49 (1982): 765–89. This admission is actually an understatement on Cohen's part, considering the massive evidence against his position. As most historians agree, the political, economic and ideological climate of England was markedly different from that of the Continent, particularly from the neofeudal states of central and southern Europe. Specifically, the monarchy's power in industrial regulation decreased in England after 1589 while it increased in France, thus lending support to the doctrine "that progress depends upon allowing free scope for individual initiative." John U. Nef, *Cultural Foundations of Industrial Civilization* Cambridge: Cambridge UP, 1958), 157.

5. See Jean-Christophe Agnew, *Worlds Apart: The Market and the Theatre in Anglo-American Thought, 1550–1750* (Cambridge: Cambridge UP, 1986), 126.

6. See Albert O. Hirschman, *The Passions and the Interests: Political Arguments for Capitalism before Its Triumph* (Princeton: Princeton UP, 1977), 102.

7. Thus according to J. H. Hexter in "The Myth of the Middle Class in Tudor England," *Reappraisals in History* (Evanston: Northwestern UP, 1963), an unambiguous, self-conscious middle class simply does not exist in sixteenth and seventeenth century England.

8. The observation is John W. Draper's in "Usury in 'The

Merchant of Venice,'" *Modern Philology* 33 (1945): 43.

9. See Stephen Greenblatt, *Renaissance Self-Fashioning: From More to Shakespeare* (Chicago: U of Chicago P, 1980) and "Improvisation and Power," *Literature and Society*, ed. Edward W. Said (Baltimore: Johns Hopkins UP, 1980), 57–99.

10. Regardless of how much initial connivance there is, both Cohen (772) and Marc Shell regard the outcome of this "tripartite unity" (Cohen's phrase) as blatantly commercial in design. See Shell's "The Wether and the Ewe: Verbal Usury in *The Merchant of Venice, "Kenyon Review* n.s. 1 (1979): 65–92.

11. Both Face and Portia are clearly actors, costumers and set designers, characters whose success depends upon negotiating rapid changes of mood and scene, and whose very names are associated with portals or doorways, liminal or boundary areas subject to reversal and change. Further, as Agnew points out, "Embedded within the idiomatic analogy between legal and social forms of identity [both of which can be regarded as 'copies'] was a new and somewhat sinister implication that the human face, like the 'skin of parchment,' was an autonomous, even alien, instrument of misrepresentation" (58).

12. However, according to Christopher Hill, in *Puritanism and Revolution: Studies in Interpretation of the English Revolution of the 17th Century.* (New York: Schoken, 1958), the shift in attitudes toward both money making and money lending can be traced to Calvin (129).

13. For a thorough examination of the multiple punning and rhyming implications contained in the literal words of this song, see Harry Berger, Jr., "Marriage and Mercifixion in *The Merchant of Venice*: The Casket Scene Revisited," *Shakespeare Quarterly* 32.2 (1981): 155–62.

14. Of course, this use of money "to beget" itself constitutes the heart of the traditional objection to usury; see, for instance, Thomas Lodge, *An Alarum Against Usurers, The Complete Works of Thomas Lodge*, vol. 1. (New York: Johnson Reprint Corp. 1966). However, as I suggest below, during this period the metaphorical basis of the objection is undergoing a subtle conversion that will twist its original distinctions to serve new purposes.

15. Knights (85) quotes Sir Simonds D'Ewes to the effect that certain of the government monopolies "furnish interesting illustrations to anyone who believes in the unfitness of government to administer industrial undertakings." *The Autobiography and Correspondence of Sir Simonds D'Ewes*, ed. James Orchard Halliwell (London: R. Bentley, 1845) 1: 171.

16. Knights quotes W. H. Price, *The English Patents of Monopoly* (Boston: Houghton, 1906), 82, 85.

17. W. R. Scott, *The Constitution and Finance of English, Scottish and Irish Joint-Stock Companies to 1720* (Cambridge: Cambridge UP, 1910) 1: 177.

18. The obvious parallel to this play on words occurs in *Hamlet,* where the prince subverts Claudius's greeting of him as both cousin and son by exclaiming, "A little more than kin and less than kind!" (1.2.65). As here, Shakespeare tends to use multilevel puns to question moral claims based upon "natural" law.

19. See Knights, 71–95, but especially his quotation from Hermann Levy, *Monopolies, Cartels and Trusts in British Industry* (New York: A.M. Kelley, 1968), 86.

20. Lodge, *An Alarum Against Usurers,* in *The Complete Works of Thomas Lodge* I: sig. B3, commented on by Agnew, 121.

21. Hence this form of exchange stands in marked contrast to the medieval one, which Agnew describes as "best understood in the restrictive, precautionary sense of a hoard or asset saved to settle, clear, or `liquidate' actual or potential liabilities" (44). Liquidity thus exists primarily to liquidate itself. Although he also points out that the medieval concept of liquidity is similarly opposed to the idea of money "begetting" itself, a major accomplishment of both comedies is in simultaneously accepting but also *altering* the basis upon which "natural" can be distinguished from "unnatural" begetting.

22. Cohen, quoting *The Death of Vsury, or the Disgrace of Vsurers* (London, 1594) Elr., 768.

23. Here Cohen's observation that much of the utopian dimension of the play, however contradictory, is paradoxically "right on the surface" of its dynamics, seems particularly relevant; see 775–76.

24. I am here appropriating Agnew's terminology; for a fuller discussion of the relationship of carnival to theater and market, and for its conversion from immanent to imminent, see 33–40 ff.

25. In this sense, verbal ability itself becomes a metaphor for the kind of "rational calculation" which, according to Hirschman is implicit in the revaluation of the concept of interest, and by extension, profit of itself. See Hirschman, 39–40.

26. In "Feudal and Bourgeois Concepts of Value in *The Merchant of Venice," Shakespeare: Contemporary Critical Approaches,* ed. Harry R. Garvin (Lewisburg: Bucknell UP, 1980), 91–105, Burton Hatlen also finds that the play contributes to the process whereby value was seen "as an ascribed rather than inherent quality"(93) and also points to the philosophical ramifications of this process in Hobbes (94). However, Hatlen rather uncritically associates Belmont with the *objective* concept of value, even though he does not find this ideology triumphant in act 5.

27. Shell is particularly observant about the implications of

these passages and its relation to Shylock's "interest," although he finds the results far more problematic; see 88–92.

28. This assessment, of course, remains essentially problematic on several counts. The most obvious of these is that the Puritan extremists whom Jonson most savagely satirizes as hoarders are also those whom Max Weber would associate with the Protestant ethic and the spirit of capitalism. See *The Protestant Ethic and the Spirit of Capitalism*, trans. Talcott Parsons (New York: Scribner's, 1958). However, Weber's thesis about the Protestant ethic is an overgeneralization that does not apply to every strand of even bourgeois Protestantism. In fact, several competing bourgeois ideologies are clearly evident during this period.

29. Thomas Cartwright, *The Second Reply against M. Doctor Whitgift's Second Answer touching the Church Discipline* (Zurich, 1575), quoted in Little 90.

30. This contract is even more explicit in the introduction to *Bartholomew Fair*.

31. I wish to thank Harry Berger, Jr., for his advice in drafting the final version of this essay, and for his early and late stimulation of my explorations of the politics of exchange.

## Notes to Chapter 7 / Kinney

1. Phyllis Rackin, *Stages of History: Shakespeare's English Chronicles* (Ithaca: Cornell UP, 1990), 2.

2. Robert N. Watson, "Tragedy," *The Cambridge Companion to English Renaissance Drama* ed. A. R. Braunmuller and Michael Hattaway (Cambridge: Cambridge UP, 1990), 301.

3. My text here and throughout this essay is the New Arden Edition of *Macbeth* edited by Kenneth Muir (London: Methuen, 1983).

4. Michael Goldman, *Acting and Action in Shakespearean Tragedy* (Princeton: Princeton UP, 1985), 101.

5. James L. Calderwood, *"If It Were Done": "Macbeth" and Tragic Action* (Amherst: U of Massachusetts P, 1986), 9.

6. Robert Hapgood, *Shakespeare The Theatre-Poet* (Oxford: Clarendon, 1988), 45.

7. David Norbrook, *"Macbeth* and the Politics of Historiography" in *Politics of Discourse: The Literature and History of Seventeenth-Century England,* ed. Kevin Sharpe and Steven N. Zwicker (Berkeley: U of California P, 1987), 101.

8. Peter Berresford Ellis, *Macbeth: High King of Scotland 1040–57* (Belfast: Blackstaff P, 1990), 43.

9. My text for Holinshed's *Chronicles* (for which Francis Thynne wrote the section on Scotland following Hector Boece and John

Bellernden) is that edited by W. G. Boswell-Stone (New York: Benjamin Blom, 1966), marginal note, 19 and marginal note, 20.

10. Jonathan Dollimore, *Radical Tragedy: Religion, Ideology and Power in the Drama of Shakespeare and his Contemporaries* (Chicago: U of Chicago P, 1984), 7–9.

11. Debora Kuller Shuger, *Habits of Thought in the English Renaissance: Religion, Politics, and the Dominant Culture* (Berkeley: U of California P, 1990), 9.

12. David Lee Miller, *The Poem's Two Bodies: The Poetics of the 1590 "Faerie Queene"* (Princeton: Princeton UP, 1988), 16.

13. Quoted in David Lloyd Stevenson, *The Achievement of Shakespeare's "Measure for Measure"* (Ithaca: Cornell UP, 1966), 151.

14. Albert H. Tricomi, *Anticourt Drama in England 1603–1642* (Charlottesville: U P of Virginia, 1989), 54.

15. Tricomi, 9.

16. *Minor Prose Works of King James VI and I*, ed. James Craigie and Alexander Law (Edinburgh: Scottish Text Society, 1982), 60.

17. Tricomi, 55.

18. Keith Thomas, *Religion and the Decline of Magic: Studies in Popular Beliefs in Sixteenth- and Seventeenth-Century England* (Harmondsworth: Penguin, 1982), 502–03.

19. As translated in C. Northcote Parkinson, *Gunpowder, Treason and Plot* (New York: St. Martin's Press, 1976), 43. The full account is in John Nichols, *The Progresses, Processions, and Magnificent Festivities, of King James the First, His Royal Consort, Family, and Court*, 4 vols. (London: Society of Antiquaries, 1828) 1: 543–44. There is some question concerning the original Latin text of this entertainment, although one is cited in 544n.

20. Steven Mullaney, *The Place of the Stage: License, Play, and Power in Renaissance England* (Chicago: U of Chicago P, 1988), 124.

21. *Minor Works*, 159–60.

22. Harold J. Laski, "Introduction," *A Defence of Liberty Against Tyrants: A Translation of the "Vindiciae Contra Tyrannos" by Junius Brutus* (New York: Burt Franklin, 1972), 41.

23. Shuger, 153.

24. Both quotations are from Shuger, 157.

25. Jonathan Dollimore, "Introduction: Shakespeare, cultural materialism and the new historicism," *Political Shakespeare: New essays in cultural materialism*, ed. Dollimore and Alan Sinfield (Ithaca: Cornell UP, 1985), 9.

26. Rebecca W. Bushnell, *Tragedies of Tyranny: Political Thought and Theater in the English Renaissance* (Ithaca: Cornell UP, 1990), 187.

27. George Buchanan, *Rerum Scoticarum Historia,* Books 18–19, trans W. A. Gatherer (Westport, Conn.: Greenwood), 114–16.

28. Stanley J. Kozikowski, "The Gowrie Conspiracy Against James VI: A New Source for Shakespeare's *Macbeth,*" *Shakespeare Studies* 13 (1980), 197–212.

29. *Sir Francis Bacon his apologie in certaine imputations concerning the late Earle of Essex* (1604). Like the Gowrie plot and *Macbeth,* witchcraft was said to be involved—and prophecy, the very conjunction of imagination and ideology.

30. Mervyn James, *Society, Politics and Culture: Studies in Early Modern England* (Cambridge: Cambridge UP, 1986), 445.

31. Laurence Michel, "Introduction," *The Tragedy of Philotas By Samuel Daniel* (New Haven: Yale UP, 1949), 36–66.

32. Quoted in Christopher Pye, *The Regal Phantasm: Shakespeare and the Politics of Spectacle* (London: Routledge, 1990), 44.

33. Annabel Paterson, *Censorship and Interpretation: The Conditions of Writing and Reading in Early Modern England* (Madison: U of Wisconsin P, 1984), 63.

34. J. G. A. Pocock, "Texts as Events: Reflections on the History of Political Thought," *Politics of Discourse,* ed. Sharpe and Zwicker, 21.

35. Michael D. Bristol, S*hakespeare's America, America's Shakespeare* (London: Routledge, 1990), 10.

## Notes to Chapter 8 / Achinstein

1. "Advertisements for the Managing of the Counsels of the Army," Walden, 1647, in A. S. P. Woodhouse, *Puritanism and Liberty* (London: J. M. Dent, 1966), 398. I wish to thank Annabel Patterson and Sarah Maza for their comments on an earlier version of this essay. The research for this essay was completed during a short-term residential fellowship at the Clark Library, and I thank the librarians and staff of the Clark for their assistance, and to the Center for Seventeenth and Eighteenth Century Studies, which made my stay there possible.

2. The degree to which ideology or interest motivated the struggles, and whether there was an opening up of political debate to admit previously excluded social groups is the crux of the current revisionist debate among historians. See J. P. Sommerville, *Politics and Ideology in England, 1603–1640* (New York: Longman, 1986) for a summary of the revisionist debates.

3. For a survey of the Royalist propaganda machines, see Lois Potter, *Secret Rites and Secret Writing: Royalist Literature, 1641–1660* (Cambridge: Cambridge UP, 1989), 7–22 and Joyce Lee

Malcolm, *Caesar's Due: Loyalty and King Charles, 1642–1646* (London: Royal Historical Society, 1983), ch. 5. On the Parliamentary side, see J. Frank, *Cromwell's Press Agent: A Critical Biography of Marchamont Nedham* (Lanham, MD: UP of America, 1980).

4. *Catalogue of the Thomason Tracts in the British Museum, 1640–1661* (London, 1908), I:xxi. This collection is not complete for the period, but gives some idea of the volume. For printing history during the English Revolutionary period, see Frederick S. Siebert, *Freedom of the England, 1476–1776* (Urbana: U of Illinois P, 1952), 166–76.

5. See Lawrence Stone, "Literacy and Education in England, 1640–1900," *Past and Present* 42 (1969): 69–139 and Thomas Lacquer, "Cultural Origins of Popular Literacy in England, 1500–1850," *Oxford Review of Education* 2:3 (1976), 55–75.

6. The larger study of which this is a part, *Milton and the Revolutionary Reader*, tracks the workings of this shift.

7. G. R. Elton, *Policy and Police: The Enforcement of the Reformation in the Age of Thomas Cromwell* (Cambridge: Cambridge UP, 1972).

8. C. S. L. Davies, *Peace, Print and Protestantism, 1450–1558* (London: Hart Davis, MacGibbon, 1976); David Cressy, *Literacy and the Social Order* (Cambridge: Cambridge UP, 1980), 177, 189.

9. A. M. Everitt, *Local Community and the Great Rebellion* Historical Association Pamphlet 70 (1969): 23; Christopher Hill, "Parliament and People in Seventeenth-Century England, *Past and Present* 92 (1981): 100–24.

10. Garth S. Jowett and Victoria O'Donnell, *Propaganda and Persuasion* (New York: Sage, 1986), ch. 2. The word's first appearance in the *Oxford English Dictionary* bore its religious heritage, and the definition referred to proselytising missionary religious activity of the 1840s.

11. Terence Qualter, *Opinion Control in the Democracies* (New York: St. Martin's 1985), 266. Qualter's chapter 6, "Propaganda: What it is," gives an excellent sketch of the history of propaganda studies in the twentieth century.

12. No mass public, or even the idea of public opinion, existed until the French Revolution, according to Paul A. Palmer, "The Concept of Public Opinion in Political Theory," in *Essays in History and Political Theory in Honor of Charles Howeard McIlwain* (Cambridge: Harvard UP, 1936), 231. In England, the "multitude" was an idea feared by elites, but was not a coherent force that could be called "public opinion." See C. Hill, "The Many-Headed Monster," *Change and Continuity in Seventeenth Century England* (Cambridge: Harvard UP, 1975), 181–204; and E. Duffy, "The Godly and the Multitude in Stuart England," *The*

*Seventeenth Century* 1:1 (1986), 31–55.

13. Jürgen Habermas, *The Structural Transformation of the Public Sphere: An Inquiry in the a Category of Bourgeois Society*, trans T. Burger (Cambridge: MIT, 1989), 58–59.

14. Ernest Sirluck, ed., *Complete Prose Works of John Milton* (New Haven: Yale UP, 1962), 2:537, 554. References to Milton's prose are to the *Complete Prose Works of John Milton*, gen. ed. Don M. Wolfe, 8 vols (New Haven: Yale UP, 1953–82), and are indicated in the text as *CPW*, with volume and page number.

15. *Mercurius Civicus*, 25 Jan.–1 Feb. (London, 1643). I have modernized spelling in all texts cited here. The location of all primary texts is London unless otherwise noted.

16. *Mercurius Elencticus Communicating the unparralell'd Proceedings*, no. 22, 17–24 Sept. (1649): 169–70; Wing M 316.

17. *The Contra-Replicant* (1643); Wing P400.

18. *England's Remembrancer of Londons integrity* (1647), no. 1: 1, 3.

19. H. Rusche, "Prophecies and Propaganda, 1641 to 1651," *English Historical Review* 84 (1969): 760; Bernard Capp, *Astrology and the Popular Press* (Ithaca: Cornell UP, 1979).

20. *Mercurius Vapulans* (1644), 7; Wing M1775.

21. George Wharton, *An Astrological Judgement upon His Majesties Present March: Begun from Oxford May 7, 1645* (1645), 8; Wing W1540.

22. William Lilly, *The Starry Messenger, or An Interpretation of that Strange Apparition of Three suns seen in London* (1645) n.p.; Wing L2245.

23. For a look at the politics of translation, see my "The Politics of Babel in the English Revolution," *Prose Studies* 14:3 (December 1991), 14–44.

24. John Booker, *Mercurius Coelicus*, Jan 25 (1644) 2; Wing W1551. Also see *A Rope for a Parrot* (1644), 2; Wing B3730.

25. *Mercurio-Coelico-Mastix* (1644), 2, 13; Wing W1550.

26. *Mercurius Vapulans* (1644), 8.

27. John Berger, *Ways of Seeing* (New York: Viking, 1972), 10.

28. *The Converted Cavaliers Confession* (1644).

29. *Mercurius Elencticus*, no. 25, 15–22 Oct. (1649); Wing 316.

30. See Strauss's analysis of writing practices of intellectuals, *Persecution and the Art of Writing* (Glencoe, IL: Free Press, 1952), 22–37. Annabel Patterson has recently critiqued Strauss in the new introduction to *Censorship and Interpretation* (Madison: U of Wisconsin P, 1990), 24–28.

31. The relation between verbal and visual wit is discussed by Ernest B. Gilman, *The Curious Perspective: Literary and Pictorial Wit in the Seventeenth Century* (New Haven: Yale UP, 1978), 28.

32. Ernest Gombrich, *Art and Illusion: A Study in the Psychology of Pictorial Representation* (Princeton: Princeton UP, 1968), 212, 252, 249.

33. So argues David Lowenstein, *Milton and Drama of History: Historical Vision, Iconoclasm, and the Literary Imagination* (Cambridge: Cambridge UP, 1990), 51–73.

34. *The Eye Cleared* (1644); *Cockoo's Nest* (1648), Wing C7459. Other pamphlets using the figure of a potion for eyes are *Eye-Salve to anoint the Eyes of the Ministers . . . of London* (1649); *Eye-Salve for the City of London* (1648); *An Eye-Salve for the English Armie* (1660).

35. Several of these pamphlets shared the same woodcut illustration: *A Paire of Crystal Spectacles . . . Counsels of the Army* (1648); *A New paire of Spectacles of the Old Fashion . . . Scots Commissioners* (1648); *Mercurius Heloconicus* (1651); *The Blind Man's Meditations* (1660).

36. *A New Invention* (1644), Wing N650.

37. *A Rhetoric of Irony* (Chicago: U of Chicago P, 1974), 91.

38. Sue Curry Jansen, *Censorship: The Knot that Binds Power and Knowledge* (Oxford: Oxford UP, 1991), 196.

39. As Thomas Corns has argued in *Uncloistered Virtue: English Political Literature, 1640–1660* (Oxford: Clarendon, 1992), 204–20.

40. John Milton, *Paradise Lost* 11.411–18, in *Complete Poems and Major Prose*, ed. Merritt Y. Hughes (Indianapolis: Bobbs-Merrill, 1957). All other references to Milton's poetry are from this edition.

41. For example, *Eye-Salve for the City of London* (1648); *Eye-Salve for the English Armie* (1660) and *Eye Salve for England* (1667).

42. This is like the position of the king at the center of the English Renaissance masque's audience: the king sat in the only position where true perspective would be possible, as Stephen Orgel has shown in *The Illusion of Power: Political Theater in the English Renaissance* (Berkeley: U of California P, 1975).

43. John M. Steadman, *Milton's Epic Characters: Image and Idol* (Chapel Hill: U of North Carolina P, 1968), ch. 5, examines "Satan and the Strategy of Illusion."

44. I am not interested in whether Milton's astronomy is Copernican or Galilean, as in Marjorie Hope Nicolson, *Science and Imagination* (Ithaca: Cornell UP, 1956), 80–110, but in the literary significance of Milton's use of this figure. Samuel Johnson saw the allusion to the telescope as Milton's striving for the sublime; Thomas Greene reads Milton's use of the telescope here as part of his mock-heroic program, an instance of the false sublime, *The Descent from Heaven: A Study in Epic Continuity* (New Haven: Yale UP, 1975), 415; Barbara Lewalski also sees the shield as typical of Satan's "declination from higher to lower heroic

kinds and models," in *Paradise Lost and the Rhetoric of Literary Forms* (Princeton: Princeton UP, 1979), 55–56; Stanley E. Fish, *Surprised by Sin: The Reader in Paradise Lost* (Berkeley: U of California P, 1971), 25, reads this passage as Milton's aim to "provide for his audience a perspective that is beyond the field of its perception," part of Milton's general assault on the reader's senses.

45. Thomas Hobbes, *Autobiography* (London: 1680), 6.

46. *The Great Assizes Holden in Parnassus* (1645), 34.

47. Mary Ann Radzinowicz, "The Politics of *Paradise Lost*," in Sharpe and Zwicker, eds., *Politics of Discourse*, 204–29, discusses the political progress of readers in "self-correction" (218).

48. The preferred revisionist term is *rebellion*. See C. Hill, a vigilant anti-revisionist and defender of the term *revolution*, "The Word 'Revolution,'" in *A Nation of Change and Novelty: Radical Politics, Religion and Literature in Seventeenth-Century England* (New York: Routledge, 1990), 82–101.

## Notes to Chapter 9 / Schleiner

1. *Seuils*, (Paris: Seuil, 1988).

2. Margaret P. Hannay, ed., *Silent but for the Word* (Kent, OH: Kent State U P, 1985), 126–48.

3. See Margo Todd, "Humanists, Puritans and the Spiritualized Household," *Church History* 49 (1980): 18–34.

4. George Ballard, *Memoirs of Several Ladies of Great Britain*, (Oxford: W. Jackson, 1752).

5. Jürgen Habermas, *Communication and the Evolution of Society*, trans. Thomas McCarthy (London: Heinemann, 1979), 2–6, 106–16.

6. Here I draw on Trevor-Roper, who notes that, just as in the 1570s and 1580s the English church had contested how far "reformed" it would become (the outcome at that border being defined by Hooker's *Ecclesiastical Polity*), in the 1610s to 1630s it was contesting how far toward a return to Catholic polity it would go (the outcome being stated by Chillingworth's *Religion of a Protestant*). The Cooke sisters were Mildred, Lady Burghley, Lady Anne Bacon (mother of Francis), Lady Elizabeth Hoby (later Russell), wife of the *Courtier* translator, and Mrs. Katherine Killegrew, close friend of the activist preacher Edward Dering and his wife, Anne Locke. See Hugh Trevor-Roper, *Catholics, Anglicans and Puritans* (London: Secker and Warburg, 1987). On their translations and verse, see my forthcoming *Tudor and Stuart Women Writers*.

7. For a vivid account of Elizabeth's participation in this scene, see Sister (of Cambray) Cary (either Anne or Elizabeth the younger), *The Lady Falkland: her life,* ed. Richard Simpson (London: Catholic Publishing Society, 1861).

8. See diagram from a contemporary report of the incident in *Publications of the Catholic Record Society, Miscellanea* 1: 92–95.

9. Habermas distinguishes strategic from communicative action as follows: "In communicative action a basis of mutually recognized validity claims is presupposed; this is not the case in strategic action. In the communicative attitude it is possible to reach a direct understanding oriented to validity claims; in the strategic attitude, by contrast, only an indirect understanding via determinative indicators is possible" (209).

10. The correct text is that of the folio, *History of the Life. Reign, and Death of Edward II ... Printed verbatim from the Original* (London: John Playford, 1680)—not that of the much shorter quarto condensation, also published in 1680, and again later by the Harleian Society (see n. 13 below). While this *History* was published as the work of Henry Cary, Lord Falkland, because found among his papers, Krontiris, building on earlier scholarship, has made a convincing case for Lady Falkland's authorship, to which I would add that the *History's* preface, like the prefatory material to Lady Falkland's published Perron translation, contains the odd, defensive claim that the work was written in only one month and thus should be read indulgently. The telling piece of explicit evidence is simply that the preface of the *History* is signed "E. F." (her husband's name was Henry, hers Elizabeth). See Tina Krontiris, "Style and Gender in Elizabeth Cary's Edward II," *Renaissance Englishwomen in Print: Counterbalancing the Canon,* ed. Anne M. Haselkorn and Betty S. Travitsky, (Amherst: U of Massachusetts P, 1990): 137–56. For further argument for Lady Falkland's authorship, see Jesse Swan, "A Critical Edition of Elizabeth Cary's *Edward II,*" Diss., Arizona State U, 1993.

11. Criticism of the play of the past dozen years, from Pearse to Beilin and others, has chosen to ignore or deemphasize this point (on which Cary is directly following her source, Lodge's translation of Josephus's *Antiquities of the Jews,* 1602, see Dunstan, n. 8 below), preferring to view Mariam as a feminist heroine: Nancy C. Pearse, "Elizabeth Cary, Renaissance Playwright, "*Texas Studies in Language and Literature* 18 (1977): 601–08; and Elaine V. Beilin, *Redeeming Eve* (Princeton: Princeton U P, 1987). Cary has indeed given her sympathetic treatment, and act 5 is devoted to Herod's fury of grief after he killed her. But her soliloquy about herself and the chorus's succeeding reiteration of its point are a clear framing endorsement of traditional wifely humility:

[Mariam] Had I but with humilitie bene grac'te,
As well as faire I might haue prou'd me wise:
But I did thinke because I knew me chaste,
One vertue for a woman, might suffice.
That mind for glory of our sexe might stand,
Wherein humilitie and chastitie
Doth march with equall paces hand in hand . . .
(4.8.1833–840)

And the chorus in conclusion to its ode on forgiveness, of
which the opening stanzas are often cited:

Had *Mariam* scorn'd to leaue a due [of revenge] unpaid,
Shee would to *Herod* then haue paid her loue:
And not haue bene by sullen passion swaide[.]
To fixe her thoughts all iniurie aboue
　　Is vertuous pride. Had *Mariam* thus bene prou'd [sic],
　　Long famous life to her had bene allowd.
(4.8.1934–939)

12. Cary, *Life*, 117.
13. See A. C. Dunstan, ed., *The Tragedy of Mariam* (Oxford:
Malone Society, 1914); Arlene I. Shapiro, "Elizabeth Cary: Her
Life, Letters and Art," Diss., S.U.N.Y. Stony Book, 1984, 43; David
Lunn, *Elizabeth Cary Lady Falkland: 1586/7–1639* (Ilford, Essex:
Royal Stuart Society, 1977); Mary R. Mahl and Helene Koon, eds.
*The Female Spectator* (Bloomington: Indiana U P, 1977), 100, and
Swan. In 1609 her first child, Catherine, was born, then in 1610
the second, Lucius, later second Lord Falkland, followed by
Lawrence, 1611–1612; but on the dates and birth order of the
middle children, the modern commentators disagree or are vague.
The pregnancy that resulted in Anne (later Dame Clementina of
Cambray) had to be in late 1613 to 1614: as entered in the Cambray
records (*Life*, 184–85), she was 24 on 8 March 1639, thus born
some time between 9 March 1614, and 8 March 1615. As the
other children can all be assigned later birth dates, this must have
been the fourth pregnancy. (My hunch is that Anne, in youth
a maid of honor to Queen Henrietta Maria and leading light of
the daughters who converted, is the author of the biography, and
thus this story of the depression during that pregnancy would
have had special significance for her.)
14. One could contend that it was only the dedicatory sonnet,
to this sister-in-law, that is referred to as having been recalled,
since the sonnet appears in some copies but not others. But this
seems an unlikely explanation, since a poem to this person of
no public importance would scarcely be matter of great offense,

or something needing to be "stolen out of her chambers."

15. This close friendship of Ladies Falkland and Denbigh, the latter being the almighty Buckingham's sister and having much influence on him, explains why the highest ranking people in the court and church, from Secretary Coke to Cousen and Archbishop Laud, personally harangued Lady Falkland, trying to pressure her back to Anglicanism and later to prevent further conversions in her family (see the *Life* and Laud's letter in its appendix, and the letter of Lady Falkland to Lady Denbigh in Shapiro).

16. The preface of the *History* is dated 20 Feb. 1627, which in Gregorian dating is 1628. The spring of 1628 is the time of official court correspondence (including a letter from the king himself) informing Lord Falkland that, as a last resort in the council's efforts to make him support his wife, money would be withheld from his salary if he continued refusing to do so. He seems to have learned in advance that this development was coming, for in January 1628, he proposed to pay her 300 pounds per year if she would stay at least ten miles from London (see the Cary *Life*, Appendix); at that time she went to live in the rundown house by the Thames of which her daughter tells, "in a little town ten miles from London" (*Life*, 37; see Shapiro, 69–70).

17. She says she has "not followed the dull character of our historians herein."

18. As noted (n 3), the eighteenth century reprint by the Harleian Society, *The History of the Most Unfortunate King Edward II*, is of the condensed 1680 quarto version, probably done at the behest of the printer John Playford by Sir James Harrington, to whom its preface is attributed (see *Dictionary of National Biography* 3:1150).

19. See *The Conceited Newes of Sir Thomas Overbury and his Friends*, 1616, xxiii ff., and my forthcoming study, *Tudor and Stuart Women Writers*.

20. B.L. MS. Egerton 2725, f.60. I take the text from Shapiro, 75.

21. Both the published prose dedication of the Perron translation, to Queen Henrietta Maria, and the handwritten sonnet in the copy at the Beinecke Library, Yale University, express Lady Falkland's devotion to and reliance on the queen, in whose chapel she was to be buried (see Shapiro, 81).

22. *The History of the Life, Reign and Death of Edward II* . . . (London: John Playford, 1680).

23. Bradbrook also notes the clear though tacit addressing of the Buckingham question through the history of the medieval favorites.

24. The *History* was, incidentally, published in 1680 for the purpose of lobbying against the great influence of Charles II's mistress; otherwise we would not have it.

25. Donald A. Stauffer made this point and was the first to suggest that it was not Lord Falkland but Lady Falkland who wrote the *Edward II:* "A Deep and Sad Passion," *The Parrott Presentation Volume*, ed. Hardin Craig (New York: Russell, 1967).

## Notes to Chapter 10 / Sondergard

1. For an example of experiential discourse (as in Bunyan's attempts to address his audiences "at the level of human empathy and experience") exploited to create an emotionally charged rapport between writer and reader/viewer, see Sid Sondergard, "The Dramaturgical Intention of Cruelty in the Cornish Ordinalia," *Mediaevalia* 11 (1985): 174–77, 184–85, n. 18. On the use of violent images for rhethorical assertion of personal authority, see Sondergard, "'Pain is perfect misery': Reading the Miltonic Discourse of Violence," *Semiotics 1988*, ed. Terry Prewitt, et al. (New York: UP of America, 1989), 380–87.

2. J. A. Froude claims in *English Men of Letters* (1880) that Bunyan must have seemed "impracticable and wrong-headed" to his opponents, who were "really aiming at his good if he had only known it" (John Brown, *John Bunyan [1628–1688]: His Life, Times, and Work*, rev. Frank Mott Harrison [1885, rev. 1928; n.p.: Archon, 1969], 155–56), and treats the prison term as "a light matter" (Harold E. B. Speight, *The Life and Writings of John Bunyan* [New York: Harper, 1928], 86). John Brown criticizes William Parry's "way of putting the case, perhaps a little sensationally" (155) in his *Religious Tests* (1790), complaining of the manner in which Parry depicted Bunyan's "damp and dreary cell, the narrow chink through which came scanty rays of light making visible the abode of woe, the prisoner, pale and emaciated, seated on the humid earth" (155). Even the *Dictionary of National Biography* remarks that "with a slight interval in 1666, he remained in prison, *not altogether unhappily*, till 1672" (3:279, my italics). While it is true that Bedford church rolls record Bunyan attending services during certain periods of his imprisonment (late 1660 and for a few weeks in 1666), "For seven years out of the twelve, 1661–8, his name never occurs in the records of the church" (*DNB* 3:279). Certainly Bunyan was indefatigable, refusing to allow incarceration to deter him from his ministry; this ability to salvage good out of a bad situation does not, however, prove that his prison experience was, in Edmund Venables's terms, "by no means so wretched." John Bubb, a prisoner in Bedford Jail while Bunyan was there, sent a petition to Charles II stating that "He hath suffered as much misery as soe dismall a place could be capable

to inflict, and soe is likely perish without His Majestie's further compassion and mercy towards him" (Brown, 157). See Brown's speculative reconstruction of the physical environment of Bedford County Jail (151–53); cf. Edmund Venables, ed. *Bunyan: The Pilgrim's Progress, Grace Abounding to the Chief of Sinners, and A Relation of the Imprisonment of Mr. John Bunyan* (Oxford: Clarendon, 1900).

3. Henry A. Talon, *John Bunyan* (1956; London: Longmans, Green, 1964), 10. Of course, Talon would also never argue that Bunyan was ever deficient in self-esteem or was insecure about his authority as minister of God; he maintains, for example, that the reason Bunyan took a horse to Reading in 1688 (and consequently caught the cold that killed him) was that "he was too manly to take the coach" (12).

4. Richard L. Greaves, "The Spirit and the Sword: Bunyan and the Stuart State," *Bunyan in Our Own Time*, ed. Robert G. Collmer (Kent: Kent State U P, 1989), 143, 145.

5. Greaves, "Conscience, Liberty, and the Spirit: Bunyan and Nonconformity," *John Bunyan, Conventicle and Parnassus: Tercentenary Essays*, ed. N. H. Keeble (Oxford: Clarendon, 1988), 26–27.

6. Christopher Hill, *A Tinker and a Poor Man* (New York: Knopf, 1989), 103.

7. James Jakób Liszka, *The Semiotic of Myth* (Bloomington: Indiana U P, 1989), 16.

8. Teresa de Lauretis, "The Violence of Rhetoric: Considerations on Representation and Gender," *The Violence of Representation*, ed. Nancy Armstrong and Leonard Tennenhouse (New York: Routledge, 1989), 240.

9. Hill, *The Experience of Defeat* (New York: Viking, 1984), 17.

10. George Fox, *The Journal of George Fox*, ed. Norman Penney (New York: Dutton, 1924), 227–28.

11. Keeble, N. H. ed. *The Pilgrim's Progress* (New York: Oxford U P, 1984), 28.

12. J. Sears McGee, ed. *The Miscellaneous Works of John Bunyan* (Oxford: Clarendon, 1987), 3:248–49.

13. Graham Midgley, ed. *The Miscellaneous Works of John Bunyan* (Oxford: Clarendon, 1980), 6:180.

14. James F. Forrest and Roger Sharrock, eds. *The Life and Death of Mr. Badman* (Oxford: Clarendon, 1988), 165.

15. In *A Being More Intense* (New York: AMS, 1984), Paula Backscheider senses the personal torment of the author as a significant factor in the characterization of *Pilgrim's Progress*'s Christian when she observes that "Christian's most accute suffering involves mental anguish combining confusion over his

present situation and of his responsibility for his suffering. The mind and the earth seem claustrophobic" (70). The intellectual conflict between the painful reality of imprisonment and an (hypersensitive) awareness of sin that deserves such punishment must be particularly agonizing for the simple Bunyan, who reveals his honesty and perplexity when recording in *A Relation of the Imprisonment of Mr. John Bunyan, Minister of the Gospel at Bedford, in November 1660* (1765) the proceedings of his pseudo-indictment. To the Justice's skepticism about writing prayers, Bunyan responds, "it is not our use," "it is none of our custom" (Venables, 411–12). The author tries to convince himself in *Grace Abounding* that his punishment cannot be too much for him to bear, because he has tempered himself to anticipate the worst (Venables, 393; cf. 295–96). Bunyan stoically insists he has not been "surprised" by the penalties of his nonconformity, and in *Seasonable Counsel: Or, Advice to Sufferers* (1684) declares that the fearless believer ultimately cannot be defeated (Owen C. Watkins, ed. *The Miscellaneous Works of John Bunyan* [Oxford: Clarendon, 1988], 10:98).

16. Nick Shrimpton, "Bunyan's Miliatry Metaphor," *The Pilgrim's Progress: Critical and Historical Views*, ed. Vincent Newey (Totowa, NJ: Barnes and Noble, 1980), 205. See also 206, 222–23. Violence (or the pain it suggests imaginatively) functions in the allegories to make doctrine refer more immediately to the reader's experience, and hence to serve as a compelling deterrent.

17. Anne Hunsaker Hawkins, *Archetypes of Conversion* (Lewisburg: Bucknell U P, 1985), 76.

18. Elaine Scarry, *The Body in Pain* (New York: Oxford U P, 1985), 52.

19. Hill explains that Spira "was notorious for relapsing from protestantism back to popery; he died in despair" (185). See Nathaniel Bacon, *A relation of the fearefull estate of F. Spira* (1638) [STC 1177.5]; and Francesco Spira, *Spira respirans: or, the way to the kingdom of Heaven, by the gates of Hell* (1695) [Wing 4986].

20. James F. Forrest, ed. *The Holy War ... Or, the Losing and Taking Again of the Town of Mansoul* (New York: New York U P, 1967), 2.

21. At the same time, the author's humility (and an awareness of his responsibility as Christian pedagogue) frequently prompts him to take himself out of the position of eyewitness and to insist on the inherent ethics of the faith, demanding accountability from the believer. An address "To the Christian Reader" in *Seasonable Counsel* deemphasizes Bunyan in favor of Bunyan's religion (Watkins, 5), while the reader of *A Discourse Upon the Pharisee and the Publicane* is openly challenged (Watkins, 111) whether

the voice of Bunyan as agent of Christianity remains audible or not.

22. Vincent Newey, "Bunyan and the Confines of the Mind," *The Pilgrim's Progress: Critical and Historical Views*, ed. Vincent Newey (Totowa, NJ: Barnes and Noble, 1980), 30. Just as Bunyan objectifies his intervention into the process of spiritual decay in the form of textual violence, he objectifies that decay through the icon of rotting flesh. Two *exempla* on rotting flesh appear in the first edition of *A Book for Boys and Girls; Or, Country Rhymes for Children* (1686), though they were excised from the 1701 edition; see Midgley (255, 260). In *The Life and Death of Mr. Badman*, see also the discussion between Wiseman and Attentive about the moral subtext of the physical deterioration caused by Pox (Forrest & Sharrock, 51–52); the discussion of the informer/spy that concludes with his being bitten by a dog (Forrest & Sharrock, 82); and the rotting condition of Badman's corpse (Forrest & Sharrock, 148–49).

23. Hill comments on Bunyan's textual companions in prison, the Bible and Foxe's *Acts and Monuments* (*Tinker*, 121). On the author's enthusiasm for martyrdom, see, e.g., Keeble, 166; McGee, 18; Watkins, 25, 41.

24. The conflict structure of the epic/romance is also the ideal vehicle for expressing the "vacillement psychologique entre le pessimisme et l'optimisme" of the author, simultaneously juxtaposing his fears of physical suffering with his celebration of the Christian rewards for patient endurance (Jean-Francois Came, "La Peur, instrument du salut dans *Grace Abounding* de Bunyan," *La Peur*, ed. Alain Morvan [N.p.: Université de Lille III, 1985], 34).

25. Keeble, "'Of him thousands daily Sing and talk': Bunyan and His Reputation," *John Bunyan*, ed. Keeble (Oxford: Clarendon, 1988), 245.

26. See Keeble, ed., *Pilgrim's Progress*, xxxi.

27. Stuart Sim, "Bunyan's *Holy War* and the Dialectics of Long-Drawn-Outness," *Restoration* 9 (1985), 95.

## Notes to Chapter 11 / Patterson

1. Galileo, *Assayer*, in *The Controversy on the Comets of 1618*, trans. Stillman Drake and C. D. O'Malley (Philadelphia, 1960), 202.

2. For a full account of the Good Old Cause in 1659, see Austin Woolrych, "The Good Old Cause and the Fall of the Protectorate," *Cambridge Historical Journal*, 13 (1957), 133–61; see also Robert Zaller, "The Good Old Cause and the Crisis of 1659,"

in Gordon J. Schochet, ed. *Restoration, Ideology, and Revolution: Proceedings of the Folger Institute Center for the History of Political Thought*, vol. 4 (Washington, D.C., 1990), 23–40.

3. Geoffrey Elton, "A High Road to Civil War?" in his *Studies in Tudor and Stuart Politics and Government*, 2 vols. (London, 1974), 2.164–82.

4. See, for example: Kevin Sharpe, "Introduction: parliamentary history 1603–29," in Sharpe, ed., *Faction and Parliament* (Oxford, 1973); Sharpe, "An Unwanted Civil War," *New York Review of Books*, 3 December 1982; M. Kishlansky, "The Emergence of Adversary Politics in the Long Parliament," *JMH* 49 (1977), 617–40; Barry Coward, "Was There an English Revolution in the Middle of the Seventeenth Century," in *Politics and People in Revolutionary England: Essays in Honor of Ivan Root*, ed. Colin Jones, Malyn Newitt and Stephen Roberts (Oxford: Blackwell, 1986), 9–40; J. C. C. Clark, *Revolution and Rebellion* (London, 1986).

5. John Morrill, *The Revolt of the Provinces: Conservatives and Radicals in the English Civil War, 1630–1650* (London, 1976).

6. Conrad Russell, *Unrevolutionary England, 1603–1642* (Ronceverte, W.V.: Hambledon, 1990).

7. Christopher Hill and Edmund Dell, eds., *The Good Old Cause: The English Revolution of 1640–60: Its Causes, Course and Consequences: Extracts from Contemporary Sources* (London, 1949). Elton referred skeptically to Hill in "A high road to civil war,?" 167.

8. *England: Studies in Religion and Poltics 1603–1642*, ed. Cust and Hughes (London and New York: Longmans, 1989), 1–46, which provides the clearest manifesto of the counterrevisionary movement. See also Johann Sommerville's *Politics and Ideology in England, 1603–1640*, which broadened the issue to constitutional theory.

9. Milton, *Complete Prose Works*, ed. D. M. Wolfe *et al.*, 8 vols. (New Haven: Yale University Press, 1953–82), 2:538.

10. Joan Webber, *The Eloquent "I": Style and Self in Seventeenth Century Prose* (Madison, 1968), 202.

11. Samuel Taylor Coleridge, Lecture 10, *Literary Remains* (London, 1836), quoted from James Thorpe, ed., *Milton Criticism: Selections from Four Centuries* (London: Routledge and Kegan Paul, 1951), 97.

12. Coleridge planned three "lay sermons," the first to the "clerisy," an alliance of the ruling and professional classes; the second to the "Higher and Middle Classes on the Existing Distresses and Discontents," that is to say, the hunger marches and demands for electoral reform that culminated in the "Peterloo Massacre" of August 1819; and a third, which he never produced, would have been addressed to the laboring classes themselves, with the goal of unmasking "our Incendiaries," the radical

spokesmen like William Cobbett and John and Leigh Hunt. See *Lay Sermons*, ed. R. J. White, in *Collected Works*, vol. 6, 35–38.

13. F. R. Leavis, "Milton's Verse," in *Revaluation: Tradition and Development in English Poetry* (London: 1936, 1964), 42–61; reprinted from *Scrutiny*, 1933; T. S. Eliot, "A Note on the Verse of John Milton," *Essays and Studies of the English Association* (Oxford, 1936), cited from T. S. Eliot, *Selected Prose of T. S. Eliot*, ed. Frank Kermode (New York: Harcourt, 1975), 258–64.

14. T. S. Eliot, "Milton," Annual Lecture on a Master Mind, read 26 March 1947 before the British Academy; *Proceedings of the British Academy* 33 (1947). Cited in Eliot, *Selected Prose*, 265–74.

15. Christopher Hill, *The Experience of Defeat: Milton and Some Contemporaries* (New York: Viking Press, 1984), 215.

16. Christopher Hill, *Milton and the English Revolution* (New York: Viking, 1977).

17. Hill found relief from the apparent conventionality of Milton's early poetry in his personal associations; for example, his friendship with Alexander Gil, who was imprisoned for libeling Buckingham in 1628 (28). Other crumbs of confort were found in Milton's commonplace book, where Milton referred to "Junius Brutus, that second founder of Rome and great avenger of the lusts of kings," (35). But the problem of the early poems had to be faced. "A masque," wrote Hill, contemplating the text we now call *Comus*, "appears at first sight rather a surprising thing for a Puritan to write if we can properly call Milton a Puritan at this time" (45). The solution, which Hill himself evidently found incompletely satisfying, was to focus on the Lady's plea "for greater economic equality" as against "lewdly-pampered Luxury" (47) and to define the spirit of the masque as being in the Puritan-individualist tradition of the lonely, heroic ordeal (49).

18. H. L. Benthem, *Engelandischer Kirch- und Schulen-Staat* (Luneberg, 1694), 58. Cited in Hill, *Milton and the English Revolution*, 391.

19. *Holinshed's Chronicles*, ed. Henry Ellis, 6 vols. (London, 1807, repr. New York, 1965), 1:497.

20. Compare Leonard Goldstein, "The Good Old Cause and Milton's Blank Verse, *Zeitschrift fur Anglistik und Amerikanistik*, 23 (1975), 133–42, who argues that neoclassical literary theory "with its emphasis on restrain, decorum, order, reason, the rules . . . constitutes counterrevolution in the form of literary criticism," (134). Goldstein's analysis is conducted, however, in terms of the history of prosody, not in terms of the political semantics of "ancient liberty."

21. Cited from *Divine Right and Democracy*, ed. David Wootton (Harmondsworth: Penguin, 1986), 110.

22. See Dryden, *All for Love, Oedipus, Troilus and Cressida*, eds. Maximilian E. Novak and George T. Guffey (Berkeley and Los Angeles: U of California P, 1984), vol. 13 of *Works*, 6–7. This equation of the 1640s and the 1680s is typical of Dryden, whose theory of the *continuity* of the Good Old Cause is the negative mirror image of my own. In 1684, he dedicated the *History of the League* to Charles II, and added a "Postscript" creating a genealogy of rebellion from Luther onwards. "Calvin, to do him right," he remarked, "writ to King Edward the Sixth, a sharp Letter againt these People; [the extreme radical sects] but our Presbyterians after him, have been content to make use of them in the late Civil Wars, where they and all the rest of the Sectaries were joyn'd in the *Good Old Cause* of Rebellion against His Late Majesty." *Works*, eds. Alan Roper and Vinton Dearing, (Berkeley and Los Angeles: U of California P, 1974), 18:398–99.

23. Dryden, *Prose 1668–1691*, ed. Samuel Holt Monk and A. E. Wallace Maurer, in *The Works of John Dryden*, vol. 17 (Berkeley: U of California P, 1971), 233.

24. Marvell himself says there, in response to Samuel Parker, "you wold fix upon me the old Martin Mar-Prelate (in one page you do it four times"). See *The Rehearsal Transpros'd*, ed. D. I. B. Smith (Oxford: Clarendon, 1971), 294.

25. Marvell complains that Samuel Parker has been making the same argument about a continuous republican movement allied with the nonconformists: "You represent them, to a man, to be all of them of Republican Principles, most pestilent, and, *eo nomine*, enemies to Monarchy; Traytors and Rebells; . . . onely the memory of the late War serves for demonstration, and the destestable sentence & execution, of his late Majesty is represented again upon the Scaffold; and you having been, I suspect, better acquainted with Parliament Declarations formerly upon another account, do now apply and turn them all over to prove that the late War was wholly upon a Fanatical Cause, and the dissenting party do still goe big with the same Monster," *Rehearsal Transpros'd*, 125.

26. Marvell, *Rehearsal Transpros'd*, 135.

27. For a similar conclusion, that Marvell wrote this passage with deliberate irony and ambiguity, see Hill, *The Experience of Defeat*, 249–50.

28. Marvell, *Rehearsal Transpros'd*, 312.

29. Marvell, *Last Instructions*, "To the King"; See *Poems and Letters*, ed. H. M. Margoliouth, rev. Pierre Legouis, 2 vols. (Oxford: Clarendon, 1971), 1:171.

30. Richard Greaves, *Deliver us from Evil: The Radical Underground in Britain, 1660–1663* (New York and Oxford: Oxford U P, 1986), 229.

# Index

# About the Contributors

SHARON ACHINSTEIN, assistant professor at Northwestern University, has published articles in *Milton Studies* and *The Journal of Medieval and Renaissance Studies*. Her book, *Milton and the Revolutionary Reader*, which discusses Milton and the pamphlet culture of the English Revolution, is forthcoming from Princeton University Press.

MICHAEL D. BRISTOL is professor of English at McGill University. He is the author of *Carnival and Theatre: Plebian Culture and the Structure of Authority* and *Shakespeare's America/America's Shakespeare*.

HEATHER CAMPBELL is assistant professor of English at York University in Ontario. Dr. Campbell has published articles on Marvell and Spenser, and she is currently working on a book-length study of autobiographical writings by women in seventeenth century England and New England, as well as an anthology of seventeenth century women's writing.

KATHERINE ZAPANTIS KELLER is associate professor of English and coordinator of Honors in English at the University of Central Florida. Dr. Keller, who has published articles on Restoration drama and ethnic literature, is also co-director of the biennial Conference on the Arts and Public Policy at the University of Central Florida.

ARTHUR F. KINNEY is Thomas W. Copeland Professor of Literary History at the University of Massachusetts at Amherst and founding editor of *English Literary Renaissance*. His latest books are *Sidney in Retrospect* and *Continental Humanist Poetics*.

CATHERINE GIMELLI MARTIN is assistant professor of English at Memphis State University, where she has just completed a book-length manuscript *The Ruins of Allegory: Tradition and Revision in* Paradise Lost. Her recently published work includes articles in *Studies in English Literature*, *Milton Studies* and in *Renaissance Discourses of Desire*, edited by C. Summers and T. Pebworth.

THOMAS S. NOWAK is assistant professor of English at Dominican College of Blauvelt in Rockland County, New York. He is currently working on a book-length study of the Gunpowder Sermons as both literature and propaganda.

ANNABEL PATTERSON is currently Andrew W. Mellon Professor of the Humanities at Duke University, and will be moving to Yale University in 1994. Her most recent books are *Censorship and Interpretation*, *Shakespeare and the Popular Voice*, *Fables of Power* and *Reading Between the Lines*. Forthcoming is a revisionary account of "Holinshed's" *Chronicles*.

DOUGLAS RUTLEDGE is assistant professor at Capital University in Columbus, Ohio. He has recently completed a book-length study of ritual, politics and Renaissance theater, *Cermony and Text in the Renaissance*. His most recent work appeared in *Medieval and Renaissance Drama in England*.

GERALD J. SCHIFFHORST, professor of English and co-director of the biennial Conference on the Arts and Public Policy at the University of Central Florida, is the editor and co-author of *The Triumph of Patience: Medieval and Renaissance Studies* and the author of *John Milton*.

LOUISE SCHLEINER is associate professor at Washington State University. She has published on topics including music and poetry, and Kristevan intertextuality in relation to Shakespeare and Milton. Her forthcoming books, from Indiana and Lehigh University Presses, respectively, are *Tudor and Stuart Women Writers* and *Cultural Semiotics, Spenser, and the Captive Woman*.

SID SONDERGARD, associate professor of English at St. Lawrence University, has published essays in *The American Journal of Semiotics*, *Mediaevalia*, *Studies in Philology* and *Theatre Survey*. He is now completing a book-length study of rhetorical violence as an authorization strategy in the work of Renaissance authors.

RAYMOND D. TUMBLESON has recently published essays in *West Virginia University Philological Papers*, *Persuasions*, *Transactions of the North-West Society for Eighteenth-Century Studies* and *Prose Studies*. His dissertation on religion and nationalism in seventeenth and eighteenth century England has just been completed at the University of Washington.